The Power and Performance of Roman Water-mills

Hydro-mechanical Analysis of Vertical-wheeled Water-mills

Robert Spain

BAR International Series 1786

2008

Published in 2019 by
BAR Publishing, Oxford

BAR International Series 1786

The Power and Performance of Roman Water-mills

© Robert Spain and the Publisher 2008

ISBN 9781407302171 paperback
ISBN 9781407332772 e-book

DOI https://doi.org/10.30861/9781407302171

A catalogue record for this book is available from the British Library

This book is available at www.barpublishing.com

BAR Publishing is the trading name of British Archaeological Reports (Oxford) Ltd.
British Archaeological Reports was first incorporated in 1974 to publish the BAR
Series, International and British. In 1992 Hadrian Books Ltd became part of the BAR
group. This volume was originally published by John and Erica Hedges in conjunction
with British Archaeological Reports (Oxford) Ltd / Hadrian Books Ltd, the Series
principal publisher, in 2008. This present volume is published by BAR Publishing,
2019.

BAR
PUBLISHING

BAR titles are available from:

BAR Publishing
122 Banbury Rd, Oxford, OX2 7BP, UK
EMAIL   info@barpublishing.com
PHONE   +44 (0)1865 310431
FAX   +44 (0)1865 316916
www.barpublishing.com

In memoriam
John Landels
amici, adiutoris, condiscipuli
Nemo solus satis sapit

FOREWORD

The writer is very much aware that in the course of this work a large number of variables have been identified, to which values have been assigned which cannot, given the limitations of the evidence, be more than tentative; some of them are 'sensitive' (i.e. a small deviation could have significant effect on the final conclusions) and where a number of variables are involved together, their cumulative effect could be important. He hopes, however, by exposing the whole of his analysis to the light of reasoned debate, to bring integrity to the findings. At the same time, the reader is given the opportunity to make an independent assessment of each of the variables according to his or her own personal opinion, and to explore the implications of any changes which may be thought appropriate. The writer apologises for not being able to adopt a strict protocol when presenting metric and imperial measurements.

CONTENTS

LIST OF ILLUSTRATIONS

ACKNOWLEDGEMENTS

The preparation of this study has benefited greatly from discussions with many friends, foremost amongst them was the late John Landels. I am greatly indebted to him for his constructive observations and editorial comment. I thank also Michael Lewis for the valuable overview that he readily gave to this work. A considerable portion of my doctoral dissertation has been embodied in this work and, for that reason I wish to acknowledge the help of Norman Smith, whose guidance in those formative years, I greatly value. None of the above is to be held responsible for the views expressed here.

My thanks to Barry Cunliffe who kindly allowed me free use of the valuable Roman water-mill material from his Fullerton Villa report, to Claude Sinter *(Musée de l'Arles antique)* for access to the Barbegal millstones, and to Jean Peire Brun *(Centre Jean Bérard)* for bringing to my attention new archaeological finds.

In preparing this technical engineering paper for more general readership, I should like to thank James Daly, Allan Spain and Diccon Spain for their numerous helpful suggestions. I also wish to thank Chris Spain, André Gautier, Heidi Kirsten and Martin Earlam for their help with translations. I am responsible for any remaining imperfections.

I am most grateful to Jackson Daly, London, Graphic Consultants, for their work in preparing the illustrations for publication.

Finally, I wish to acknowledge my great debt to Ann, my wife, for her constant support and encouragement, especially during many visits to Provence.

Robert Spain, Boxley, 2007

PART ONE

1. Introduction

During the last few decades the remains of several water-mills have been discovered, and they have provided new evidence of Roman water-power technology. At the same time new studies of some previously known sites have helped to increase our knowledge and understanding of the buildings, which housed them, their hydraulic arrangements and the working machinery. This growing body of knowledge has been particularly strengthened by new finds in the north-west provinces of the Empire. Until recently Britannia had the largest number of confirmed and probable Roman water-mill sites[1], but now the number found in Gaul and Italy has markedly increased, and so too have the identified sites in North Africa[2], followed by Germania, and Helvetia[3]. Roman Iberia is disappointingly barren in this respect, although we can hope for more evidence in view of a recent increase in archaeological activity[4]. Within Europe, virtually all the archaeological evidence of Roman water-mills relates to vertical water-wheels, and it is with that type that this paper is particularly concerned.

The writer believes that it is possible to make use of modern theoretical knowledge and experience of water-power generation and of its applications in order to learn more about the performance and behaviour of Roman machines. (The fact that the Romans did not have any such theoretical knowledge is irrelevant; they used standardized designs, which had been tested through many years of practical experience, and their innovations were almost all empirical. But they were, after all, dealing with a physical substance, which behaved 2000 years ago in exactly the way that it does today.) To achieve this it is necessary to subject the archaeological evidence to functional analysis, in contrast to the static, descriptive analysis made by the archaeologists; this can provide information which cannot be found by any other means of enquiry. The study of water-mills lends itself very well to this analysis technique.

Functional analysis may be divided into two distinct phases, in which two different modes of treatment are used. The first mode is theoretical or *dynamic* analysis, which involves the application of mathematics or theoretical mechanics to investigate function and evaluate performance. In this analysis the artefact itself, or a replica, does not feature. The second treatment is analysis of function by *practice*, where the artefact, or a replica, is examined under probable working conditions and its performance assessed.

Theoretical analysis is particularly well suited to those ancient artefacts that had mechanical functions, such as the components of the machinery found in water-mills, whose behaviour can be accurately envisaged. It provides us with a better understanding of how the machine was constructed, how it worked and what it could do, especially where there was an interaction of several mechanisms or forces that influenced each other. Nearly all these either had moving parts or they moved, and therefore provide opportunities for analysis related to the physical laws of motion. Of special relevance in this study are those artifacts that involved water (static or in motion) and so offer the opportunity for theoretical analysis by using the laws of fluids and hydrodynamics. Thus the historian of technology uses the laws and language of physics to progress towards probability and reality by quantifying and qualifying.

But retrospective analysis brings with it two insurmountable difficulties. Our knowledge of an artefact's original environment is always less than complete, and our view of the ancient world is liable to distortion because of the preoccupations and prejudices deriving from modern experience. It is very easy for the historian of technology to become so entrenched and immersed in theoretical calculations that his vision of the ancient reality becomes impaired or lost altogether. Moreover, as Smith has said, the Romans attitude to efficiency and productivity, and the values they set on the factors that influenced them (especially labour and materials), were by no means the same as our own[5]. One of the typical dangers that we face when examining ancient technology through modern eyes is the assumption that the Romans had a concept of efficiency as we have (i.e. the relationship between energy input and work output). The values that they placed on the factors of production, especially labour and materials, were clearly different from ours. So too were their attitudes[6].

---

1 Spain 1984a.
2 Wilson 1995. Most of the North African sites appear to be horizontal-wheeled machines, but none of these are securely dated.
3 For a comprehensive list of pre-A.D. 700 Roman or Byzantine water-mill sites see Wikander 2000.
4 Keay 2003.
5 Smith 1983/4, 80.
6 Wilson 2002. Concerning Roman intellectuals disparaging views of technology.

Nonetheless, we need to identify critical points within the development of technology. A good example of this in Roman corn-milling is the development of the dressing of millstones with furrows, which improved the efficiency of the process.

The historian of technology also needs to relate his findings with the technological and social background of the Roman period, and in doing so to express himself in language which is familiar to disciplines other than his own; if not, his contribution will not take its rightful place in socio-economic history. But how do we assess the validity of the results achieved? We know how to do this in physics or biology or astronomy, but how in history?[7] It was Droysen who said that historians must know what they wish to seek; only then will they find something. One must question things correctly, and then they give an answer[8]. Theoretical and operational analyses are surely the historian of technology's best diagnostic tools. Their application takes us towards realism and the experience of the original artisans and craftsmen, which we can approach but not reach. If this work leads to a fuller appreciation and a better understanding of their machinery design, operation and performance, it should lead to the identification of improvements and innovations, and providing we have a representative corpus of evidence over time, this will facilitate our understanding of technical evolution. But that will take time. As Wilson says, specialist research work on particular branches of history takes a while to filter through the consciousness of mainstream history[9].

The use of theoretical analysis in the study of Roman water-power is not a recent development. It has been a diagnostic tool used by historians of technology for many decades in the continual search for the better understanding of performance of these early prime-movers. In Part Two of this work, where individual Roman water-mill sites are examined, the contributions of theoretical analysis made by other historians in their published works are identified, evaluated and commented on. Particular attention has been given to *Barbegal*, the best known and most examined Roman water-mill. In the context of Roman water-power, virtually all of the archaeological site evidence relates to corn-milling, although we do have two sites where there is evidence that the power was used for marble-sawing[10]. Thus we are concerned primarily with the generation of water-power by vertical water-wheels powering millstones using gears.

Landels twenty years ago lamented the little progress made by historians to envisage mechanical contrivances in action, a statement he later attempted to answer[11]. The writer will demonstrate, that certainly in the study of water-power, our knowledge of the performance of these machines has advanced little. In some earlier examinations of water-mills the need to assess potential power and productive output has been the dominant aim. But hitherto, no attempt has been made to measure the power necessary to drive Roman style millstones, nor to calculate their production/power rate. This study includes a report of the replication and testing of a pair of millstones that has provided us with critical comparators that can be transposed to different Roman water-mills, thus removing a major factor of ignorance influencing our interpretation of their performance. Nevertheless, the reader will discover below that there still remain some areas within the theoretical analysis where assumptions have to be made, or degrees of uncertainty have to be accepted in order to progress. In many cases the influence on the result is considered to be relatively insensitive to the range of variation that can confidently be applied. In others, values and interpretations have been adopted to avoid forcing an interpretation from the evidence that invites criticism and weakens the integrity of the work.

The writer considers that the corpus of evidence of vertical-wheeled Roman water-mills has now reached a strength and quality that offer this particular examination, using *hydro-mechanical* analysis, where the disparate sites that have appropriate evidence can be evaluated and the results synthesized to provide us with a clearer picture of technical development and achievement and, if possible, evolution[12]. This is the aim of this paper.

2. The dynamics of a water-mill and the limitations of evidence and analysis.

Of the machines that occur in the Ancient world, the water-mill is surely one of the simplest in construction, but the analysis of its behaviour and performance may be quite complicated. The horizontal-wheeled water-mill has only one rotating integral mass, comprising water-

7 Finley 1985, 56.
8 Droysen 1958, 4, 22, 35-6.
9 Wilson 2002.
10 Seigne 2002a, 14-16; Seigne 2002b, 36-7; Seigne 2002c. One mill is at Jarash, Jordan, and has been provisionally dated to A.D. 527-565. See below site number 5. Another stone-sawing mill has been identified at Ephesos, but is not included within this study.
11 Landels 2000, 7.
12 Much of this work forms the basis of an unpublished dissertation. Spain 1992.

wheel, shaft and top millstone, and its performance is determined by the interaction of the power generated by the wheel and the work involved in overcoming the friction of the millstones and the bearings[13]. In a vertical-wheeled water-mill the machinery and its behaviour is somewhat more complex. There are two rotating masses connected by gears of different sizes so that the masses rotate at different speeds directly related to the mechanical ratio (MR) of the gears. The presence of a geared drive encouraged the exploitation of millstone speed variations. In a relatively slow-moving vertical water-wheel, for example a river mill, the MR would have been made greater in order to increase the speed of the top millstone for effective operational work[14]. Thus the greater rotating mass (the water-wheel, shaft and driver gear) would be moving much slower – in proportion to the MR – than the lighter mass which consisted of the vertical millstone spindle, the driven gear and the top millstone[15]. Of course, with a fixed gear ratio these two rotating masses can be treated as one mass, but the difficulty is in determining the MR, which has to be considered as a variable of unknown quantity in the initial stages of the analysis.

Provided the water flow rate and the dimensions, arrangements and construction of the wheel and head-race are known, or can be reasonably ascertained, the water-wheel can be subjected to theoretical analysis, and its performance can be ascertained for certain conditions. But it is with the determination of the friction losses that we meet with greater difficulty. Bearing resistance, both for the wheel-shaft journals and the footstep bearing, whether of iron or bronze resting in hardwood or stone, present no difficulty and can be calculated using known and established coefficients for sliding friction. The resistance of the gears is more problematic.

Archaeological evidence of Roman gearing systems is rare and consequently our present knowledge of their design and arrangement is very limited. Aside from the fortuitous friction marks of iron-shod gear rims giving us information

Fig. 1.

The Zugmantel Roman lantern gear.

rjs 2005

about their diameters[16], we have the well known Zugmantel six-stave lantern gear published in 1912[17] (See Fig. 1.) that would have been driven by a face gear with wooden contrate pin-type cogs. The next valuable contribution discovered at *Hagendorn*, Switzerland in 1944 but not published until 1991, was the remnants of a wheel-shaft in the end of which were the remains of a spur gear. This spur gear had radial projecting tapered wooden cogs morticed into the shaft and must have engaged with an identical spur-type driven gear[18]. This design of gear is cruder and mechanically less efficient than the contrate face gears that existed at Zugmantel, the mills of the *Athenian Agora* and those at the *Baths of Caracalla*. More recently the remains of a considerable number of Roman wooden gears were found at the bottom of a large well at Barzan, Charente-Maritime, France, apparently related to water-lifting machinery[19]. The fragmented evidence of numerous wooden hubs and cogs suggests that radial spur-gears with round section wooden cogs prevailed at this site. Some of the gears showed evidence of having long radial cogs morticed into the shaft or hub and strengthened by an annular wood ring, through which the engaging ends projected.

There are no known coefficients of sliding friction for the crude rudimentary types of gears that we are dealing with. However, the best projections that can be made show that the combined friction losses for the bearings and gears represent a small part of the whole friction in the mill[20]. (See

13 Primarily the footstep bearing carrying the vertical shaft, but there would be some resistance caused by the neck seal, where the shaft passes through the lower millstone.

14 The speed at which the Romans operated their water-powered millstones is an interesting question. The millstone speed of a horizontal water-wheel is more predictable because the machine was gearless and there are fewer variables to deal with. Lewis considers that they normally rotate at around 60 rpm and Smith suggests that under a 4ft head a three foot diameter wheel would revolve at 50 rpm. Lewis 1997, 47; Smith 1983/4. Whilst they must have varied, these speeds are probably of the right magnitude. In vertical -wheeled geared water-mills the option for greater millstone speed was always available, no matter what the hydraulic arrangement was. The writer has always favoured the concept that in these geared mills the miller would have been influenced by the obvious prevalent comparator, the quern and the ungeared horizontal mill, both perhaps rotating at 60 rpm. This speed he would surely match and probably exceed to gain greater production.

15 See Appendix Three for illustrations of general terminology.

16 Found at the mills in the Athenian Agora and the Baths of Caracalla. Parsons 1936; Schiøler and Wikander 1983.

17 Jacobi 1912, 89-90, Text abb. 44, Taf. xvii. This was a complete specimen still attached to its vertical iron millstone spindle with a two-winged rynd on the top, dated to the second half of the 2nd c. A.D. The spindle was found at the bottom of a well of a *vicus* house associated with a Roman hill-top fort by the German *limes* and was probably not water-powered, but its design is of singular value to the historian. *Pers. comms.* Prof. D. Baatz of the Saalburgmuseum.

18 Gähwiler and Speck 1991, 48, 49 and 62. See below site number 20.

19 The writer is indebted to Prof. Alain Bouet for this information. Coadic and Bouet 2005, 37.

20 This appeared to be confirmed by the full-scale replication of a Roman water-lifting machine built and operated at the Museum of London during 2003, co-designed by the writer. The machine has two similar sized contrate face gears with peg-type cogs and iron journals in oak bearings that can be moved very easily.

below, Section 3). It is the millstone that absorbs perhaps 90% of all friction losses and in the calculation of the power necessary to drive a pair of millstones, the coefficient of friction of motion[21] is critical, having great effect upon the result. Millstones have a complex behaviour influenced by several variables, some embodied in their design and others in the condition and flow rate of the grain. Unfortunately our knowledge of millstone behaviour, especially the earlier cruder profiles and dressing styles of Roman stones, is virtually nil. It is strange that there appears to be no established theory for the behaviour of working millstones. Even when the corn milling industry reached its peak, when the energy forms of water, wind and steam power were widespread and much in evidence to the enquiring minds of Victorian engineers, the subject of the performance and power requirements of millstones appears to have been more or less ignored.

Because of its vesicular nature, hardness and tenacity, lava stone is a first class material for grinding grain. Before the discovery of quartzose stones in the La-Ferte-Sous Jouare region of the Department of Seine, these lava stones were considered to be the best available. There were several ancient quarries yielding trachytic basalt lava, which the Romans exploited for centuries in Italy[22] and especially Germany, in the Rhine valley, near Mayen[23] west of Coblenz. In later periods the Mayen quarry and others in the area continued to provide millstones and querns for English corn mills; this grey/black lava stone became known as 'Cullin' stone after Cologne. Of all the different stones used for grain milling, lava stone was probably the most used and has been found in many provinces of the Empire. It was for this reason that the writer decided that lava stones should be used in an experiment to determine the coefficient of friction for Roman-style millstones.

3. Hydro-mechanical analysis.

The modern history of technology classifies the vertical water-wheel into three broad types, the undershot, breastshot and overshot[24]. For the student of Roman water-mills these terms are imperfect and can be misleading. In the modern overshot, water approaches the wheel level with the top or slightly higher, so that its velocity is similar to that of the wheel's rim, and enters the buckets, passing over the wheel-shaft – hence its name. The power developed is due solely to the weight of the water, with the buckets designed to hold as much water for as long as possible. The distinction between breastshot and undershot is much less clear. If we adopt the simplified method of classifying by water flow relative to the wheel-shaft as a datum, then the breast type is an undershot. This confusion is increased where the head of water approaching a wheel is much lower than the wheel-shaft. At what point does a breast wheel become an undershot? Theory would suggest that distinctions could be based on the question whether the power is generated by weight or by impulse, but the modern terminology of classification does not reflect this. In fact, in relation to Roman vertical water-wheels it is misleading and often inappropriate. We have several examples of Roman wheels where the head of water is so high above the wheel that we have doubts as to whether it passed below or above the wheel-shaft. Furthermore, a classification using the direction of flow relative to the wheel-shaft tells us nothing about how the water was applied and harnessed. Within this study the terms overshot, breastshot and undershot have been used only when there is certainty of the arrangement. To avoid confusion, the classification of water-wheels used in this study is based upon the two components of water-power, the impulse (caused by velocity) and the weight (caused by gravity) of the water. Having regard to the known Roman water-mills, it is suggested that the study of the water-mill sites should progress from those using weight of water only, to those using impulse, moving from low-head to high-head accelerated head-races.

To facilitate a full hydro-mechanical analysis of a vertical-wheeled water-mill, the archaeological evidence needs to provide us with **first**, the *hydraulic data* including (a) head, bed inclination, cross-sections and material of the head-race (b) depth of water flow (c) the size of the water-wheel and its position relative to the head-race, and **second**, the *mechanical data* including the diameter, thickness, inclination of the grinding face, and material of the top millstone. An indication of the gear sizes would indicate the MR that would render the analysis more accurate, but such information is rarely provided from the archaeology. In the absence of this information, different MR's can be entered into the calculations as can an allowance for the friction of the gears and bearings. From the hydraulic data, the power

21 As distinct from the friction of rest, where a greater force is required to start a body from a state of rest than merely to keep it in motion.
22 A vesicular grey leucitite lava, having white inclusions, which appears to have been popular in Italy. Wilson 2003, 87-8.
23 Röder 1972, 35-46; Crawford and Röder 1955, 29, 68-75.
24 Within these divisions there are other variations, such as pitch-back and Poncelet, which need not concern us.

developed at different wheel speeds can be determined; and from the mechanical data, the friction absorbed, again at different wheel speeds and MR's, can be assessed. When these are combined on one graph of power v. speed the balance of power can be identified. Unfortunately, few ancient water-mill sites provide sufficient evidence to allow a complete hydro-mechanical analysis. However, several other sites provide limited evidence that nonetheless allows us an insight into the design of the machinery and its potential performance.

For water-wheels that are powered by weight only, where the water is applied to the top of a bucket wheel, simplified calculations can be made concerning its potential power. Bearing in mind that in this type of wheel as much water as possible is held by the wheel for as long as possible, one approach we can use is to simply limit our calculation of potential power using the fall or head of water[25], the rate of the water flow and an efficiency factor applicable to such wheels[26]. But we need to be cautious with the efficiency factors we apply to wheels driven solely by weight, because they have been evolved from late eighteenth and nineteenth century experiments undertaken by Victorian engineers. Reynolds provides us with an excellent summary of the history of the theoretical and experimental analysis of the efficiency of the vertical water wheel[27], which demonstrates the bewildering variations in the coefficients proposed by numerous engineers. For 'traditional' wooden water-wheels a consensus would appear to be 15-35% efficiency for undershot wheels and 50-70% for overshots[28]. The writer suggests that a figure of not more than 60% might be appropriate for Roman wheels driven by weight only. A far more reliable and detailed determination of potential power can be calculated using a space diagram where the wheel and its buckets are drawn to scale. The torque for each bucket is evaluated by the position and magnitude of the downward force from the weight of water acting vertically downwards from the centre of gravity of the water. The total torque generated is the summation of all the elements[29]. The disadvantage of this method is that the number and shape of the buckets has to be assumed, as does the speed of the wheel. A further assumption is that the water is laid on the wheel at roughly the same velocity as that of the perimeter

of the wheel, for a higher water velocity would create impulse from the kinetic energy. In recent centuries, experimentation showed that there was an advantage when the water entered the top of the wheel at a slightly greater velocity than the rim[30].

Where there is a head of water above the wheel the velocity of free-falling water can be determined easily but where there is a substantial head above the wheel, there will clearly be an impulse effect upon the wheel in addition to the gravity effect of the buckets, and other methods of analysis have to be used. The revolving wheel is also affected by centrifugal force, so that the surface of the water is curved following a radius from an origin on a vertical line above the axis of rotation. This can be used on a scale drawing of the wheel to determine the spillage losses due to centrifugal force at a known speed. Having determined the torque we may then, knowing the wheel speed, calculate the horse-power.

For water-wheels that are powered solely by impulse, where the water strikes radial floats or paddles at any position on the wheel's rim, the calculations to determine power are well known and suitable equations can be found in most text books devoted to hydraulics[31]. Essentially impulse power is related to change in the velocity of the water, that is, the difference between the velocities at entry to and exit from the wheel. According to theory the best velocity for the wheel is when the floats are travelling at half the water speed, for the efficiency is then at a maximum of 50%. But this formula for under-shot or impulse wheels does not allow for such things as back pressure on the floats, hydraulic jump before the wheel, or the effectiveness of applying and limiting the water to the floats and reducing leakage or bypass to a minimum. In practice, the most efficient mean velocity for the floats has been found to be slightly less than half the water velocity. Many eighteenth century engineers conducted their own experiments to establish the optimum velocity but the results of John Smeaton's work was probably the most reliable. He found that the wheel velocity averaged 0.4 of the water velocity and approached 0.5 with the sluice wide open[32]. This optimum wheel speed, which has been taken as 0.425, at which we assume maximum power was generated, affects

25 Strictly speaking, the head is the fall from the bed of the head-race immediately in front of the wheel, to the water surface below the wheel in the tail-race. The larger the wheel between these limits, the more efficient it is in generating the potential power.
26 As an example, Landels used this simple method to calculate the potential power of the Barbegal wheels with a realistic result. Landels 2000, 21, 22.
27 Reynolds 1983.
28 The engineer John Smeaton apparently obtained a 65% mechanical efficiency on overshot water-wheels; Coles-Finch suggests 60% and Bradley 68%. Test cases are rare but John Farey quotes a water-wheel installed by Smeaton at Griff in Warwickshire, which proved to have a mechanical efficiency of nearly 66%. Smeaton 1759; Coles Finch 1928, 147; Bradley 1912; Farey 1827, 300-304.
29 The result can also be determined by graphical resolution using a polar diagram and funicular polygram. Industrial Archaeology of Watermills and Waterpower, 1975, 56-60.
30 Lea 1916, 285.
31 Lea 1916, 268; Weisbach 1877, 205.
32 Smeaton 1759, 101-124.

Fig. 2.

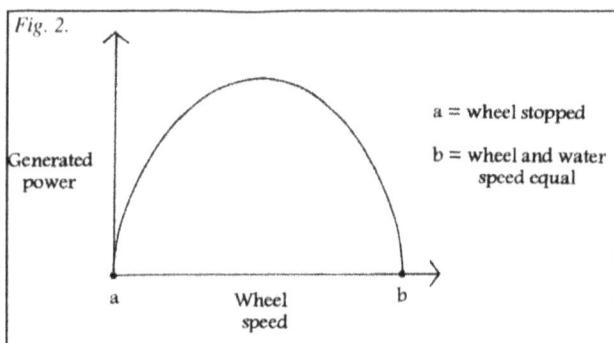

Fig. 2.

our calculations in two ways. First, it influences the assumed depth of water in front of the wheel[33] that is used in the hydraulic equation sequence in order to determine velocity and flow rate. Secondly, it will provide the speed of the water-wheel when determining the power generated. The impulse effect is greatest when the wheel is stationary and the water fastest. But then the speed of the wheel is zero, and therefore so is the horsepower, which is proportional to the product of torque and rotational speed. So we have the following relationship between power and wheel speed (see Fig. 2).

An important factor where the power is generated by impulse is the velocity of the water striking the wheel, especially when there is a high hydraulic head or the head-race is designed to promote an acceleration of the flow. All accelerated head-races have inclined beds whose declivity can either be a constant or variable gradient. When the head-race is delivered by an inclined wooden trough[34] the analysis is concerned with that portion of the race between the point where critical flow[35] occurs, and where deceleration occurs at the tangential intercept. This provides us with the final velocity of application into the wheel allowing for specific energy in the head-race, resistance to flow and acceleration due to the free drop between the trough and wheel. For convenience and simplification of the hydraulic calculations it is sometimes possible to limit the enquiry to the flow rate that provides the maximum effect on the wheel – the capacity of either the head-race or the wheel. But where there was a variable gradient the calculations to determine the velocity of application can be complex. The equation sequence uses several hydraulic formulae and determination of the effect

of head-race friction on the velocity involving trial and error feedbacks.

An alternative and slightly simplified method of calculating the power generated by impulse on a submerged paddle is provided by the formula;

$$\text{Horsepower (HP)} = 1.341 \text{ A V (V-}v\text{)} \, v \text{[36]},$$

where A is the area of impact (m²), V the velocity of the water at impact (m/s), and v is the average velocity of the paddle (m/s) which is taken as 0.425V.

To establish the magnitude of typical bearing losses a detailed analysis was undertaken by the writer of the *Haltwhistle Mill*, to the extent of designing the entire wheel (both clasp-armed and radial-armed options), shaft, journals and gears in order to obtain realistic bearing reactions[37]. Allowances were made for the different moisture contents of the wheel and shaft, and alternate materials for the journals (bronze and iron) and bearings (wood and stone) were considered. The total friction losses for all three bearings[38] represented between 3 – 4% of the total wheel-shaft power transmitted.

The power lost through transmission via wooden gears is most difficult to calculate. An efficiency figure is normally employed for modern gearing[39] that is applied to the torque being transmitted, but these coefficients are for gears with high precision machine-cut profiles moving at a much higher velocity than those that we are dealing with. It is considered that a 5% transmission loss would be reasonable to allow for the rudimentary form of gearing involved in our analyses.

The absence of established theory for millstone behaviour[40] means that predicting the performance of Roman or other early style millstones is very difficult. However, the study of the power absorbed by millstones can be calculated by using formulae associated with clutches, where the surfaces under consideration occupy an annulus. Where the surfaces are inclined to a plane normal[41] to the axis of rotation, as in Roman millstones and querns, the formula derived for cone clutches is particularly relevant. Using this formula it is possible to calculate the torque required to power a pair of millstones knowing the size and weight of the top stone, the

33 If we assume that the body of water striking the float is slowed down by the float so that its cross-section expands to match the face area of the float, then theoretically, its depth when approaching will be 0.425 that of the float. Some allowance has to be made for leakage underneath and on the sides of the float.
34 Rarely found but we can confidently assume they existed due to the physical arrangements e.g, Athenian Agora, Baths of Caracalla etc.
35 Critical flow occurs where there is a change from laminar to non-laminar conditions, where the law of resistance changes. This means that the gradients and sections upstream of this point do not affect the hydraulic conditions downstream.
36 Industrial Archaeology of Watermills and Waterpower, 56.
37 Spain 1976.
38 Friction coefficients were used assuming that the wheel-shaft journals were iron on hard wood bearings and the iron footstep spindle rested on a stone bearing. Simple lubrication of either water or animal fats was allowed for.
39 Machinery's Handbook, 1944, 12, 502.
40 For a discussion on the theory of millstone design and behaviour see Spain 1992, 46-57; Schoonhoven 1978, 269-283.
41 At right angles or perpendicular to.

inclination of the grinding face and most important, the coefficient of grinding. The clutch formula can be expressed in one of two ways. The first has been derived on the basis that constant wear occurs across the friction faces, and the second method is based on constant pressure existing across the friction faces. In theory, the formula for constant pressure produces a higher torque (T_P) result than the constant wear method (T_W). For example, when the rim diameter is five times greater than the eye diameter, a typical relationship for Roman millstones, T_P is 14.8% greater than T_W. However, the question as to whether or not working millstones suffer constant pressure or constant wear (or some other mode of mechanical behaviour) is most difficult to resolve[42], and it is therefore suggested that an average value (T_A) be taken. When the average torque for the millstones is established this can be related to power by using the standard formula.

Therefore for a given pair of millstones whose diameter, coefficient of grinding and surface inclination can be assumed as constant, horse power is proportional to the product of speed and weight, thus;-

$$H.P \propto speed \times weight$$

We must also be aware of another dominant influence on the power required to drive a millstone. Roman discoidal top millstones have been found over 20 cm thick and we have examples of them being used until they were discarded at between 3 and 6 cm thick[43]. Because the torque necessary to power a millstone is directly proportional to its weight, it would be misleading to limit a power analysis using a millstone that was at or near the end of its useful life. As a top-stone became thinner and lighter[44], the same water-wheel would create a potentially faster machine, which gave the miller the option of increasing millstone speed and thus output. Our analyses must therefore pay regard to millstone life cycles.

We have recognized that the coefficient of grinding is

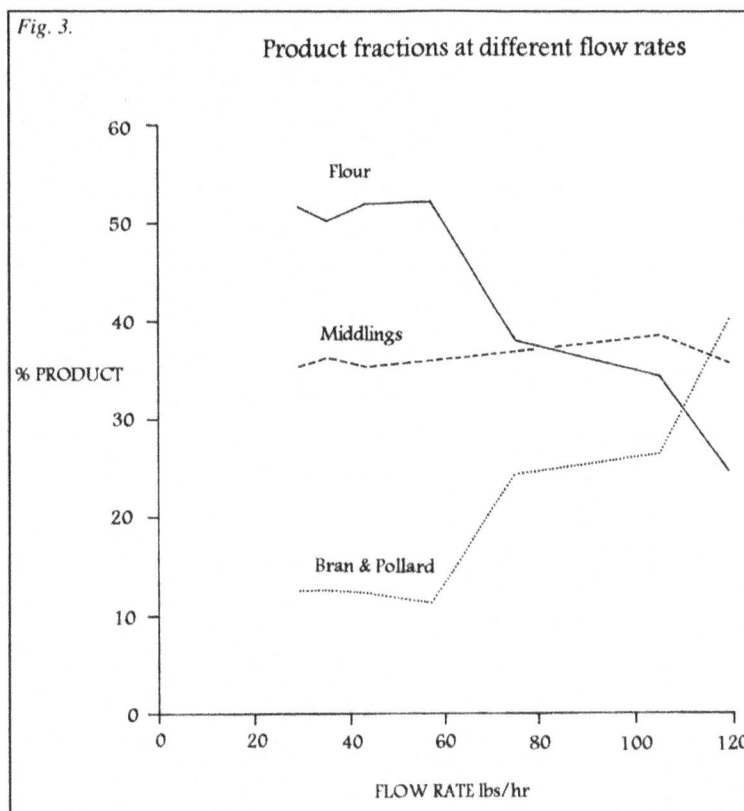

Fig. 3.

Product fractions at different flow rates

% PRODUCT

Flour

Middlings

Bran & Pollard

FLOW RATE lbs/hr

important because it is the dominant component of the power necessary to maintain motion of the mill machinery. During 1976 the writer undertook friction tests using fragments of furrowed Roman lava millstones in non-rotary experiments with grain and meal[45]. The crude nature of these tests and the limitations imposed by the fragments of stone left much to be desired. The writer therefore resolved to undertake a more refined laboratory test using 600 mm diameter rotary lava millstones replicated in design to match typical dressed Roman stones[46]. During 1985 he designed and commissioned the making of a pair of millstones from Mayen near Coblenz[47]. These are the lava fields that the Romans exploited for centuries for their millstones and querns. At Mayen the porosity of the lava varies according to the depth and position of the deposits; the deeper the deposits the less the porosity and the smaller the gas cavities become. The millstones were taken from the same strata that the Romans used, and the design of the grinding faces was influenced by extant Romano-British stones and specimens in the Saalburg Museum.

42 For a discussion on this see Spain 1992, 49-51.
43 Parsons 1936. In the Athenian Agora mill, all of the six stones found were remarkably thin, taken to the limit of their strength and grinding effectiveness.
44 The implication of these machinery life-cycles, with millstones changing much more frequently than water-wheels and head-races is that a miller could gradually change the size of his stones and his gear ratio to suite the power of his wheel.
45 Experiments conducted during March 1976 at Mid-Kent College of Further and Higher Education Maidstone. Spain 1976, 5-8, unpublished report. The coefficient of friction was calculated at 0.4309 using dressed Mayen lava stones and English wheat. The coefficient for grain was 0.231 and meal 0.532. The arithmetic average was 0.382 but the coefficient was calculated at the radius where the surface area outside was equal to that area inside.
46 For a report of the experiment and the results see Spain 1992, 75-119.
47 The writer was fortunate in gaining the help of Frau Röder, wife of the late Dr. Röder, an acknowledged expert on the history and development of the Mayen lava quarries.

The grinding experiment was facilitated by a rig-table, on which the millstones sat, driven from a 1.5 h.p. motor and integral gear box, via pulleys and gears. The driver gear was a contrate face gear with pin-type wooden cogs engaging a six-stave lantern gear[48]. The millstone spindle with a two-winged rynd,[49] was supported via a footstep bearing carried on an adjustable bridge-tree to allow gap adjustment between the stones[50]. British wheat was used for the grinding experiment. Its moisture content was measured during the experiment and found to be 16%. Various samples of meal were taken at different feeding rates[51] at constant speed and with the full weight of the top stone. The results were analysed[52]. Fig. 3 shows the product fractions at different flow rates.

Table A below provides a comparison with typical modern products. The natural capacity of these stones was 60 lbs/hr so this can be recognized as their critical or optimum flow rate above which the product becomes rapidly coarser. This comparison shows that the meal coming from the Roman type lava stones is much coarser than modern millstone products and that the product of Roman millstones was likewise undoubtedly coarse and probably not returned to the stones for refinement, a conclusion supported by the coarseness of the sieves used and the lack of evidence of grinding more than once[53].

Table A comparisons with typical modern products

PROCESS	% PRODUCT		
	Flour [Dunst & flour]	**Middlings** [Semolina & fine middlings]	**Bran & Pollard** [Bran & wheatings]
Modern stoneground wholemeal (English wheat)	75.7	15.7	8.6
Modern roller mill wholemeal (English & Canadian)	83.5	12.5	4.0
Roman-style millstones (English)	52.4	36.2	11.4

The modern classification of products is shown in brackets.

During the grinding experiment one sample was ground twice and failed significantly to reduce the general coarseness of the product, suggesting that the stones impose a natural limit on the fineness of the product and that the dress of the stones needed to achieve further reduction was different from that required for whole grain. With the normal dress the throat of the stone, which is used to crack and reduce whole grains, would have no effect on meal. If the coarser fraction were put through the milling process again, the stones needed to be a different pair dressed accordingly. Although it is possible that in those corn milling establishments having more than one set of millstones, sieving followed by further grinding of the coarser products may have occurred, it seems unlikely, for as Jasny points out, repeated grinding is far too important not to have been mentioned in the sources. He reasons with conviction that the grades of product given by Pliny were uncommon, indeed rare, probably found only in the largest cities, and that the dominant product was wholemeal[54].

Using a laboratory wattmeter connected into the power circuit, separate induction tests were conducted to determine no-load and loaded conditions. The output power of the shaft was then calculated at 0.51 H.P. (381 w) at a speed of 84.6 rpm. Using the constants relating to the Westree top millstone of weight (143 lbs), rim diameter (1.968 ft.), eye diameter (0.164 ft.) and grinding face inclination of 9°, the values of T_W, T_P and thereby T_A, the average torque, were determined. Substituting these values into the horsepower formula we established that the coefficient of friction (μ) has the value of 0.351. It is interesting to compare this result with the average coefficient determined from the non-rotary grinding experiments conducted earlier by the writer. In that experiment the coefficient for grain was 0.231 and for meal 0.532, suggesting that the figure 0.351 is in the right order.

There are apparently no recently published values for the coefficient of friction of corn grinding although two or three earlier sources provide figures and it is possible to derive values from published engine tests[55]. However, these figures relate to modern millstones, of different materials and dress from those of the Roman period. This coefficient of 0.351

48 Based on the unique Zugmantel Roman lantern gear. See Fig. 1 above. Jacobi 1912, Taf xvii. The rectangular cog form shown by Jacobi on the driver gear is considered by the writer to be based on relatively modern gears and is not Roman.
49 The Zugmantel and Romano-British specimens and numerous millstones with rynd cavities confirm the design.
50 The operation of the Westree rig was most interesting but the various minor problems encountered need not be related here.
51 Seven different feeding rates from 29 – 117 lbs/hr.
52 By Dr. Simon Hook, Principal Scientific Officer of the Flour and Baking Research Association at Chorleywood, Hertfordshire. For more information on the analysis of samples see Spain 1992, 106-11.
53 Jasny 1944, 150, 151. See also White 1984, 67.
54 Jasny 1944, 138, 151 and 155.
55 For example, Sutcliffe states that a 30 hp engine will power five pairs of constantly working French burr stones, four foot eight inches in diameter at a speed of 95-100 rpm when the grain is moderately dry. Making assumptions concerning stone thickness, density etc, this equates to a coefficient of grinding of 0.069. Sutcliffe 1816, 285, 384. Kozmin also states 1/20 (0.05) to 1/22 (0.045). Kozmin 1921, 193. Fabrè, as quoted by d'Aubuisson, from his work upon the mills of Provence, estimated the resistance for milling wheat, supposing it to act at two-thirds of the radius of the runner stone, as 1/22 (0.045) of its weight. d'Aubuisson also quotes Belidor as establishing a coefficient of 0.0286. d'Aubuisson 1852, 447.

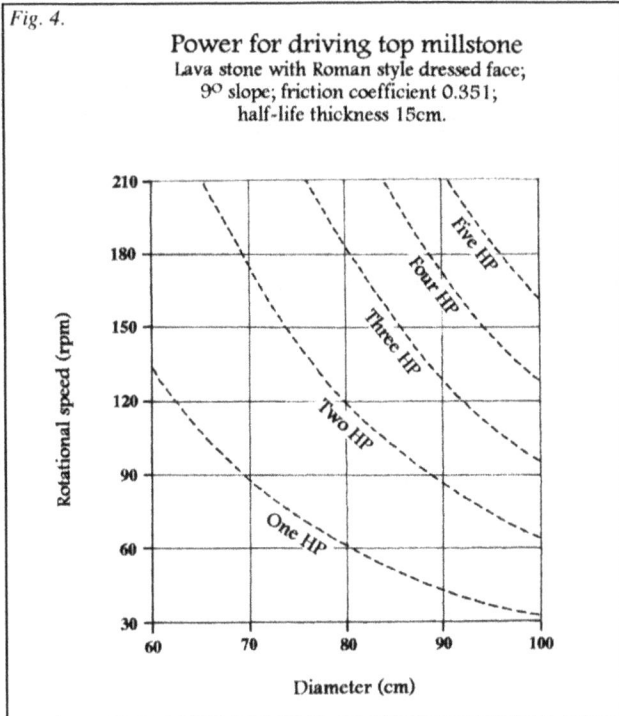

Fig. 4.

Power for driving top millstone
Lava stone with Roman style dressed face;
9° slope; friction coefficient 0.351;
half-life thickness 15cm.

relates to lava stone; how it would vary for other types of stone is unknown. However, the writer would venture to suggest that other grinding stones having similar coarseness and homogeneity of structure suitable for reducing grain to meal, probably have similar coefficients of friction.

The Westree experiment was conducted with a pair of millstones whose grinding faces had been recently dressed with furrows. Thus the coefficient determined relates to a pair of stones in good condition, 'young' in the dressing life-cycle. As the furrows of a stone wear away, their cutting action and contribution to the reduction process diminishes[56]. If the furrows were allowed to disappear the product fraction would shift markedly towards a coarser output, and recent milling experience tells us that the overall output would be reduced[57]. Despite the fact that some sites yield well-worn Roman millstones, many without any signs of furrows, the writer holds the view that most millers, certainly those using water-mills with discoidal millstones, would probably have regularly dressed their stones with furrows to increase their efficiency and produce a finer product using less power[58].

Having established a reliable coefficient of friction of grinding for lava millstones, and noting that the working millstones absorb some 90% of the water-wheel's generated power, we can now take an overview of the power necessary to drive typical Roman millstones. In the following analysis for discoidal lava millstones, the horsepower is expressed in terms of stone speed and rim diameter. See Fig. 4. The calculations allow for an inclined grinding face of 9°, an eye to rim diameter ratio of 1.0 to 5.0[59], and the coefficient of friction derived from the Westree experiment using typical Roman style dressed grinding faces. Allowance also has to be made for the major variable of weight of the top stone, which varies from a maximum when new to a minimum when discarded. The power curves shown are based on the weight of a top stone having half-life, that is a thickness occurring mid-way between new and abandonment[60]. The half-life thickness has been chosen as 15 cm[61]. The great majority of Roman millstones range in diameter from 65 – 90 cm, with a mean of 80 cm[62]. The average thickness of approximately 50 abandoned top millstones found at various sites was 8 cm. For illustration purposes, if we assume that a top millstone varied in thickness from 21 cm (new) to 8 cm (discarded, broken or moved to the bottom as a bed-stone), then an 80 cm diameter stone revolving at 60 rpm would require 1.4 HP (new), 1.0 HP (half-life) and 0.53 HP (end of life).

The Westree experiments showed that the millstones absorbed 0.51 h.p. when their throughput was 60 lbs/hr. (27.2 kg/hp.hr.). Their product/power ratio is therefore 117.0 lbs/hp.hr. (53.0 kg/hp.hr.) It is interesting to compare this product/power ratio against modern millstone figures. The following information, which relates to the stone milling of wheat using disc stones, is associated with experiments undertaken by millers of different nationalities, nearly all during the nineteenth century. For most of these experiments the operating conditions are not declared and information on the type of wheat, moisture content, fineness of product, millstone speed, dress and size is invariably missing. The type of stone, except in one or two instances, is not declared, but the customary stone used for wheat throughout this period, confirmed by many of the texts in

---

56 Schoonhoven provides a most appropriate analogy; fresh cut furrows are like a sharp knife cutting through bread; when the furrows become worn, it is like using a blunt knife on bread. Schoonhoven 1978, 276.
57 Freese 1971, 112.
58 The practice of dressing stones may have developed when the inclination of grinding surfaces became flatter as discoidal millstones evolved from Pompeian.
59 An average for Roman top stones from the Agora, Ickham, the Palatine Hill in Rome (See Wilson 2003) and others from the writer's records.
60 Cessation of use as a top stone can occur when either (a) it becomes too thin to provide sufficient weight for grinding, or (b) when the rynd cavity breaks through the top surface so that the rynd can no longer support the stone, or (c) the stone breaks, or (d) it is moved to act as a bed-stone. It should be noted however that we do have some unusual and rare Roman top millstones that have been found in Britannia with the rynd cavity cut right through.
61 The average thickness of top millstones that have apparently been discarded at numerous Roman sites including Agora, Ickham, and the Palatine Hill in Rome is 8.25 cm. If we assume the thickness of new stones ranged from say 20 – 25 cm, their half-life thickness is close to 15 cm.
62 The mean diameter has been based on a sample of over 70 Roman millstones, including those from the Janiculum, Barbegal, Ickham, Agora and Palatine sites plus specimens from the Saalburg Museum and Museum of London.

which these figures feature, was French burr[63]. The use of these figures for comparison purposes must therefore be treated with some caution[64]. A summary of these comparisons is given in Table B.

We should note that the few writers who addressed the subject of flour milling were often describing exemplary examples of best practice which the great number of mills, especially rural wind, water and steam powered, were striving to match. The figure given by Freese, which probably relates to a production/power ratio at the millstone spindle of, say 25 lbs/hp.hr, could be said to represent flour milling at its peak. This low production/power ratio is supported by the evidence from a miller who operated 1.067 m. diameter wheat stones in the early twentieth century that could process 168 lbs of wheat in an hour,

which equates to between 33 – 42 lbs/hp.hr[77]. One final comparison is that provided by Wulff who declares product/power ratios ranging from 29.7 – 33 lbs/hp.hr.[78]

These lower product/power ratios can be considered to relate to modern millstones from say c.1850 onwards when millers were seeking increasingly refined products using carefully designed and dressed grinding faces. It is interesting to note that it is only some of the older figures that approach the Westree ratio of 117 lbs/hp.hr. Jasny appears to have anticipated the Westree result when he concluded the coarse meal coming from Roman stones needed 'no more than 1/2 hp. per bushel' i.e, 118 lbs/hp.hr.

Although some of the modern figures are difficult to confirm as being accurate comparators in view of our ignorance of the operating conditions etc, their general

Table B Production/Power Ratios (Water-powered stones unless stated)

Source	lbs/hp. hour	Conditions if known
Westree Rig	117.0	
D'Aubuisson de Voisins[65]	55.1	Wheel-shaft power[76].
D'Aubuisson de Voisins	over 82.7	Power at the millstones.
Freese[66] (England)	16.8	Windmill – gross power.
Belidor & Navier[67]	108.4	
M.Hashette[68] (Nr. Paris)	73.2	Wheel-shaft power.
Tardy & Piobert[69] (Toulouse)	5.6 – 59.1	Power at the millstones.
M.Egen[70] (Westphalia)	46.5	
Kozmin[71] (Russia)	94.5 – 126.0	From 35 –56 ins. Dia. Stones.
Buissan[72]	30.3	Burrs, no exhaust.
Dedrick[73]	51.0 – 78.5	Power at millstones.
Farey[74]	approx. 59.0	Steam; grinding & dressing.
Usher[75]	59.0	

63 A freshwater quartz found among beds of freshwater limestone in the Paris basin at La Ferté-sous-Jouare east of Paris and Epernon west of Paris. The stone was quarried in small pieces, trimmed, fitted and cemented together in plaster of Paris, and considered the best for grinding wheat. It was very popular in the last three centuries but we have no evidence that it was used in Roman times for milling.

64 We must beware of making comparisons between ancient and modern practice; eg, Wilson compares the output of Barbegal. millstones with modern Swedish and Bosnian mills – an innocent but misleading exercise. Wilson 2002.

65 d'Aubuisson de Voisins, see Bennett 1852, 448.

66 Freese 1971, 111.

67 d'Aubuisson, see Bennett 1852, quoting Belidor & Navier 1819, 464.

68 d'Aubuisson de Voisins, 448.

69 d'Aubuisson de Voisins, 448.

70 d'Aubuisson de Voisins, 448.

71 Kozmin 1921, 190.

72 Freese 1971, 112.

73 Dedrick 1924, 309. Derived from a modern mill power requirement varying between 0.26 – 0.40 hp. per 196 lbs. in 24 hrs and allowing that 40% of the power is needed by the millstones. The writer disagrees with Jasny's calculations using Dedrick's figures. See Jasny 1944, 157.

74 Farey describes several trials made between the years 1806 and 1811, made with steam engines powering millstones, in most cases declared as French burrs, dressing wheat. In nearly all cases Farey adopts a power rating of one bushel of wheat (59 lbs) an hour per hp. rather than the declared nominal rating of the engine. Farey 1827, 33-75. The same production/power ratio seems to have prevailed in the millwright trade; see Box 1882, 63.

75 Reynolds quotes Usher who writes of studies made around 1800, indicating that it took approximately one horsepower to grind a bushel of wheat (59 lbs) per hour. Reynolds 1983, 173. Usher 1954.

76 Where the power ratio is related to the wind-shaft or the wheel-shaft the production/power ratio for the millstones will be greater than shown, because the gross power will include not only bearing and gear friction losses, but also ancillary machinery including bolting and dressing machines, elevators and conveyors. The proportion of wheel-shaft power taken by millstones will vary from mill to mill and most certainly through time as more machinery appeared during the nineteenth century to help millers to produce increasingly refined products. In the hey-day of flour milling, say from approximately A.D. 1870 onwards, a typical well-fitted flour-mill would have perhaps one half or less of the wheel-shaft power devoted to the millstones, particularly in large mills.

77 Allowing that this pair of stones would be absorbing 4 h.p at most. See Spain and Fuller 1986, 166.

78 Wulff 1966, 398-401. The figures relate to 1.2 m diameter disc stones operating in Persian arubah-style horizontal mills, but they need to be treated with caution.

magnitude shows beyond reasonable doubt that the Westree production/power ratio is considerably higher than that achieved by modern millstones. The analysis of the meal samples shows that this is essentially a reflection of the coarseness of the product. The relationship between power and coarseness of product is disproportionate, so that for a reduction in fineness the power required is proportionally much less, a phenomenon recognized early last century[79]. Thus we may conclude that power required for grinding is proportional to Q (quantity)/f (fineness of particle size)[80].

What factors might influence this product/power ratio accuracy and its application to other Roman mills? The most obvious influence on the production/power ratio is the flow rate itself. From Fig 3, which shows the product fractions at different flow rates, we have identified what appears to be a natural capacity, a flow rate limit, up to which the fractions are fairly constant. Above this there is another range of flow rates where the fractions remain more or less constant, but where the product is very much more coarse. This variation in product refinement relates to a production/power ratio of 147 – 206 lbs/hp.hr. Although the change from the lower flow rate to the greater would be very noticeable to a miller by virtue of the sudden increase in the coarseness of the meal issuing from the stones, we cannot take for granted that the product refinement associated with the lower flow rate was generally adopted. For the purposes of this study the production/power ratio of 117 lbs/hp.hr. has been adopted for lava stones, but if a coarser product was accepted then the production could have been increased by up to 75% using the same power. This fact has great implications for our study.

The other obvious influence on the production/power ratio is the coefficient for grinding.

The size of millstones chosen for the experiment was at the bottom end of the size range for water-powered Roman millstones and this raises the question, would the grinding coefficient have been different with larger diameter stones? During the Westree grinding experiments a sample of meal that had passed through the stones twice showed that no further refinement had taken place, suggesting that the stones had reached the limit of reduction[81]. If this is correct, it also suggests that if the stones had been larger, the product would have been the same. In other words,

refinement is not dependent on size of stone but material and dress. Thus we come to the conclusion that the porosity and nature of lava stones which the Romans employed produces meal that is coarse by modern standards; in other words they are unable to produce fine flour. We can also conclude that if a much larger pair of stones produces the same coarseness of product at the rim, the average coefficient of grinding would be the same as for a smaller pair, such as was used in the Westree experiment.

On the subject of wheat type, it would have been appropriate to have conducted the milling experiments using the unique strains of Emmer and Spelt wheat grown and harvested at Butser Ancient Farm Trust, but this was not possible. What difference this might have made to the results is not clear. From the power formula discussed earlier, theory tells us that provided there is always meal between the stones' faces, and the diameter, speed, dress, weight and other factors remain constant, then the amount of power required is also constant. Under these conditions the work being done at the stone faces on the grain or meal does not change, and greater throughput simply means that the thickness of meal between the stones is greater, and the product spends less time in contact with the stone, resulting in a coarser meal. Thus the same power can be used to produce greater throughput of less refined meal. It has been recognized that a pair of millstones running at constant speed can grind twice the quantity of corn if it is produced as coarse meal for animal food rather than meal containing fine flour[82]. For this to happen, and for the relationship Power α speed x weight to hold true, means that the throughput (Q) must be directly related to the fineness (f) or particle size of the product i.e, an increase in coarseness would facilitate an increase in throughput. A particular pair of millstones will produce a meal whose fineness is limited by the inherent grinding properties of the stone, but determined by the throughput flow rate within limits[83]. Thus if throughput is increased and all other factors are constant, the product will become generally coarser.

So the coefficient of grinding is not a function of product fineness or flow rate, but a property of the stones relating to work done upon the product. A change in grain type or, say, moisture content, should be viewed as affecting the flow rate rather than the coefficient of grinding, i.e, a higher

79 Annales Institut National Agronomique 1910, 2nd series, lx, 309-310.

80 Jesperson has proposed that the grinding capacity of millstones can be related to the peripheral speed of the stone, but the concept does not appear to take account of the effect of weight, dress and product refinement. Smith 1983-4, 82, correspondence from Anders Jesperson to The Newcomen Society.

81 During 1971, the late Dr. Hugh Chapman of the Museum of London conducted milling experiments using a Mayen lava quernstone. He found that it was not possible to re-grind the products following the removal of the finest flour (sieved by a 0.25 mm grid sieve), they were 'too fine already and did not go through the quern'. A second separate experiment confirmed that a very coarse product resulted, which rather perplexed the investigators. The writer concludes that these results indicate a natural limit of reduction for lava stones. (Pers. comms.).

82 Industrial Archaeology of Watermills and Waterpower, Project Technology Handbook, 11, 35.

83 There is clearly a minimum flow limit to keep the stone faces apart, and a maximum flow when the capacity of the stones is exceeded and proper grinding action ceases to take place.

moisture content would require more power and therefore the production/hp.hr. would be reduced. Within the Westree experiments the effect of the grains' moisture content on the power requirements was not determined. Although the 16% moisture content of the wheat that was used was slightly high by modern standards it can probably be compared to the moisture content of grain coming straight from the field or storage[84]. When corn drying was practised, the power requirement for milling would have been somewhat less, though by how much is unknown. As Moritz suggests, for climatic reasons, Roman wheat probably contained less moisture than English wheat[85].

In conclusion the writer considers that taking all things into account, it would be prudent to view the coefficient of grinding provided by the lava stones of the Westree rig as being of the right order of magnitude, although not necessarily exact. The Westree production/power ratio allows us to estimate the production rates of those Roman mills where it is possible to determine the power absorbed by the millstones.

84 English wheat cannot be stored in bulk above a moisture content of 16% or in sacks above 18% without risk of overheating and mould occurring. Simmons 1955, 101.
85 Moritz 1958, 222, Note U.

Fig. 5.

Roman vertical-wheeled water-mills
Location of sites

Chesters Bridge
Willowford Bridge
Haltwhistle
Burn Head
HIBERNIA
BRITANNIA
Nettleton Fleet Tide Mill Lösnich
Ickham GERMANIA
Fullerton
Dasing
Hagendorn
München-Perlach
Saint-Doulchard DACIA
GAUL
Avenches
Martres-de-Veyre ILLYRICUM THRACIA
Barbegal Les Mesclans ASIA
La Bourse Baths of Caracalla MACEDONIA
Saint Pierre Venafro Ephesos
Janiculum Hill Agora
Nahal Tanninim
TARRACONENSIS
Jarash
MARE INTERNUM
NUMIDIA
MAURETANIA

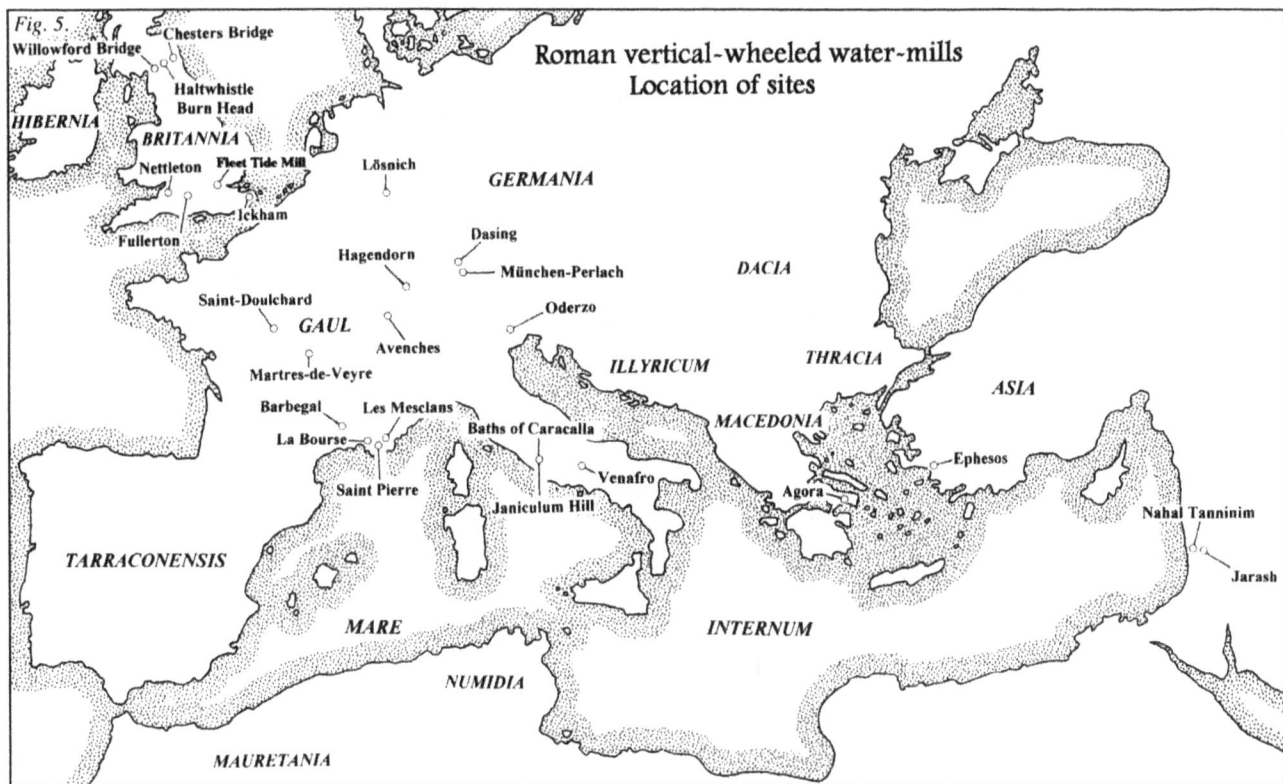

PART TWO – THE SITES

Fig. 5 shows the location of the sites that are discussed below. The general order in which these sites are presented is, first, sites that generated power only by weight of water (often called bucket wheels) followed by those sites where the power is generated by impulse using wheels with radial paddles. Within these two broad categories, there are many sites having little difference in their hydraulic arrangements, so that the order in which they are given is unimportant. Not all Roman water-mill sites are included in this study. Some of those excluded are sites where the evidence, be it a combination of watercourse, millstones or building remains, do not reach the threshold of certainty – and there are many of these, especially in England. Others have been excluded because they contribute little to the objectives of the work, usually because the site evidence is vague or lacks sufficient detail to allow a meaningful interpretation. Two or three sites have been included which may contribute little or nothing to the subject of generated power but their inclusion is merited for the incidental information that they contribute to the overall picture of the technology. At a few sites, where analysis

shows that there have been different phases of building (e.g, *Fullerton*, *Ickham* and the *Baths of Caracalla*), the phases have been separated and presented as individual case studies. Finally, and with some trepidation, the writer must admit of the possibility that he may have overlooked, or simply not found, a Roman vertical-wheeled water-mill, published or un-published, that merits inclusion in this study. Shortly before this work was printed, the writer learnt of five recently found Roman vertical-wheeled water-mill sites[86]; [1] *St. Michel La Garde*, Var (2nd c. A.D.); [2] *Vareilles Pauchan*, Hérault (1st to 2nd c. A.D.); [3] *L'Auribelle-Basse*, Pézenas, Hérault (1st to 3rd c. A.D.); [4] *de la Paludi*, Celano (Aq.); [5] *St. Romain-de-Jalionas*, Isère. The reader will see below that some archaeological discoveries take time to surface into the public domain (e.g, *Haltwhistle Burn Head* (69 years) and *Hagendorn* (47 years) for a variety of reasons. But it would be a misplaced and unfair criticism to complain of such delays; the fact is that without the energies and indomitable spirit of the professional and amateur archaeologists of all nationalities, this study could not have been written.

This study of sites commences with *Barbegal*, the most published and surely the best known of all Roman water-mills. The writer makes no apology for the rather detailed

86 Sites [3] and [5] were the subject of papers presented at Colloque International D'archeologie at Site Pont du Gard 20-23 September 2006; sites [1] [2] and [4] *pers. comms.* from J-P Brun.

and lengthy examination of this site, because certain historical interpretations need to be clarified and developed. *Barbegal* also acts as an exemplar of many of the diagnostic methods used at other sites. In the early parts of the impulse section, wheels having relatively low velocity impacts are presented first, followed by faster wheels. The order towards the end of the section then becomes more distinct as increasingly fast impact velocities occur, leading to high-head, accelerated head-races. The unusual *Venafro* wheel provides a fitting finale to this study of archaeological evidence.

1. Barbegal, Provence, France.

These most impressive remains of a Gallo-Roman corn mill near Arles have understandably attracted the attention of a number of archaeologists, and historians both of economics and technology. Constructed in early 2nd c. A.D. and working until the early 4th c. A.D.[87] the building housed sixteen water-wheels arranged in two parallel cascades down the scarp slope of a hill. (See Fig. 6.) Its limestone walls and aqueduct, hewn from the ancient quarries in the nearby Chaine des Alpilles, have withstood the kind Provençal climate and the stone-robbing of man to leave us enough indisputable evidence, especially in the lower mill chambers, to allow a theoretical reconstruction of its building and machinery. First we need to agree the size and arrangement of the wheels and then the water flow rate.

The depth of the wheel chambers varies from 2.42 m (EIII) to 2.65 m (EII)[88] with an average for the five that can be measured of 2.59 m[89]. Assuming that all wheels were the same diameter, it is wheel chamber EIII that suggests that a wheel diameter of 2.1 m was the probable size, allowing for reasonable underside clearance and an incline for the wooden head-race trough. The width of the wheel chambers

Fig. 6.

Barbegal - General Plan

Fig. 7.

Barbegal – Plan of the lower East side mill chambers   rjs 1989

Fig. 8.

Section through wheel chambers EII and EIII looking East

between the stone walls varies from 1.11 m (EIII) to 1.33 m (EIV), with five of the seven measuring within 1.21 m ± 2 cms[90]. (See Fig. 7.) Of the wheel chambers remaining, two (EII and EIII) have massive calcareous encrustations on the upstream ends of the walls. At the northern end of both chambers the deposits have reduced the clear width between the walls to 0.95 m (EIII) and 0.97 m (EII), a total build-up of 24-28 cm. As Benoit comments[91] there are no rubbing marks of the wheels on the deposits, unlike those that Parsons observed in the *Agora Mill* in Athens[92]. Allowing for side clearance, a wheel width of 0.75 m (0.7

---

87 Leveau 1995, 116-144. Originally thought to have been built in the 4th c. A.D. now identified as early 2nd c. A.D. work.
88 All measurements and observations are the result of a site examination made by the writer in 1986.
89 Benoit says that they are all constant at 2.60 m deep, which they are not. Benoit 1940, 46.
90 Benoit records their width as 1.10 m and presumably only measured EI, whilst Sellin states that the stone chambers were 1.0 m wide, clearly an error, unless he measured between the calcareous encrustations that occur in chambers EII and EIII. Sellin 1981, 420.
91 Benoit 1940, 50.
92 Parsons 1936. Similar evidence occurs at Ephesos and Les Mesclans.

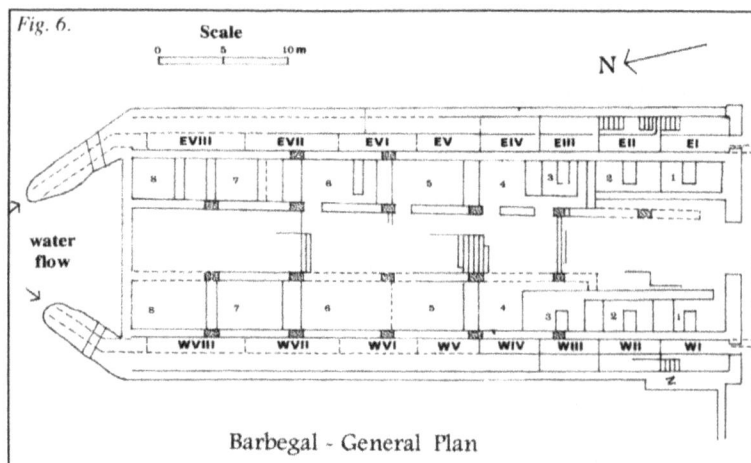

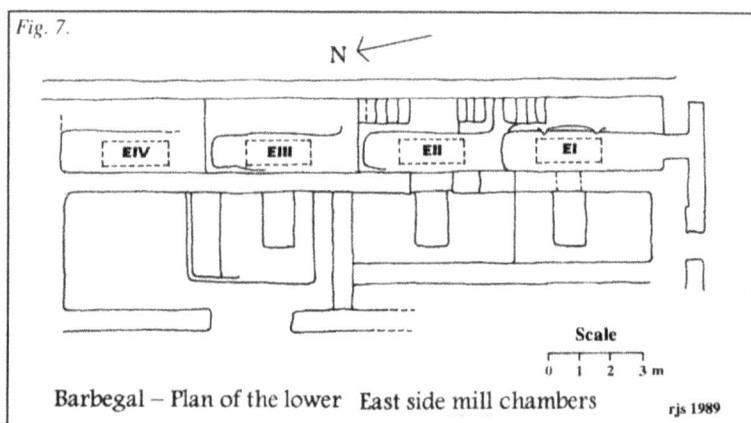

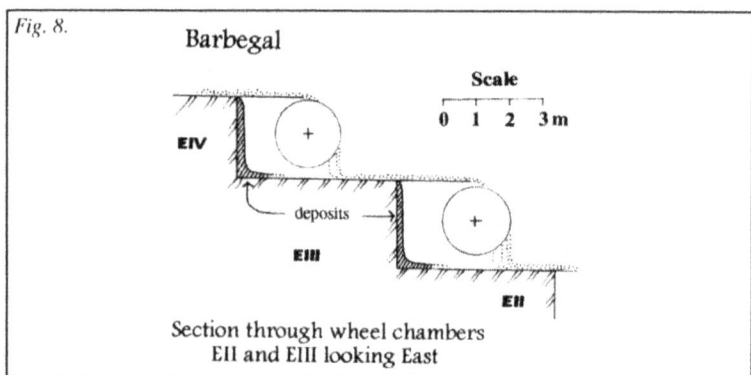

m inside the shrouds) would have been appropriate[93].

The consensus of historians is that the water passed over the shafts of the *Barbegal* wheels[94], although one or two express a reservation[95]. (See Fig. 8.) If the water passed below the wheel-shaft, then it must have been directed onto the wheel via a steeply inclined wooden trough. The velocity of application would be something approaching 4 m/s, which would rule out a gravity wheel with buckets; it would require a wheel with radial floats whose power would be generated solely by impulse. Whilst this arrangement would probably provide satisfactory power, the site evidence indicates that it was improbable for two reasons. First, the geometry of the wheel-pit shows us that the trough would need a declivity of approximately 50-55° from the horizontal[96], virtually a tangent to the rim of the wheel for effective impulse on the radial floats. Secondly, even if this arrangement prevailed, which is most unlikely, how did they divert the water in order to stop the wheel? It could not have been done by raising the lower end of the trough, for the water would not clear the wheel. Neither could it have been achieved by dropping the end of the trough to a near-vertical position, for the volume and the velocity of the water approaching would have probably thrown it forward so as to strike the wheel. Neither of these alternatives would have created the build-up of deposits that we now witness on the north wall of the wheel chambers below the trough. If impulse wheels had been installed, surely the builders would have inclined the last metre or so of the chamber floors, to accelerate the water towards the next wheel?

With the water being applied to the crown of the wheel via a trough, there seem to be two possible alternatives for controlling the volume using a bypass arrangement. One way would be to use an extension that slid forward from the underside of the trough to project the water over and clear of the wheel. Another method suggested by Sellin was to deflect the water through an opening in the trough. It is unnecessary to go into detail about these alternatives because they have no influence on the power calculations, but the writer tends to favour the latter method because of the substantial calcareous deposits in the north end of the chambers[97].

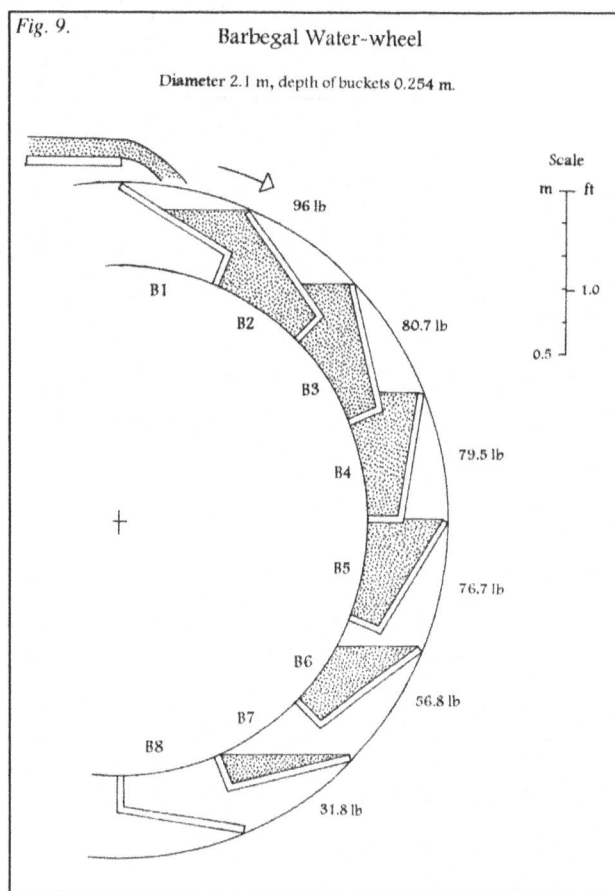

Fig. 9.

Barbegal Water-wheel

Diameter 2.1 m, depth of buckets 0.254 m.

One other dimension has to be settled before we can advance an analysis, namely the depth of the buckets in the wheels. Sellin has suggested '*an equivalent uniform depth of bucket*' of 0.2 m. He uses this as the *swept volume* to determine the flow rate, and it is not to be taken as an indication of bucket size. The writer considers that a bucket depth of 0.25 m is reasonable having regard to the water flow rate (see below), and the effect of centrifugal force acting on a fast moving water-wheel, of relatively small diameter. Next we need to agree the water flow rate entering each cascade of water-wheels. A section of the mill aqueduct just north of the mill shows it to have been constructed 0.8 m wide, but the depth of the water is more difficult to ascertain. Lewis[98] measured it above the deposits as 0.56 m, which compares with Sagui's figure of 0.5 m[99]. Sellin demonstrates that Sagui's estimates of flow rate in the mill aqueduct is high[100] and initially proposes a lower, more realistic mean velocity of 1.0 m/s rather than Sagui's 2.5 m/s. Sellin then adopts a wheel speed of 10 rpm[101], and

93 Sellin suggested 0.7 m width 'that could be accommodated with safety', but as noted above, he recorded the stone channels as 1m wide. Sellin 1981, 420.
94 Forbes 1956, 589-622; Sagui 1947, 225-31; Sellin 1981.
95 Reynolds 1983, 40; Blaine 1966, 25.
96 The angle varies from one wheel chamber to another.
97 Spain 1987, 337-340. The writer discusses the various alternatives as to how the water may have been controlled in a similar wheel at the Athenian Agora.
98 *Pers. comms.* from Dr. Michael Lewis.
99 Sagui 1947, 226.
100 Sellin 1981, 418.
101 It will be seen below that this is slow for a loaded wheel of this size.

using a simplistic but effective calculation of the theoretical swept volume of the wheel's annular, calculates the throughput of the mill aqueduct as 0.3 m³/s resulting in a mean velocity of 0.8 m/s[102]. Having regard to the substantial sinter accretions in the aqueduct, the writer has adopted Sellin's figure of 0.15 m³/s as the flow rate applied to each cascade of mill wheels, as being the minimum reasonable flow rate that existed during the *later phase* of *Barbegal's* operational life.

Using a flow rate of 0.15 m³/s the total potential power available to each wheel chamber with the average head of 2.59 m is 5.11 hp (3.81 kw). Although we can assume that most, if not all of this water, was available to each wheel, it is not clear how the water was restrained and collected into a trough 0.7 m wide from the chamber floor width of *c*.1.2 m. In chamber EI there are substantial calcareous accretions from 10-15 cm thick, in the north-east corner of the 'maintenance' platform next to the four stone steps, showing that water must have bypassed the wheel. Whether or not this occurred whilst the mill was working, or perhaps following abandonment, we do not know.

Using the critical dimensions of a water-wheel 2.1 m diameter and 0.7 m wide between the shrouds, and a bucket depth of 0.25 m, a space diagram, drawn to scale, helps to resolve the torque components for each bucket. (See Fig. 9.) Sixteen buckets have been provided for the wheel[103]. The following Table C shows the theoretical torque generated by each bucket and the total torque generated by the wheel.

Table C - Torque analysis of wheel

Bucket	Weight of water (lbs) (Load)	Distance from vertical axis to c.g. of water mass (ft) (Moment)	Torque (ft.lbs)
1	0	-	-
2	96.0	1.42	136.3
3	80.7	2.29	184.8
4	79.5	2.81	223.4
5	76.7	2.81	215.5
6	56.8	2.33	132.3
7	31.8	1.48	47.1
8	0	-	-
TOTAL	421.5		939.4

This provides us with the maximum theoretical torque that

this size and design of wheel can generate from gravity acting on the water. With the maximum bucket capacity of 96 lbs and a flow rate of 0.15 m³/s, the fastest speed that the wheel can revolve for each bucket to initially receive 96 lbs, allowing for a 10% loss, is 11.6 rpm. Above this speed therefore the torque generated reduces. Before we can use this figure in a power calculation, we need to consider the following;- (i) operational speed of the wheel (ii) the efficiency of transfer and (iii) the effect of centrifugal force. Let us examine each of these in turn.

A fully loaded working wheel driven solely by weight usually has a rim velocity ranging from 4.0 – 7.5 ft/s. The smaller the wheel, the faster its rim velocity. Sellin adopted a figure of 10 rpm (3.6 ft/s rim velocity) but does not qualify the assumption[104]. A reasonable figure for the rim velocity of the *Barbegal* wheel is 6.6 ft/s (2.01 m/s) which is an average coming from several sources[105]. This represents a wheel speed of 18.3 rpm. At this speed and with a flow rate of 0.15 m³/s the maximum theoretical volume of water that a bucket can receive without spillage is 67.8 lbs. This means that the above table of torque analysis has to be modified, because buckets nos. 2 to 5 inclusive can only receive 67.8 lbs of water. But before we can do this we need to consider the efficiency of transfer.

To assume that all of the water leaving the head-race trough will enter and remain in a bucket until the next bucket presents itself for filling is unrealistic. An allowance has to be made within our calculations for losses due to splashing, turbulence and water missing the wheel. We might call this *transfer efficiency* but we should admit that this is something of an inspired guess. We have very little to guide us on this question, but the following observations should influence our thoughts. On the 'negative' side, the transfer is taking place at a fairly high velocity because it is a relatively small wheel. On the 'positive' side, we can be confident that the water was delivered in a trough of similar width to the wheel. Furthermore, it seems likely that the water was delivered at a velocity similar to that of the rim, having regard to the available head in the wheel chambers[106].

Benoit thought that the head-race trough was held up by drawstrings[107] the evidence of which is difficult to find now.

102 Sellin correlates this with his survey of the extant section and gradient of the mill aqueduct using Manning's equation with an n value of 0.015. Sellin 1981, 420. For aqueducts the writer has used a surface coefficient value of 0.10 for smooth cement and plaster as proposed by Kutter and Jackson. Gibson 1930, 288-91. The value of 0.15 used by Sellin seems excessive, approaching the value of 0.17 used for rubble masonry set in cement or brickwork in an inferior condition.
103 Different numbers and shapes of buckets could be tried to vary the efficiency of water entry and retention but within practical limits, the effect on the volumetric efficiency is considered to be insignificant. The head-race trough and water entering the wheel are shown to remind the reader of the delivery arrangement. The position of the end of the trough should be considered approximate.
104 Sellin 1981, 420.
105 Bradley, 1912, 6.75 ft/s – an extrapolated value; Buchanan, 1814, 7.2 ft/s – extrapolated from a range of mean figures; Fairburn 1871, 142, 6.25 ft/s extrapolated from a graph based on several working wheels.
106 Reynolds assumes a velocity or impact head of 0.98 ft, not an unrealistic figure that would be nearly 8 ft/s. Reynolds, 41.
107 Benoit 1940, 49.

If this interpretation were correct it would have provided an easy method of accelerating the water to match the rim velocity. Although theory suggests that the whole of the velocity head is lost in the eddies in the buckets, and there would be a further loss due to the shock if the leading edge of the bucket is not parallel to the incoming water flow[108], it is suggested that we simplify our approach and use the concept of *volumetric transfer*. It is suggested that we assume a 10% loss of volume on the transfer to allow for the mis-direction and spillage of water, and that this should be applied to the total flow leaving the head-race trough. Accepting this theory, the maximum weight of water that a bucket can receive when the wheel is moving at its operational speed of 18.3 rpm is now 67.8 x 0.9 = 61.02 lbs. This revised figure is used for buckets nos. 2 to 4 inclusive.

As the wheel revolves, the surface of the water in the buckets takes up a curved form due to centrifugal forces. The radius of the curvature[109], whose origin lies on a vertical line through the axis of rotation, can be calculated knowing the position and velocity of the centre of gravity of the water in the bucket in question, which will vary slightly from bucket to bucket. Fig. 10 shows the effect of centrifugal force on the water when the wheel rotates at 18.3 rpm[110]. Measurement of the cross section area of the water in each bucket and the position of the centre of gravity allows us to calculate the revised torque components as follows. (See Table D.)

Table D – Torque analysis of wheel allowing for centrifugal force

Bucket no.	Load (lbs)	Moment (ft)	Torque (ft.lbs.)
2	61.02	1.48	90.3
3	61.02	2.31	140.9
4	61.02	2.75	167.8
5	58.0	2.79	161.8
6	33.6	2.29	76.9
7	4.0	1.40	5.6
Total	278.66		643.3

The total power generated by this torque is 2.24 hp. From the total power generated (shaft power) we must subtract an allowance for the resistance of the wheel-shaft's two bearings, the footstep bearing and the gears. If we allow 4% of the shaft power for the three bearings[111] and 5% for the gears as recommended above, the available power for the millstones is 2.24 x 0.91 = 2.038 hp. We can now generate

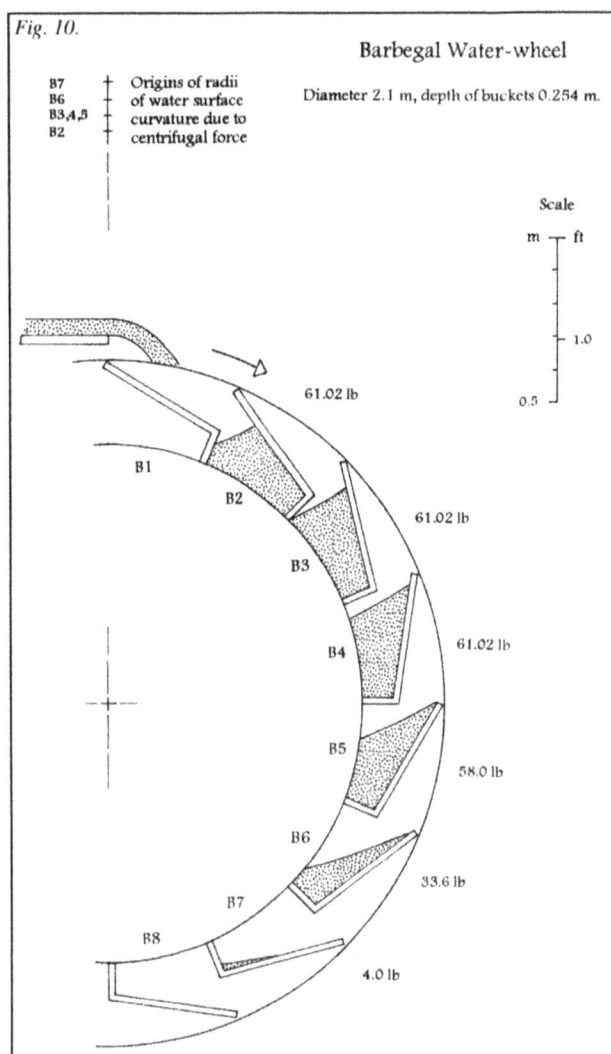

Fig. 10.

Barbegal Water-wheel

Diameter 2.1 m, depth of buckets 0.254 m.

B7, B6, B3,4,5, B2 Origins of radii of water surface curvature due to centrifugal force

a power/wheel-speed graph. (See Fig. 11.) Point z is 2.038 hp at 11.6 rpm. Point z is the fastest that the wheel can revolve and still receive a maximum bucket capacity of 96 lbs with a head-race flow of 0.15 m³/s and allowing for a 10% loss of water on transfer[112]. Point y is the shaft power generated at the operational speed of 18.3 rpm. The efficiency of this wheel is the total power generated divided by the total available potential power i.e., 2.24/5.11 = 43.8%[113]. This illustrates the danger of using modern wheel efficiency figures, such as the often quoted 65% for a bucket wheel as used by Sagui, Sellin and others. This apparently low efficiency figure is mainly the result of the proportion of the available head occupied by the wheel, and the relatively small diameter wheel that brings disproportionate losses due to centrifugal force at its operational speed. For example, the weight of water carried

108 Lea 1916, 287.
109 In theory, the radius of the curvature will vary slightly within each bucket, each element of water being affected by the radius of rotation. For our purposes this is ignored and a constant radius is generated for each bucket. Vapeur 1894, II, 31-34.
110 The position of the trough should be considered approximate. Having regard to the velocity of the rim, a more realistic position would be several inches upstream of the crown of the wheel.
111 See p. 6 above. The 4% is a comfortable figure because the Haltwhistle Burn Head wheel from which the figure was derived, was larger than the Barbegal wheels.
112 The losses due to centrifugal force, with a radius of curvature on the water surface of 16.12 ft above the axis of rotation, are imperceptible.
113 The writer admits to being surprised by the figure of 43.8%. Prior to the analysis he thought that no more than 60% was realistic as stated on page 5 above.

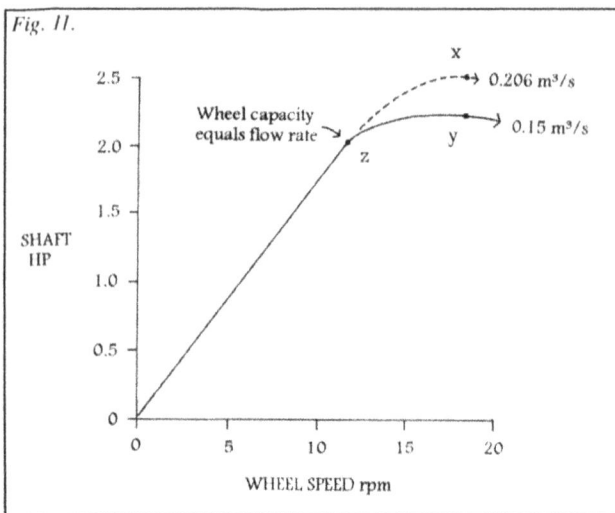

Fig. 11.

at 18.3 rpm is 279 lbs compared with 421 lbs at speeds unaffected by centrifugal force, only 66% of the maximum capacity. If the wheel was full at 18.3 rpm, and allowing for centrifugal force, the power generated would be 2.52 hp and its efficiency would be 2.52/7.02 = 35.9%. To achieve this, the flow rate, including 10% for spillage etc, would have to be 0.206 m³/s to each water-wheel (point x on Fig. 11), which would require a mean velocity within the mill aqueduct of 1.10 m/s. Sellin has modified Sagui's power assessment of *Barbegal* in light of more realistic aqueduct flow rates (see above), and using a 65% wheel efficiency, concludes that each waterwheel could have generated 2 KW (2.68 HP)[114]. Whilst this is in the same order as the writer's figure, the factors that have been used in the calculation are insecure and not supported by evidence.

There are the remains of ten millstones in the *Musée de l'Arles antique* that have been identified as probably coming from the *Barbegal* site[115]. The most complete, a broken but re-assembled *meta*[116] on display, is confidently identified by the museum as coming from *Barbegal*, and this could well be the specimen depicted in Benoit's drawing because its height of 45 cm agrees with his drawing and text. However its diameter is 75 cm and not 90 cm as given in the drawing. This is the only tall *meta* and all others are badly worn and broken. The writer has identified fragments of nine other lava stones, amid numerous querns

within the basement store, as most probably *Barbegal* millstones because of their diameter and inclination of grinding face[117]. An examination of all the remains shows that the diameters vary from *c.*66 to 88 cms, with an average of 78 cms, and we must therefore conclude that Benoit's statement and depiction of the 90 cm diameter stones is at least misleading, if not in error[118]. Furthermore, the slope of the grinding face depicted (24° from the horizontal) is not accurate – the one on display is *c.*35° and all ten specimens vary from *c.*28-35° with an average[119] at 32°.

During the 1993 excavations, several fragments of millstones were found apparently having characteristics of Early Empire stones[120]. Benoit does not inform us of the shape of the top stones (*catilli*) a factor that could have considerable effect on their weight and consequently on the power required to turn them. If the upper stones were flat topped they would have been heavy for their diameter, a consequence of their steep grinding faces creating a deep rim. With this shape, a top stone 200 mm thick at the eye would weigh 330 kg and when absorbing 2.0 hp would rotate at 45 rpm, an MR of 2.46 to 1.0[121]. If the top face was inclined parallel to the grinding face with the same thickness at the eye of 200 mm, the stone would weigh 201 kg and the same power (2 hp) would drive it at 74 rpm, an MR of 4.03 to 1.0. Thus the shape of the top stone is critical to its speed and thereby the gear ratio. Three of the millstone fragments can be identified as top stones but all of them have subsequently been used as bottom stones[122] thus obliterating their original top faces. We should take note that an interesting collection of late 1st c. A.D. millstones, found at *Avenches, En Chaplix*[123], all show the top stones as having conical top faces, roughly parallel to the steeply inclined grinding faces, as did two top stones found at *Les Mesclans*[124]. Other examples of conical shaped top millstones exist in various museums[125].

Let us explore the relationship between the weight and speed of the top millstone during its life cycle and the MR of the gears. Assume for the moment, that the weight of a new top stone is 201 kg as above – the figure does not matter for this exercise – and the MR is 4.03 so that it

114 Sellin 1981, 421.
115 The writer is most grateful to Claude Sinter, Director of the museum for his help and allowing access and recording to take place.
116 The lower stationary stone of a Pompeian mill. The writer considers that it is appropriate to use this term in view of the similarity of the Barbegal stones to Pompeian style mills.
117 These early non-discoidal millstones are worthy of closer examination and measurement, but this is not the place to explore them.
118 Benoit 1940, 59. So too is Sellin's statement. Sellin 1981, 421. The museum is also aware of this perplexing discrepancy. The diameter of 90 cm has been quoted by others e.g, Sellin 1981, 421; Roos 1986, 332.
119 The slope given for the nine stones within the basement store are approximate due to the conditions of measurement.
120 Leveau 1996, 149. The writer is attempting to obtain the publication that was proposed by Amouric to see what additional information these stones might provide.
121 All of the stones are basalt and so the coefficient of grinding determined by the Westree experiment can be used for the power calculation.
122 Examples of this practice were found at two other Roman water-mill sites, at Ickham, Kent and Fullerton, Hampshire.
123 Castella 1994. See below, site number 9.
124 See site no. 2 below.
125 Musée romain d'Avenches; Musée romain de Lausanne-Vidy; Martigny, inv. MY89/4684-11; Römermuseum Augst, inv. 1978.7026.GSTL-848. See Castella 1994 for other examples.

Fig. 12.

Barbegal Water-mill

Artist's reconstruction of mill
chamber East 1. Building
fabric omitted for clarity.

absorbs the net 2.0 hp available from the wheel-shaft and revolves at 74 rpm. (18.3 x 4.03)[126]. As the stone wears away becoming thinner and lighter it would continue to rotate at the speed dictated by the water-wheel and the MR of the gears. Whilst its speed would remain more or less constant, the power that the stones absorbed would get less, proportional to its reducing weight. And so its throughput of grain decreases, being directly related to power according to our interpretation of the Westree experiments. Thus, unless the operators increased the speed of the top millstone towards the end of its useful life by changing the MR of the gears[127], it might only be harnessing perhaps a quarter of the potential wheel-shaft power. If the same new stone was given an MR of 6.38 and initially rotated at the same speed of 74 rpm, the water-wheel would revolve at 11.6 rpm, where a balance of power still exists at 2.0 hp. Now, as the stone becomes lighter, the water-wheel would speed up towards its natural velocity dictated by gravity acting on the buckets, but still delivering a net 2.0 hp. Thus the production for this MR gearing would be at a maximum until the wheel in time reached the speed of 18.3 rpm when the top stone would be revolving at 117 rpm. Thereafter, the

stone would continue to work at this speed until it was abandoned[128]. Therefore this MR enjoys the advantage of enabling the water-wheel to provide constant power for a particular speed range and time period.

This raises the very interesting and pertinent question, did the Roman millers seek to optimize throughput? This extraordinary factory with its sixteen independent corn-milling units would have provided a concentrated environment of maintenance and production. As time passed, all of the primary machinery elements, water-wheels, gears, millstones, bearings etc, would have evolved their own life cycles of maintenance and replacement. The awareness of the operators of opportunities to improve and innovate was surely heightened, if not intensified, by the duplication and ever-present comparisons facing them. In such an environment, surely some degree of technical evolution would have occurred during the 200 years of *Barbegal*'s existence? The writer would propose that we do have one example of the builders seeking optimization of throughput. As *Barbegal* was being built, from the top of the scarp slope of the Rochers de la Pene downwards, the builders initially created the wheel chambers more or less

126 Sellin holds that a millstone 0.9 m diameter requires 3.6 kw (4.824 hp) for a speed of 53 rpm. Sellin 1981, 421. Modern corn-milling experience suggests that this is a high figure. A pair of four foot diameter new millstones weighing over 800 kg absorbed no more than 4 hp when rotating between 100-120 rpm. This is four times the weight and twice the speed of the example given!
127 See Appendix One for the implications concerning gear ratio changing options.
128 Until the production rate or quality became unacceptable, or the stone broke.

parallel to the slope[129]. But from mill V downwards, the slope of the wheel series becomes steeper than the hillside itself so that the lowest two mills I and II have their wheel and gear chambers cut into the rock face of the hillside. The writer has explored the various building developments and the reasons that may have precipitated this change in design[130], but the inescapable conclusion is that the builders wished to maximize the exploitation of water-power and thereby output. The writer is therefore inclined to believe, that in order to maintain production potential, the operators, having discovered the advantages of having different MR's throughout the sixteen mills, either coupled new top stones to an MR that caused the water-wheel to rotate at close to 11.6 rpm, or moved the stones when they had become lighter to enjoy higher stone speeds. This could have been achieved by decreasing the size of the driven gear[131].

Our calculations of just over 2.0 hp being available for millstone work from each water-wheel suggests that it was most unlikely that each wheel powered two pairs of millstones as suggested by Sagui[132]. The speed of the stones would be much slower, probably close to 30 rpm, and the limited space indicated by the lowest mill chambers (viz., EI – EIII and WI – WIII) makes the gearing arrangement difficult. [133] An artist's view of a mill chamber is given in Fig. 12.

We have now arrived at the point where we can estimate the output of *Barbegal*, the meal production coming from the sixteen water-mills. The writer believes that the scale and nature of the *Barbegal* factory indicates that a continuous operation probably existed, and considers that the factors which affect production (maintenance, water and grain supplies, management and labour disruptions etc.) can be combined into a single load factor of 60% working (40% downtime)[134]. Using the production/power ratio determined by the Westree experiment (117 lbs/hp.hr) and the net

power available for millstone work (2.038 hp/mill) the total output from *Barbegal* would be 25.0 tonnes/day which is considerably higher than Sellin's estimate of 4.5 tonnes/day[135]. This equates to 108 kg/hr from each mill, ten times as much as Sellin's proposed output. Using a consumption rate of 900 g/person day[136] and assuming that 90% of the product was used for human consumption[137], the *Barbegal* output of 25.0 tonnes/day would have supported approximately 27,500 people[138]. If this figure is accepted, Sellin's contention that this mill supplied only Arles with flour, needs to be reviewed[139].

Before we leave this fascinating subject of *Barbegal's* production, the writer would wish to remind the reader of the following major influences;

i   if a coarser product was accepted the production could have been increased by up to 75% (see p. 11 above);

ii   Provencal wheat probably contained less moisture than the English wheat used in the Westree experiment and therefore required less power (see p. 12 above);

iii   the mill aqueduct's estimated flow rate made allowance for the existing substantial sinter accretions. The greater flow of earlier periods would have facilitated fully loaded water-wheels that would have produced approximately 12.5% more power (see p. 16 and 18 above);

iv   if the aqueduct flow calculation allowed for a surface coefficient for smooth cement and plaster rather than a rougher surface value, the velocity and thereby the flow rate through the wheels would be greater.

129 The writer interprets the position of the top three wheel chambers differently to Benoit, but it does not affect the following conclusion. Historians should not be confused by Benoit's slope of 30% mistaken by some as 30°, observed by Roos. Roos 1986.
130 Spain 1992, 177-181.
131 When the number of cogs became less, the gear probably took the form of a lantern gear, similar to the Zugmantel specimen. The work implications of changing the gear size are interesting but beyond the scope of this paper.
132 Sagui 1948. Kiechle and Klemm also accept Sagui's interpretation. Kiechle 1969; Klemm 1954, 39. Fleming's perspective drawing used by Sagui, showing each wheel driving two pairs of millstones, incorporates a vertical shaft with a great spur wheel engaging lantern pinions on the millstone spindles. This is a modern corn-milling drive arrangement and the MR depicted is something like 25 to 1, totally unrealistic. Fleming 1983, 68.
133 Recently evidence of at least six duplex-drive water-mills has been found in Israel dating from the early 4th c. A.D. to mid 7th c. A.D. From the remains of the millstones found on these sites it appears that each water-wheel drove two pairs of small Pompeian-style millstones. Ad *et al.*, 2005.
134 For a discussion on this see Spain 1993, 196-199. The writer is rather inclined to propose a higher load factor than 60% on the basis that the rare interruptions to supplies of water and grain are abnormal and external to the factory.
135 Using Sellin's flow rates, and Sagui's figure of 45 kg/hr for each pair of Barbegal stones.
136 *Pers. comms.* The writer is grateful to Dr.M.Lewis for the figure based on rations for slaves, soldiers and plebs given by Cato, Seneca, Polybius and various ancient legal codes and laws. The consumption rate of 350 g /person.day hitherto accepted and used in these calculations by Sellin, Casado and others is much too low. See Appendix Four. André 1961, 73-4.
137 The proportion for human consumption is very speculative. See Jasny 1944. Sagui, Sellin and others made no allowance for non-human consumption.
138 This compares with Sellin's figure of 12,500 people, that has been quoted by many historians such as White 1984; Wilson 2002, 12; Maróti 1975, 268; Kiechle 1969, 125; Hodge 1990, Scientific American 265, 5, 58-64; see also The Times 15th August 1991. Casado calculated the output could support 80,000 people, but his consumption rate at 35 g/day is unrealistic. Casado 1983, 653.
139 Leveau 1996, 149.

20

2. Les Mesclans, Provence, France.

This Roman water-mill site was uncovered in 1996 during a rescue excavation in the Department of Var, southern France[140]. The site, which is dated from the 2nd c. A.D. is thought to have been in use until the mid 3rd c. A.D. It is associated with a nearby villa that was producing wine, oil and cereals. The water was taken from a nearby aqueduct that served the villa, in a stone-lined head-race to the mill that had stone foundations, walls, and wheel-pit. A bypass channel was found close to the mill that joined the tail-race some 7.5 m downstream of the mill. (See Fig. 13.) The wheel was overshot, and its diameter of 3 m was ascertained from the marks made by its rim scoring the calcium deposits on one wall of the wheel-pit. The narrow wheel-pit shows that the width of the wheel was no more than 0.25 m and Brun and Borréani have interpreted an earlier phase of machinery arrangement involving a shorter wheel-shaft that was later lengthened to c.3.3 m long. The ground above the wheel-pit was lost to post-Roman erosion but a reconstruction of the mill shows a low head of water above the wheel[141].

Fragments of four different millstones were found, belonging to a pair of basalt lava stones and a pair of rhyolite stones. The basalt stones were 0.58 m diameter, and with the top stone having a rim thickness of 11 cm, we can calculate that the complete stone would have weighed 129 lbs. (58.5 kgs.). Its top face was parallel to the grinding face, which had a 20° slope, indicative of an early stone. The rhyolite top stone had a diameter of 0.59 m and a thickness of 14 cm at the rim, and when complete probably weighed c.164 lbs (74.5 kg). If we assume that the basalt top stone was close to mid-life, then a new basalt top stone would weigh, say, 176 lbs (80 kg). This would absorb 0.46 hp to drive it at 60 rpm.

A bucket wheel 3 m diameter has a rim velocity of 5.7 ft/s (1.74 m/s), which equates to a wheel speed of 11.0 rpm. At this speed and diameter the origin of the curvature of the water surface in each bucket due to centrifugal force is 5.8 m above the top of the wheel. We need not concern ourselves with the velocity of application. A slight declivity of the head-race trough combined with a small drop onto the wheel could have been used to produce a similar velocity to that of the rim. If we assume a bucket depth of 0.25 m, we can generate a wheel design and calculate the

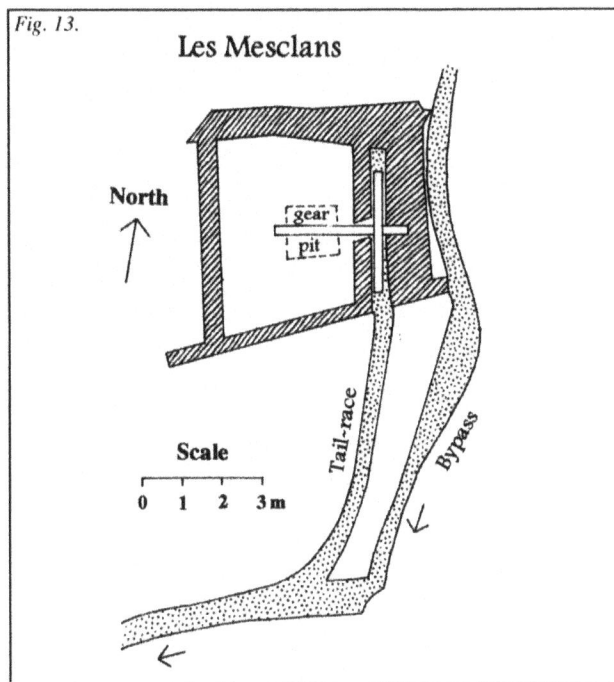

Fig. 13.

Les Mesclans

load and moment for each bucket allowing for centrifugal force. (See Figure 14.) This informs us that the maximum water flow that this wheel receives – determined by bucket number 1 that has the greatest capacity – is 2.37 ft³/s (0.067 m³/s) including 10% for water losses. With a water head of

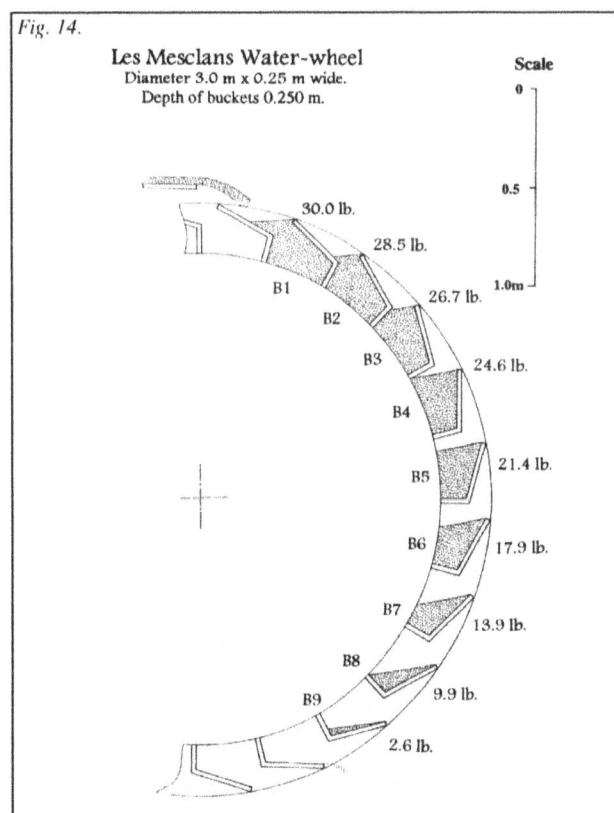

Fig. 14.

Les Mesclans Water-wheel
Diameter 3.0 m x 0.25 m wide.
Depth of buckets 0.250 m.

140 Brun and Borréani 1998.
141 Brun and Borréani 1998, 300, Fig. 27.

21

3.6 m in the wheel-pit the total kinetic energy available is 3.18 hp. The following Table E schedules the loads, moments and torque for each bucket. With this torque the power of the wheel when rotating at 11.0 rpm is 1.24 hp. In comparison to the total kinetic energy available this represents an overall efficiency of 39%. If we allow 9% of the generated power to overcome friction of the bearings and gears in accordance with our earlier calculations, the power available for the millstones is 1.13 hp. This shows us that the wheel was quite capable of driving the lava millstones at say, 120 rpm, when they would absorb 0.92 hp.

Table E – Torque analysis of wheel

Bucket no.	Load (lbs)	Moment (ft)	Torque (ft.lbs.)
1	30.0	1.69	50.7
2	28.5	2.75	78.4
3	26.7	3.54	94.5
4	24.6	4.10	100.9
5	21.4	4.39	93.9
6	17.9	4.33	77.5
7	13.9	3.96	55.0
8	9.9	3.29	32.6
9	2.6	2.42	6.3
Total	175.5		589.8

3. Saint-Pierre/Les Laurons, Provence, France.

This site was probably established in the 2nd c. A.D. and may have been in use until about the middle of the 3rd c. A.D. The excavation revealed an oil-mill and, 25 m to the west, the foundations of a water-mill, including the lower part of the wheel-pit, gear-pit and tail-race[142]. (See Fig. 15.) The wheel-pit was approximately 3.0 m long and its width and depth suggests that a wheel not more than 2.60 m diameter and probably c.0.5 m wide operated here. Although the position and length (c.3.10 m) of the wheel-shaft could be determined from the evidence, all of the upper layers of the original ground have been lost, together with all traces of the head-race, so that it is not possible to determine with reasonable certainty the wheel arrangement. However, the modern environs would suggest that this was probably an overshot water-wheel. The gear-pit was of a

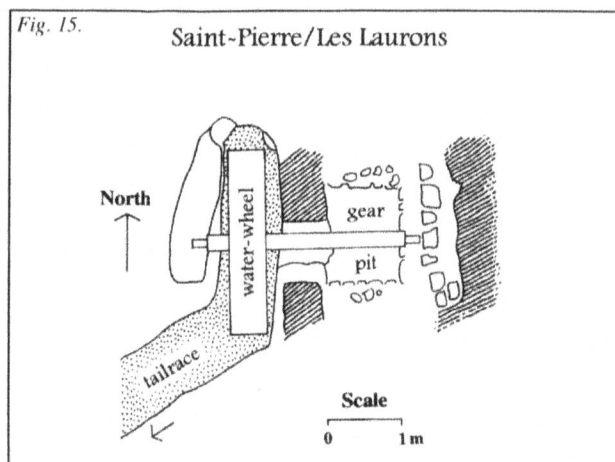

Fig. 15. Saint-Pierre/Les Laurons

size that would have allowed a 1.0 m diameter pit-gear to operate, and which in turn suggests an MR to speed up the millstones for satisfactory operation.

4. The Baths of Caracalla, Rome, Italy. [Early Mills]

In 1983 Schiøler and Wikander produced a theoretical reconstruction of the water-mills that existed under the *Baths of Caracalla*[143]. Their comprehensive study embraces both archaeological and engineering analyses and provides an excellent balance of descriptive and illustrative material so essential for the visualization and understanding of reconstructed machinery. This analysis concerns the two earlier water-wheels that, it is proposed, existed in the centre of the subterranean room, prior to the later phase involving two new water-wheels that were the subject of the Schiøler and Wikander's report. The reasons for concluding that earlier wheels existed have been examined in some detail by the writer, but in summary, it is the symmetry, size and position of earlier chambers in relation to the later mill chambers, in conjunction with informative calcareous deposits that support this interpretation[144].

A detailed survey of all three extant wheel chambers[145] has shown that all of the wheels were very similarly sized in diameter and width, which prompts the suggestion that they all had a common design. The width of the wheel-pit for wheel A is 0.61 m, and allowing for side clearance, it is suggested that the wheel was 0.53 m wide, which is the

142 Brun and Borréani 1998.
143 Schiøler and Wikander 1983.
144 Spain, forthcoming publication. See also Schiøler and Wikander 1983, 50, Fig. 2, chambers VI and VIII.
145 The observations for both the Early and Later mills come from a visit and survey made at the Baths by the writer during April 1988.

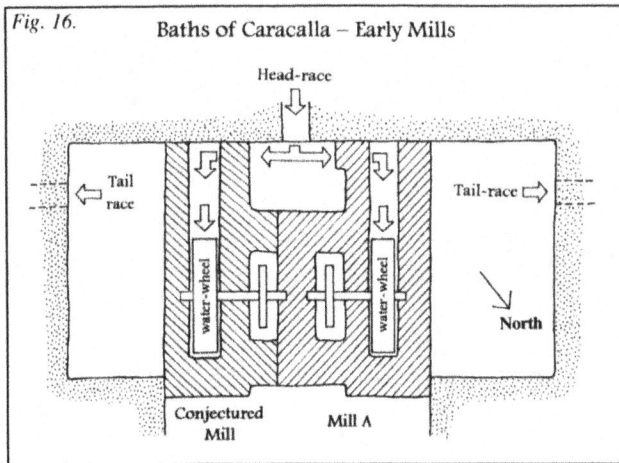

Fig. 16.

Baths of Caracalla – Early Mills

same width as the two later wheels. (See Fig, 16.) Schiøler's section of the wheel and gear-pits suggests that the earlier wheel was c.2.28 m diameter[146]. This allows for the same underside clearance that the later wheels had, and a drop of 0.125 m from the bed of the head-race entering the chamber to the crown of the wheel. It is suggested that the water was delivered over a distance of 4 m at a velocity similar to the rim of the wheel. This head-race arrangement confirms that the power was generated solely by weight of water.

Schiøler proposed that the water flow through the later two mills was 3.5 ft³/s (0.1 m³/s), which, we can presume, related to the total flow entering the chamber[147]. An inspection of the head-race tunnel shows that it enters the mill chamber with a declivity of c.9°, and a few metres upstream turns through 90° and rises, perhaps more steeply, towards the ground surface. Immediately on entering the chamber, the flow divided in the earlier arrangement, with each water-wheel having its own branch carried on the back wall. The dimensions of the earlier head-race channels within the chamber are unknown to us. Although there are calcareous deposits on the back wall of the chamber they are not very helpful to us because they relate to the later wheel arrangement. There are no deposits in the head-race tunnel that might indicate water levels, but the declivity of the approach and the three abrupt changes of direction before reaching either of the wheels, must have created a fast and very turbulent flow with much surging and splashing[148]. When we come to examine the later wheels (see below site number 22), we shall need to assume flow rates and velocities to advance the analysis, but with this bucket wheel we can reverse the process, and see if this can shed light on the probable flow rates.

146 Schiøler and Wikander 1983, 52, Fig. 7.
147 Schiøler 1986.
148 Within the headrace tunnel supercritical flow existed, with hydraulic jumps and entrained air causing 'bulking' (an increase in flow cross-section) that would require complex computations beyond the writer's basic knowledge of hydraulics.

From our previous research this diameter bucket wheel would have an operational rim velocity of c.6.5 ft/s (1.98 m/s), that is a wheel speed of 16.6 rpm. Using the major dimensions of 2.28 m diameter and 0.47 m inside the shrouds, a 16 bucket wheel has been drawn to scale. (See Fig.17.) Allowing for centrifugal force, measurements from the drawing show that the following torque is generated. (See Table F.)

Table F – Torque analysis for wheel allowing for centrifugal force [Flow 0.17 m³/s]

Bucket no.	Load (lbs)	Moment (ft)	Torque (ft.lbs.)
2	75.6	1.56	117.9
3	68.1	2.50	170.2
4	63.7	3.04	193.8
5	48.1	3.08	146.2
6	28.8	2.60	74.9
7	5.6	1.69	9.5
Total	289.9		712.5

This wheel would generate 2.26 hp at 16.6 rpm when fully loaded. Calculations show that this would require a water flow of 0.17 m³/s including 10% for losses, which compares with Schiøler's 0.1 m³/s. With this flow rate the total kinetic energy available is 6.23 hp, which tells us that the efficiency of this loaded wheel is 36%.

We must now make an assumption on the water flow rate. First let us allow that the flow entering the chamber fed two wheels simultaneously, no doubt with similar volumes. If we apply this volume 0.085 m³/s (3.0 ft³/s) to each wheel revolving at 16.6 rpm the maximum weight per bucket, allowing 10% for losses, is 39.51 lbs (17.9 kgs). This means that in the torque table buckets 2 to 5 inclusive can only carry 39.51 lbs. The revised torque analysis is shown in Table G.

Table G – Torque analysis for wheel allowing for centrifugal force [Flow 0.085 m³/s]

Bucket no.	Load (lbs)	Moment (ft)	Torque (ft.lbs.)
2	39.51	1.71	67.6
3	39.51	2.58	101.9
4	39.51	3.04	120.1
5	39.51	3.08	121.7
6	28.8	2.60	74.9
7	5.6	1.69	9.5
Total	192.44		495.7

23

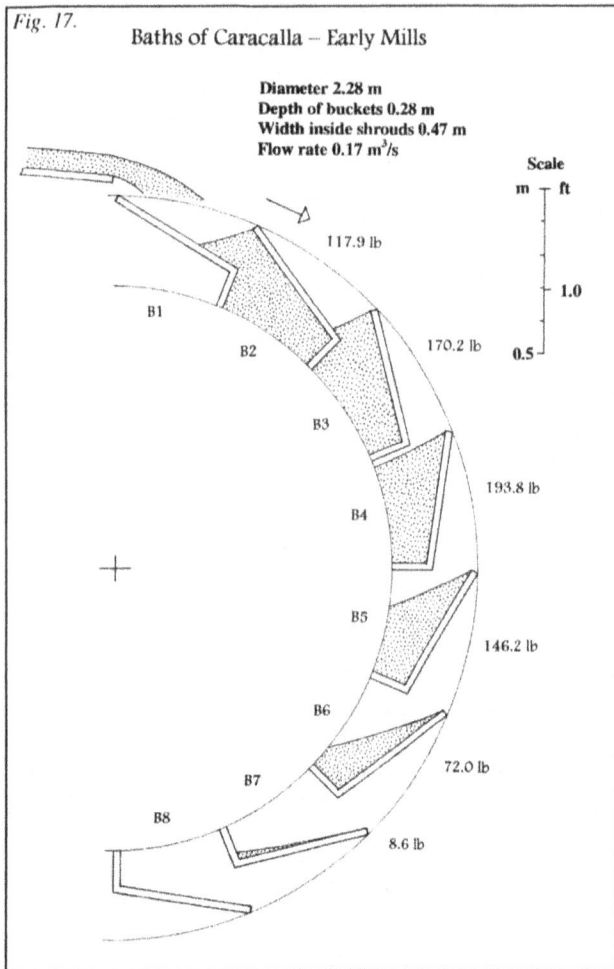

Fig. 17.

Baths of Caracalla – Early Mills

Diameter 2.28 m
Depth of buckets 0.28 m
Width inside shrouds 0.47 m
Flow rate 0.17 m³/s

Scale
m — ft

117.9 lb

B1

B2   170.2 lb

B3

193.8 lb

B4

B5

146.2 lb

B6

B7   72.0 lb

B8

8.6 lb

At 16.6 rpm this torque develops 1.57 hp shaft power and allowing for 9% for bearings and gear friction, leaves 1.425 hp for the millstones. Schiøler's 0.1 m³/s relates to the phase two arrangement of machinery, where the water outlet from the common wheel-pit serving the two later wheels is considerably smaller than the earlier drain, indicating that a diminution of supply had occurred. It is therefore proposed that the water supply for each of the earlier wheels was *c*.0.17 m³/s and that one or both of the bucket wheels had a capacity similar to that drawn in Fig.17, which would have provided flexibility of operation. This bifurcated supply arrangement would allow greater power to be generated when one wheel was idle for whatever reason, including a continuous milling operation involving a shift system of both wheels. It would also solve the problems that arose from the changing life cycles of millstones when heavier new stones required more power. As to the operational speed, we have no evidence that can shed light on gear sizes and we can only conclude that the shaft power available would have allowed the stones, for

most of their life, to run several times faster than the water-wheel. The early mill is considered to have commenced operations with the building of the baths dated to A.D. 212-235 and was destroyed by fire at some time around or shortly after mid. 3rd c. A.D[149].

Although millstones were found in earlier excavations they cannot be traced[150], but one millstone can be seen embedded in the bottom of a wall and its projecting segment tells us that it is 0.76 m diameter. It is a bottom stone and appears to be lava stone with a convex grinding face. Calculations show that a 0.152 m (6 in) thick top stone of the same diameter would weigh 324 lbs (147 kg) and would require 1.024 hp when rotating at 60 rpm.

5. Jarash, Jordan.

In 1926 the remains of a water-mill were found in the Temple of Artemis, *Jarash*, but were apparently not studied or published until 2002 by Seigne[151]. The remains, which included two abandoned partly-cut stone column drums, have been confidently identified as a water-powered mechanical sawing installation. Seigne's examination of the evidence considered alternative mechanical arrangements as suggested by other scholars, but he proposed that on each side of the water-wheel, a wooden disc was mounted having an eccentric metal pivot pin connected to a long rod. Each rod drove a horizontal wooden saw-frame carrying four close-set iron saw blades. (See Fig.18.) The remains of two emplacements for the wheel-shaft bearings, one on each side-wall of the wheel-pit, shows that the driving discs were overhung on the shaft ends. Score marks made by one of these discs helped to determine the axis of rotation, and also showed that it had moved up or down at some time by 0.14 m. The water-wheel has been determined as being *c*.0.5 m wide and between 4.0 and 4.5 m diameter.

Water came to the wheel from a shallow cistern set slightly above the top of the wheel outside the west wall of the mill chamber. The diameter and arrangement of the wheel shows that it was most likely a bucket wheel served by an inclined wooden trough fed by a short 0.4 m wide channel from the header cistern. Seigne's proposed reconstruction of this machine, especially the wheel, is convincing. (See Fig. 19.)

149 Schiøler and Wikander 1983, 62-3.
150 *Pers. comms.* Orjan Wikander 10 March 1988.
151 Seigne 2002a; 2002b; 2002c.

24

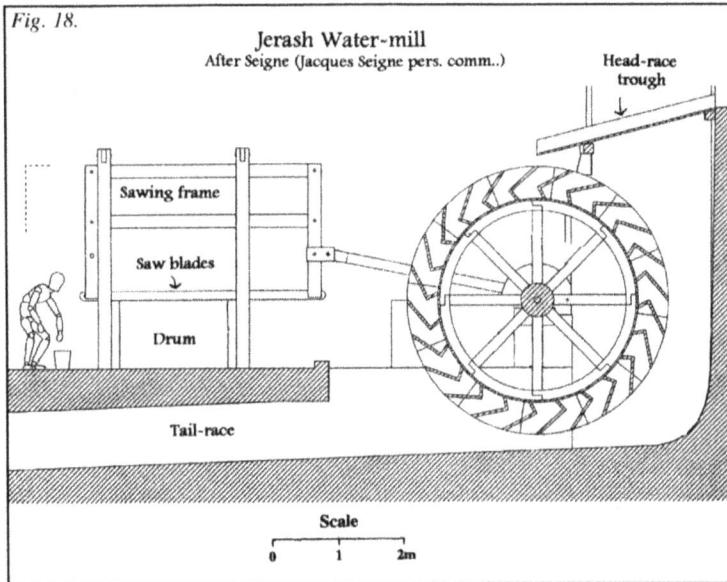

Fig. 18.

Jerash Water-mill
After Seigne (Jacques Seigne pers. comm..)

Head-race trough

Sawing frame

Saw blades

Drum

Tail-race

Scale
0   1   2m

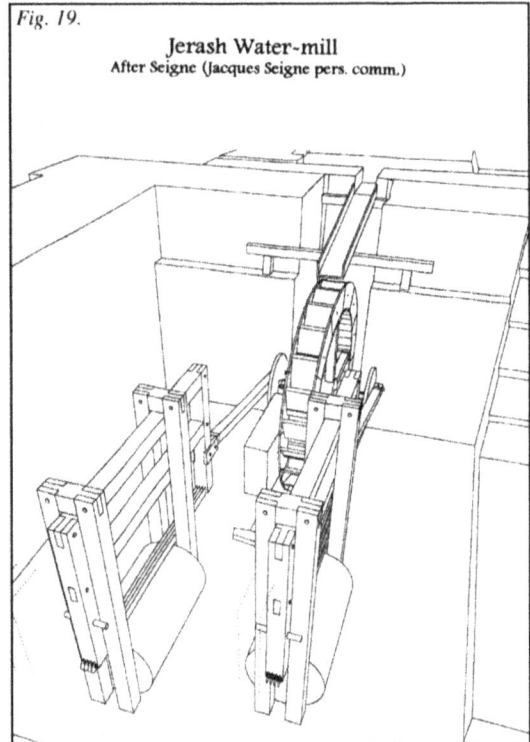

Fig. 19.

Jerash Water-mill
After Seigne (Jacques Seigne pers. comm.)

The design of the iron saw-blades, their lubricity and the forces involved in working them are beyond our experience. The position and shape of the wheel-shaft bearing foundation blocks, with their square cut recesses well below the axis of rotation, suggest that this may have been designed to counter the thrust reaction of the saw-frames. If the eccentrics drove in-phase, a force diagram would show that the torque on the water-wheel was cyclical, and so the writer favours them driving out of phase, with the pins displaced 90° in their relative positions to minimize the surging that would occur with a varying wheel rim velocity[152]. With the probable variation in wheel diameter and the uncertainties concerning water flow rate and sawing forces, it is not worthwhile attempting further hydro-mechanical analysis. It has been proposed that construction of this water-mill probably took place at the time of Justinian A.D. 527-65 or shortly after and may have worked for some while but not later than A.D. 749 when an earthquake destroyed *Jarash* causing its progressive abandonment.

6. Fullerton, Hampshire, England.

During 1965 excavation work associated with Fullerton Roman Villa, near Wherwell, Hampshire, traced an ancient watercourse leading to two narrow leats choked with rubble together with fragments of millstones, which was identified as a probable water-mill[153].

In 2000/01 further excavations undertaken by Cunliffe[154] revealed the remains of two Roman water-mills served by a head-race at least 250 m long coming from the nearby River Anton. Both mills were timber framed and supported from earth-fast posts and ground plates. The *older* mill, which was probably constructed as early as the 3rd c. A.D. was powered by an undershot wheel up to 2 m diameter and 0.8-0.9 m wide, protected by a debris grille[155]. (See Fig. 20.) Site levels indicate that this wheel probably enjoyed a maximum hydraulic head of 1.16 m, so that the head-race water was approaching the wheel at near shaft level. Structural analysis suggests that the wheel-pit was probably timber-lined on the base and had wattle panels on the sides, although we have no positive evidence due to post-Roman erosion. The radial floats of the wheel were probably not shrouded and sole boards may have been absent to avoid up-thrust[156]. Three of the primary post holes were found with fragments of millstones serving as foundation stones, indicating a high probability that a water-mill existed here or close by prior to the building of the older mill.

The *later* mill, which was still in active use in the decades A.D. 360-80, was built upstream and confirms the abandonment of the earlier mill. The old head-race was

152 It is interesting to note that heavy millstones can also cause a surging action as they rotate. Box 1882, 63.
153 JRS 1965, 217.
154 Cunliffe, forthcoming publication. The writer is grateful to Prof. Cunliffe for providing full details of the evidence prior to publication.
155 A feature probably common to Roman water-mills but rarely found in excavations. Another example was found in the common headrace serving the Janiculum mills in Rome.
156 When water is surging into an under-shot wheel where sole boards exist, an up-thrust can occur if the rate of flow exceeds the capacity of the wheel. Such a condition would tend to lift the wheel-shaft from its bearings, a potentially dangerous situation for the water-wheel and the gearing.

substantially widened and deepened, creating a potential cross section three times the area of the earlier head-race, and a new bypass was created adjacent to the later mill. Post-Roman erosion makes it difficult to determine the head-race water level but the scale of the improvement work suggests that the hydraulic head may have been increased. Analysis suggests that this wheel was the same diameter as the earlier wheel but narrower at 0.6 m wide, and again the water probably approached at wheel-shaft level. The foundation 'footprint' suggests that this wheel-shaft was shorter than the early mill's shaft. In this mill the builders adopted an improved foundation design using transverse ground plates that facilitated framing and lining of the wheel-pit, suggesting that the wheel was not shrouded. This narrower wheel with its shorter shaft meant that its rotating mass was less than that of the earlier mill, and with an improved wheel-pit lining the water transfer was probably better. Thus, the later mill was somewhat more efficient both mechanically and hydraulically than the earlier mill. (See Fig. 21.)

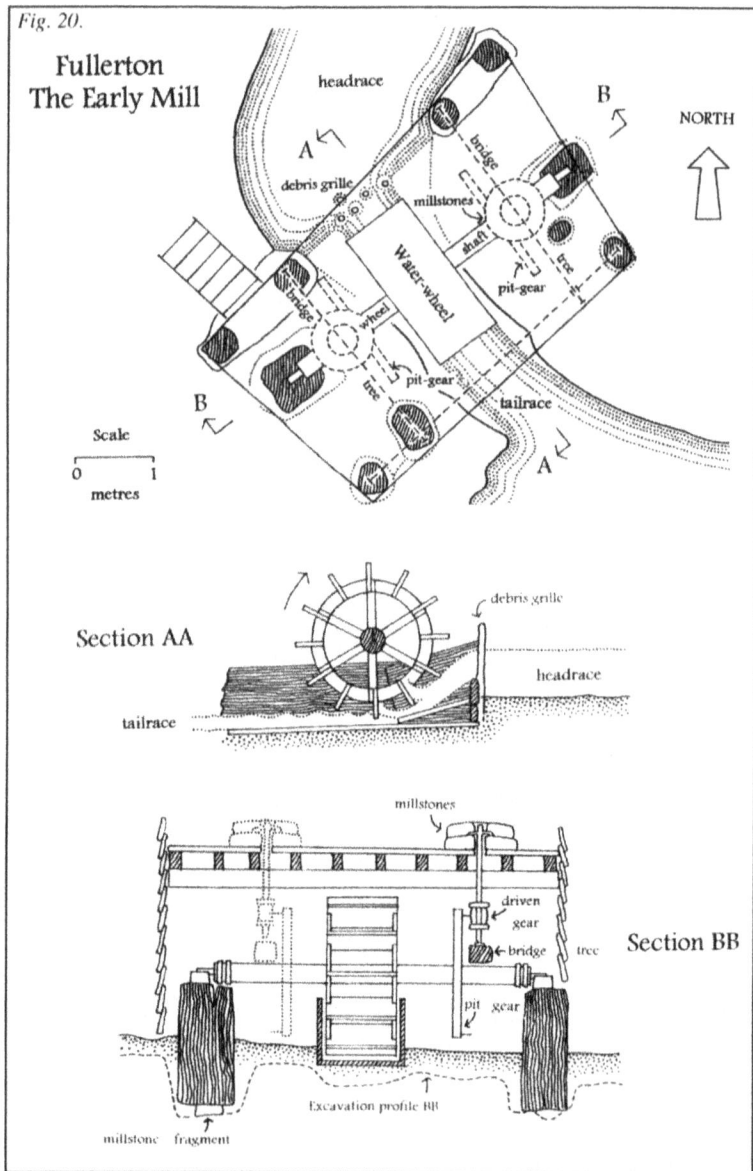

Fig. 20.

Fullerton
The Early Mill

Section AA

Section BB

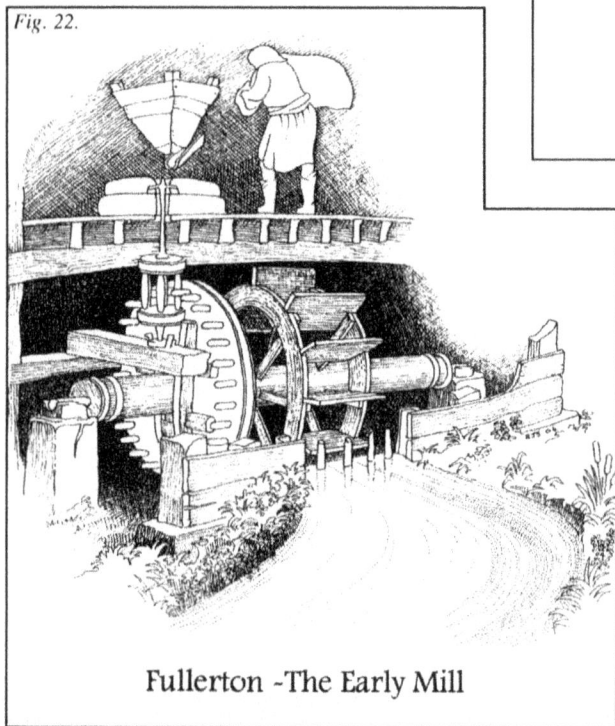

Fig. 22.

Fullerton -The Early Mill

Fragments of twelve millstones were found, and of those that could be measured, the range in diameter was from 75-86 cms, suggesting a reasonable uniformity of size. One top-stone associated with the later mill was 0.23 m thick and 0.84 m diameter, and if we assume a coefficient of friction the same as for lava stone[157], this stone would require 2.40 hp to rotate at 60 rpm. The absence of well-defined water levels makes it impossible to do an accurate hydraulic analysis, but the adequate headraces, especially in the later mill, would have provided ample water to both wheels. However, some basic calculations can be made.

We can calculate the flow that would occur over the sluice-gate cill of the later mill, assuming it to act as a suppressed weir with two end contractions. (See Table H below.)

157 All the stones were either Greensand or Old Red Sandstone, a quartz conglomerate. The writer is grateful to Ruth Shaffrey for the petrology data.

26

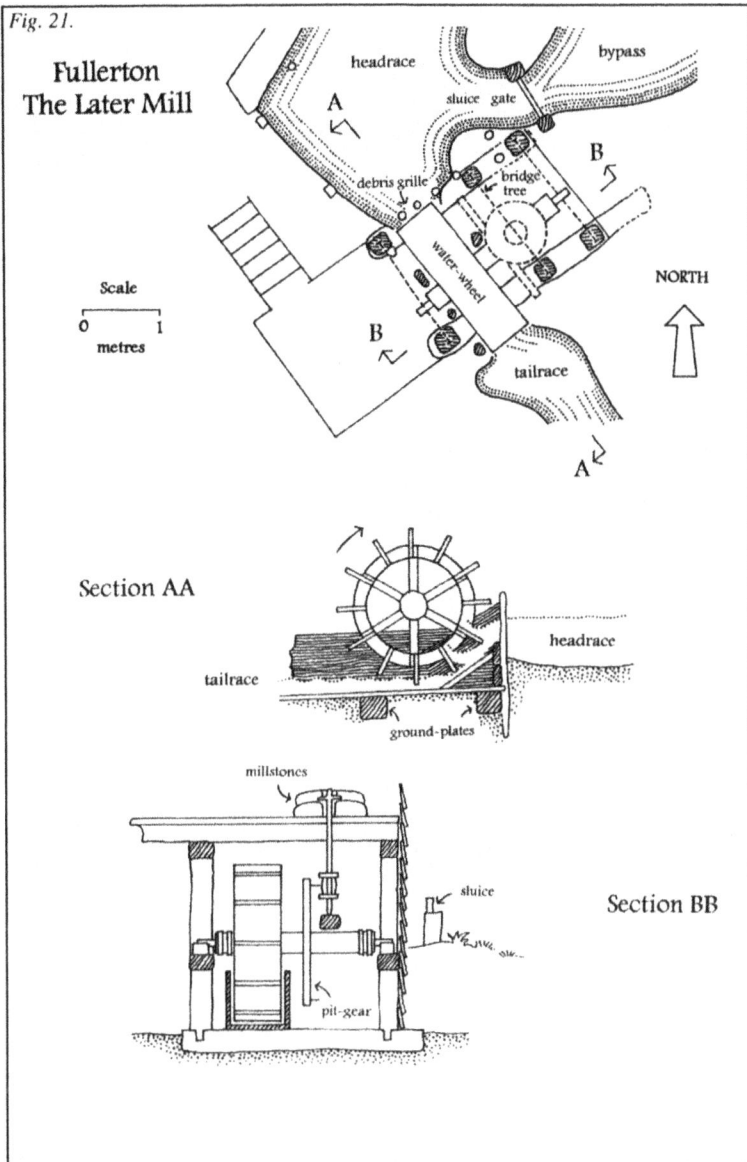

Fig. 21.

Fullerton
The Later Mill

Section AA

Section BB

Table H – The potential power from different flow conditions

H = depth of water over the cill (ft) [m]	Q = flow ft³/s [m³/s]		Kinetic Energy for 1.0 m drop (hp)	Horse power at 30% efficiency
0.5 [0.15]	2.44	[0.07]	0.91	0.27
0.75 [0.23]	4.48	[0.127]	1.66	0.5
0.1 [0.3]	6.9	[0.195]	2.62	0.78
1.25 [0.38]	9.64	[0.273]	3.61	1.08
1.50 [0.46]	12.7	[0.36]	4.7	1.41

Let us compare for the moment the power required by the heaviest top stone that was found, (2.4 hp for 60 rpm) which we can assume relates to a fairly new stone. The total kinetic energy (KE) for a 1.0 m head generated from the

different depths of water flowing over the sluice-gate has to be multiplied by a factor of say, 30%, to allow for the efficiency of the undershot arrangement. Even if we allow for a depth of water of 1.25 ft entering the wheel, which is probably excessive having regard to its diameter, theory tells us that this heavy millstone could not have rotated more than 25 rpm. As the top millstone became lighter with age, it would have rotated faster at a speed inversely proportional to its weight. Although this analysis is very basic it indicates that to obtain a reasonable shaft horsepower a fairly large flow rate would have been required. Thus, this relatively small wheel needed to have a high *volumetric capacity* that was unlikely to have been met by using buckets. It is concluded therefore that this wheel probably had fairly deep radial floats with the power generated by both weight and impulse facilitated by a sloping trough in front of the wheel. (See Fig. 22.)

The 'footprint' of the earlier mill's earth-fast posts and ground-plates has facilitated a reconstruction of the building and machinery frames. This has revealed that both of the wheel-shaft bearings were at such a distance from the wheel as to invite the suggestion that the wheel powered two pairs of millstones simultaneously. If the wheel had driven two pairs, each pair would absorb approximately one half of the total power available. In theory therefore, very little is to be gained in terms of greater output by duplicating the stones. There is however, one advantage with duplication. If the mill's products required two different functions, for example if the miller wished to process different grains or, that the process needed two different treatments prior to reduction into meal, then two sets of millstones would be an advantage. Of these alternatives, perhaps the most significant is the treatment of the grain, knowing that the spelt or emmer widely used in Roman times required the husks to be removed prior to reducing the grain to meal. De-husking can be done manually before milling, or it can be achieved by passing the grain through the stones with them set slightly apart. It is interesting to note that at a slightly later period, doubleflumed horizontal-wheeled mills, both Irish and Anglo-Saxon, have been proposed as possible examples of process milling, where the products of one pair of stones are passed through a duplicate pair[158]. Nonetheless, we have no evidence at present that this practice of processing grain consecutively through two sets of millstones occurred in the Roman period. However, recently evidence has appeared of several Late Roman duplex-drive water-mills in Israel[159]. These drove two pairs of small Pompeian-style millstones.

In conclusion, having regard to the theoretical power calculated above for these wheels, it is unlikely, though not impossible, that there was sufficient power for working two pairs of stones simultaneously, even though the power required for de-husking was probably less than that needed for milling. There is one other alternative operational arrangement, which is that two pairs of stones could be driven from the same wheel-shaft, but not necessarily simultaneously. This arrangement would require some means of disengaging the individual drives, most likely by moving the lantern-gear away from the driver gear. Whilst not beyond the ingenuity of Roman millwrights, the extra work and machinery to achieve this is probably no greater than simply coupling up a different pair of millstones to the millstone spindle in order to undertake a different grinding process.

The scale of the enlarged head-race for the later mill, at 5-7 m wide and over 250 m long, is enigmatic, and whilst this supports the notion of increased flow rate, it is excessive and unnecessary for the size of wheel. Such an increase in head-race surface area invites the suggestion of water storage, but the great size of the nearby river tapped by the head-race, negates this. Moreover, we have found little evidence that the Romans stored water for their vertical-wheeled water-mills[160].

7. Nettleton, Wiltshire, England.

An unusual water-wheel site was discovered in 1968 following a severe storm that caused flooding and denuding of river banks to reveal a narrow water-wheel emplacement, c.0.36 m wide, formed of well-cut and dressed limestone[161]. (See Fig. 23.) The intake to the mill

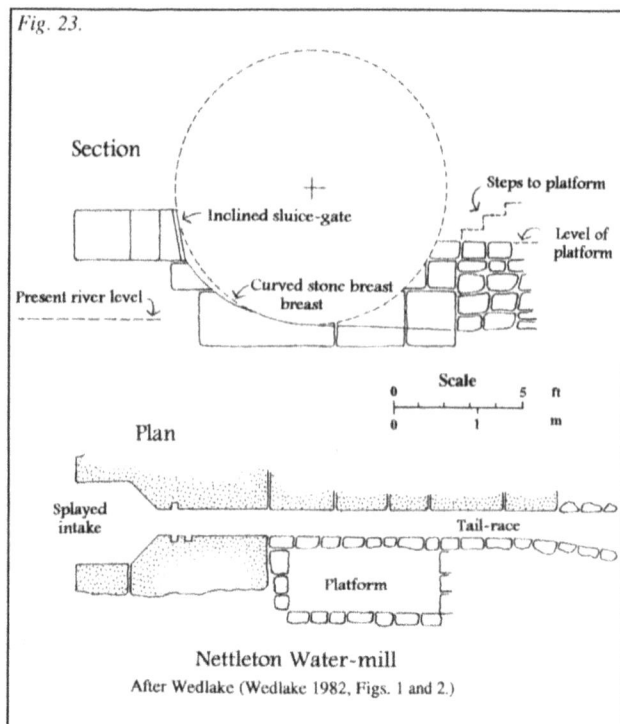

Fig. 23.

Nettleton Water-mill
After Wedlake (Wedlake 1982, Figs. 1 and 2.)

channel is splayed and the wheel emplacement has provision for an inclined sluice-gate and a curved breast that enables us to determine the diameter of the wheel as 2.6 m. A stone-lined tail-race was traced for 5.5 m downstream. The arrangement suggests that an impulse wheel with radial floats, and without shrouds, existed here. Wedlake considered this stonework to be coeval with other 3rd c. A.D. work on the site[162], but the evidence is entirely circumstantial, and in the writer's opinion, the Roman dating is weakened by the following observations.

Opposite the water-wheel position the river bank takes a prominent indent landwards with what appears to be a

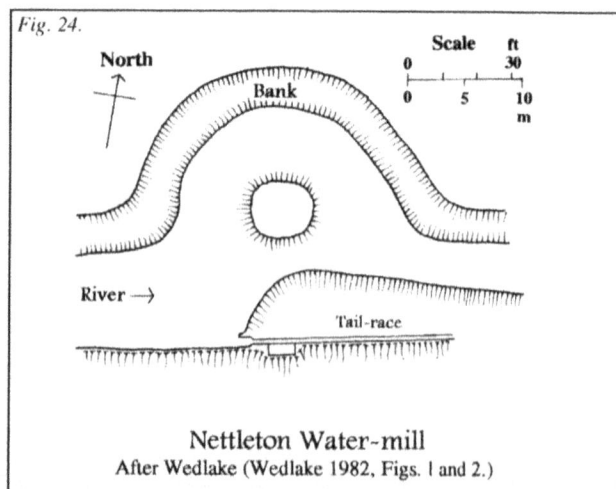

Fig. 24.

Nettleton Water-mill
After Wedlake (Wedlake 1982, Figs. 1 and 2.)

---

158 Watts 2002, 71. In these mills each pair of stones is driven by a separate horizontal water-wheel.
159 Ad *et al.*, 2005. See site 25 below.
160 With the possible exception of a probable Roman tide-mill. See site no. 28 below. Spain 2004. See also Lösnich, site number 26 below.
161 Wedlake 1982, 95-98, Figs. 1 and 2.
162 A view shared by Michael Lewis (*pers. comms.*).

28

channel passing around an island. (See Fig. 24.) This feature must surely be man-made and associated with the building of the wheel emplacement, but for what purpose? The writer had earlier suggested a weir[163] but the flow required by the wheel was infinitely small compared with the river volume, and could easily have been diverted, if needed, by using stakes and boards. The very scale of this river deflection rules out water control for the wheel, and we are left with the worrying possibility that these are the remains of perhaps an eighteenth-century romantic landscape with an impressive weir and ornamental water-wheel[164]. The second observation is that the splayed intake and *inclined* sluice-gate, which our modern experience tells us was to admit water below the lifting gate, are both presently unique in the Roman corpus.

8. La Bourse, Marseille, France.

During excavations from 1967-77 in the ancient port of La Bourse in Marseille, some unusual remains of a late 5th c. A.D. Roman water-wheel were found[165] which provide us with valuable insight into the design and construction methods of a bucket wheel[166]. A considerable portion of the wooden rim was found that shows that the wheel had a single set of radial arms supporting L-shaped buckets between segmented shrouds[167]. (See Fig. 25.) Sole boards were morticed into the flanks of the radial arms and nailed through the shrouds. An additional and rare feature was the remnant of a curved wheel-trough, carved from solid wood that lay beneath the wheel. A reconstruction of the wheel shows that it had 30 buckets, was 2 m diameter and 0.2 m (0.3 m?) wide, and it is thought to have operated with a hydraulic head of close to 1.0 m.

Varoqueaux and Gassend have made a valuable study of the wheel including a reconstruction of its design and a torque analysis by resolving the load and radius components of each compartment[168]. (See Fig.

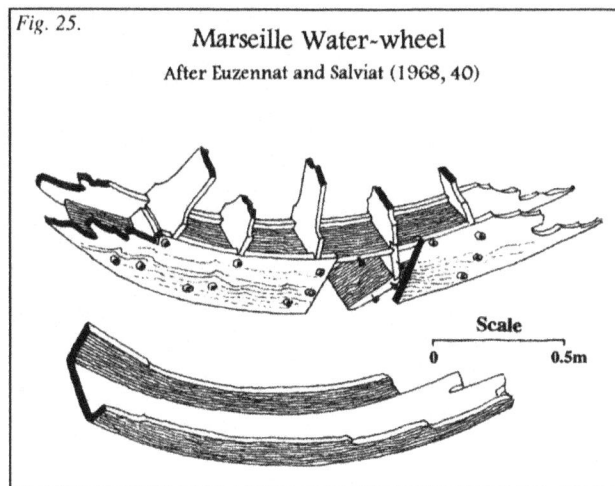

Fig. 25.

Marseille Water-wheel

After Euzennat and Salviat (1968, 40)

Scale

0   0.5m

26.) Such theoretical power calculations are commendable and rare for Roman water-wheels. The reconstruction drawing shows the wheel to have been a low-breast application with the water entering well below the level of the wheel-shaft at about four o'clock (viewing the side of the wheel as the face of a clock). The shapes of the L-shaped buckets provide supporting evidence to the design adopted by the writer for calculating the power of other bucket wheels (e.g *Barbegal, Baths of Caracalla (Early)* etc.). The suggested design of the wheel hub is practical and appropriate, with the radial arms morticed into boarded hub flanges or discs held by half-lapped clasp-arms around a

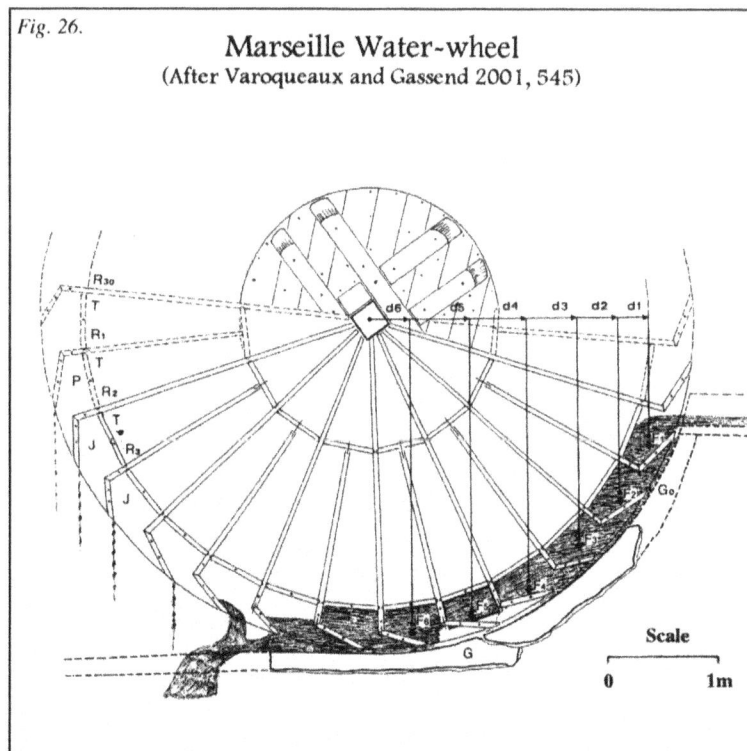

Fig. 26.

Marseille Water-wheel

(After Varoqueaux and Gassend 2001, 545)

Scale

0   1m

163 Spain 1984a, 119.
164 This suggestion is weakened by the fact that the site appears to be miles from any stately home.
165 Guéry and Hallier 1987, 265-282. The excavations also revealed evidence of a series of three successive water-raising wheels serving a 'tank-dock'.
166 This wheel had apparently replaced two earlier wheels occupying this site, the earliest dating from the beginning of the 2nd c. A.D.
167 Euzennat and Salviat 1968; Varoqueaux and Gassend 2001, 538, Fig. 9.
168 Varoqueax and Gassend 2001, 545, Fig 13.

square shaft[169]. However, in view of the transverse narrowing of the radial arms, and in absence of other evidence, there is an alternative arrangement for the hub construction, with the arms being morticed into a solid hub similar to the *Venafro* wheel. (See below site no. 25.) But this debate has little value and a negligible effect on the power calculations.

Varoqueaux and Gassend have produced a table of the torque generated by each bucket, using the moments d_1 to d_6 and a bucket volume of 7.37 litres which they have taken as 7.30 kg, presumably to allow for spillage[170]. See Table I.

Table I – Torque generated by the La Bourse wheel (after Varoqueaux and Gassend)

Bucket	Moment (m)	Weight (kg)	Torque (kg.m) [ft.lbs]	
d_1	1.3	7.3	9.49	[68.4]
d_2	1.2	7.3	8.76	[63.2]
d_3	1.0	7.3	7.3	[52.6]
d_4	0.75	7.3	5.47	[39.5]
d_5	0.47	7.3	3.43	[24.7]
d_6	0.2	7.3	1.46	[10.5]
		Total	35.9	[327.3]

The total torque calculated by Varoqueaux and Gassend is 36 kg.m, but the figure should be treated with caution for several reasons. First, there is some doubt about the hydraulic head, although 1.0 m is probably in the right order. But the assumptions on the bucket water loads and velocities need qualification. With the head-race trough of the same or similar width as the wheel, the average velocity in the trough will be (R2 - R1)/ y[171] times the velocity of the buckets in order to deliver enough water to theoretically fill the wheel. From their drawing y is one fifth of (R2 - R1) which would produce a very high velocity. Even if we take what may be a low provisional rim velocity of 1.0 m/s, the head-race velocity is extremely high at 5 m/s. The energy and head required to achieve this would have been wasted and it would have been more fruitful to increase the existing hydraulic head of 1.0 m and gain a higher efficiency for this weight-driven wheel. In other words the depth of water entering the wheel should be much greater than illustrated.

Varoqueaux and Gassend's drawing and their calculations assume the rim compartments to be completely full of water immediately in front of the intake, an unrealistic assumption. With a bucket wheel, a load diagram would normally assume that the water in each bucket would be level with the outer lip of the bucket. However, with this undershot wheel having shrouds and sole boards working within a curved trough, more water could be fed into the wheel to flood the compartments and maximize the weight of water carried, and thereby the generated power. To achieve this, the flow rate can be greater than the capacity of the moving compartments; this would help to allow for splashing and the inevitable leakage between the wheel and its breast (the wheel trough). Increasing the flow rate would no doubt add to the weight of water carried but it would not entirely flood the compartments, there would be air-locks above the heel of each descending bucket in addition to air trapped by the buffeting and agitation of entry. Moreover, the whole process of filling and carrying would be subjected to centrifugal force by the moving wheel, which would tend to throw the water out of the buckets against the wheel-trough. This force would combine with gravity, and cause the water to leak out of the compartments as they move downwards. Thus, the *volumetric efficiency*[172] of the compartments would be a maximum at position d_2 and decrease to d_6, the last bucket to have a torque affect on the wheel-shaft. What value to put on these volumetric efficiencies is unknown – perhaps a range from 80% to 60%, less or more. Whatever values are used, they need to be applied to the compartments to help determine the volume and weight of water, so that each torque component can be measured.

Another and more difficult problem is what velocity to give the wheel rim in order to use rpm and the total torque to calculate the horsepower generated. The wheel speed cannot be calculated theoretically; this is one occasion when our only guide is modern experience coming from Victorian and early 20th century water-wheels. At other sites in this study, where the water has been applied into the tops of bucket wheels, rim velocities have been adopted based on evidence of Victorian overshot working wheels. Such figures hold good for overshots and high-breast wheels where the water is applied well above the level of the wheel-shaft, but they are questionable when the water is carried only in the lower portion of the wheel. In very low-breast wheels the proportion of the wheel loaded with water is much less than in other types and so the rim velocities will be less. If we assume a wheel speed of 5 rpm (a rim velocity of 0.73 m/s) and the volumetric efficiency as 90%, then the power generated is 0.28 HP. Different figures can be applied but the result is well below the power for operating a pair of millstones and we can confidently

---

169 On a minor detail the writer favours all of the radial arms being morticed into the discs rather than intermediate ones springing from an inner ring of sole boards. This conforms to the design of some Roman mine-drainage wheels – but this is not important.
170 Varoqueaux and Gassend 2001, 549, note 24.
171 Where R2 is the outer rim radius and R1 the inner radius and y the thickness of the entering water stream.
172 Completely full compartments represent 100% volumetric efficiency.

suggest that the wheel served some other purpose. Guéry and Hallier have suggested that the wheel powered forge bellows, and in absence of any evidence of what arrangement existed, this is entirely plausible[173].

9. Avenches, En Chaplix, Switzerland.

The remains of this watermill were discovered in 1990/91 on the banks of an ancient river outside the nearby Roman city[174]. A plan of the excavation that extends 12 m upstream of the mill shows a 4 m wide head-race approaching the mill. The shape and the section of both head and tail-races suggest that these were probably natural channels with little evidence of canalization. It is thought that the head-race was not timber-lined, although beside the mill the wheel emplacement and the tail-race were timber-lined for several metres downstream. Close to the area where the water-wheel operated, there were substantial remains of two timber-lined mill-races, an earlier one overlain by a later structure taking a different alignment. On one bank appear the remains of a platform with a planked floor where the mill building stood. (See Fig. 27.)

The older lower tail-race was 1.7 m wide and had a planked floor supported by transverse ground-plates and timber walls. The later tail-race, built on top of the remains of the earlier tail-race floor, shows an improved design. Once again transverse ground-plates are used but these have recesses cut into their top faces, 1.34 m wide, to facilitate the erection of a planked trough. An important feature is the remains of a 7 m long plank found nailed in the recesses of several of the ground-plates. One edge of the plank was 7 cm away from the shoulders of the recesses, showing that a vertical side plank would have been positioned in this gap, nailed and wedged against the shoulder. This provides us with an important example of construction of an early Roman mill-race. This evidence can only indicate the probable width of the water-wheels but not their diameters. The earlier tail-race suggests that the older wheel could have been c.1.4 m wide, whereas the later wheel, working within a mill-race 1.2 m wide, was probably c.1.1 m wide. Both water-wheels were probably un-shrouded, certainly the later one operating in a well constructed mill-race

173 Guéry and Hallier 1987, 265, 272-4.
174 Castella 1994.
175 Castella 1994, 47, Fig. 31.

indicates this, and there is no doubt that both wheels had radial floats. The large natural shape of the head-race and absence of any evidence of acceleration – except for the contraction into a narrower mill-race – tells us that these were fairly low velocity impulse wheels having relatively high flow rates.

The construction of the mill has been dated to A.D. 57-58 and the end of its activity at A.D.c.80. Although we cannot be certain, the different alignments of the mill-race, together with their different widths and construction methods, suggest that a new water-wheel was built to replace an earlier one, which is rather surprising in view of the very short life (20 years) of the site.

The remains of 22 basaltic lava millstones were found in the environs of this site with diameters varying from 0.6-0.73 m with an average of 0.65 m. This collection of stones provides an excellent example of steeply inclined grinding faces that are now accepted as indicative of early discoidal millstones. The other interesting feature of these stones is the shape and drive arrangement of the top stones[175]. Their top faces are convex and the evidence shows that the mill

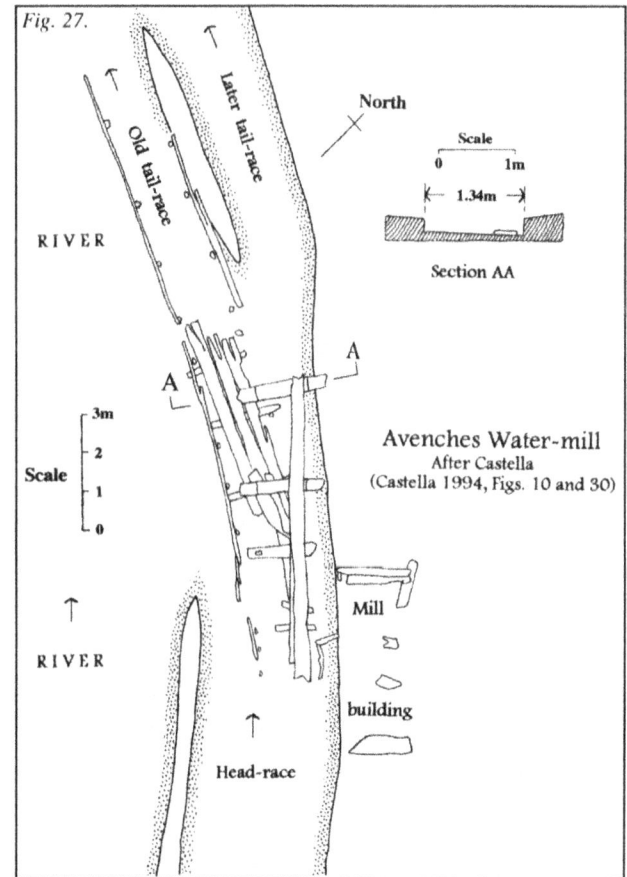

Fig. 27.

Avenches Water-mill
After Castella
(Castella 1994, Figs. 10 and 30)

31

rynds, attached to the top of the millstone spindle, curve over and down engaging diametrically opposite cavities on the top surface of the top stone, rather like cramp-irons.

10. Ickham, Kent, England. [Early Mill]

In the early 1970's, extraction of river-gravel by the wet-pit method using floating dredgers brought to light an ancient course of the River Little Stour passing through the remains of timber structures which were subsequently recognized as water-mills. The sites of the water-mills, at Ickham, near Canterbury, Kent, were part of a large area of Roman occupation where numerous Romano-British finds had been made since 1958. Three structures were found, two of which were sites of vertical-wheeled water-mills, and the third has been interpreted as having ground-plates for a possible double-penstock horizontal-wheeled water-mill[176].

At the site of the *Early Mill*, numerous post-ends were found well preserved by the water-logged soil. This high concentration of earth-fast posts facilitated a reconstruction

of the building and its machinery[177]. Evidence for dating the mill comes from 95 coins found within or close to the structure, that were identified and compared with histograms both of the entire site and of Arles, France. The conclusion from this investigation is that the mill was probably built and in operation close to A.D. 225 and had ceased working by A.D. 270. The remains of most of the larger posts were found to have their buried ends roughly hewn by adze or axe, but obtuse and not sharp, indicating that they had been dug in and not driven as some of the smaller posts and stakes probably were. The mill was apparently sited on the edge of the marshes, but the large posts would not have been placed much below the water-table, so the building conditions were probably better than the excavating conditions, when the water-table was well above the post ends. Although the mill must have stood very close to estuarine land margins, the tidal waters would not have been permitted to create backwater and thereby affect the working of the wheel.

An examination of the foundation plan (See Fig. 28.) has identified several groups of posts, and established that within each group nearly all posts have quadrilateral sections and axes parallel to each other. In addition to these cluster groups other linear groups have been identified where the posts have common minor axes all parallel to the group's major axis. Unfortunately, the salvage and rescue nature of the excavation did not reveal the levels and gradient of the head-race, but its position and that of the tail-race, were readily identified. A structural analysis of the plan suggests that the wheel-shaft and the millstone platform were supported by separate post and truss frames. The proposed reconstruction shows the wheel-shaft bearings were carried by transverse beams A and B, the millstone platform supported by beams F and G, and the bridge-tree C (carrying the millstone spindle), supported by beams D and E. There are two alternative positions for the driver gear, but the writer favours option A mainly because of improved access. The width of the water-wheel is determined by posts on either side of the wheel emplacement, which would have been planked on the walls. Its width could not have been much more than 0.56 m but the diameter is not so readily

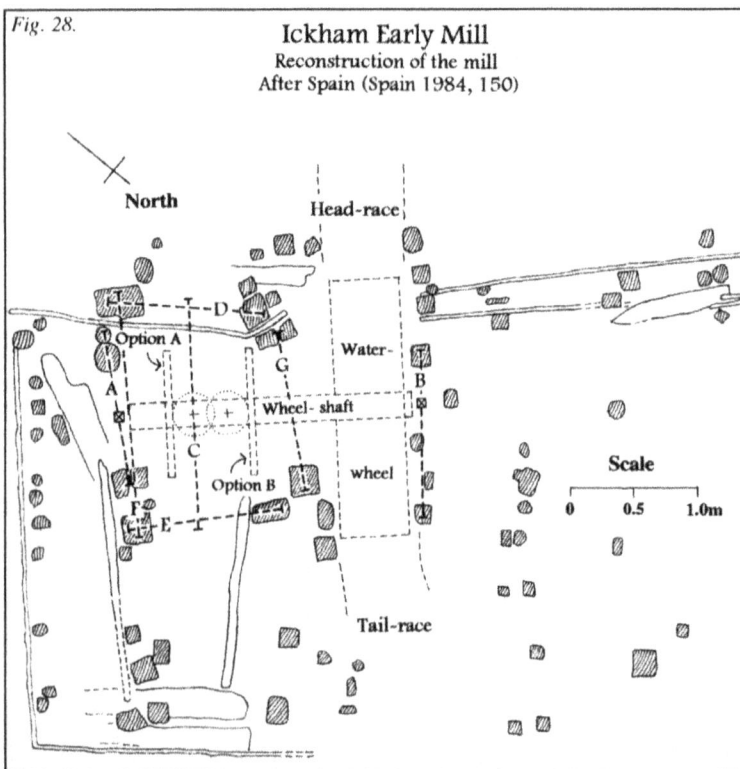

Fig. 28.

Ickham Early Mill
Reconstruction of the mill
After Spain (Spain 1984, 150)

North

Head-race

Water-

Wheel- shaft

wheel

Option A

Option B

Scale

0   0.5   1.0m

Tail-race

---

176 Spain, *et al*, forthcoming publication prepared by the Canterbury Archaeological Trust under the auspices of English Heritage.
177 Spain 1984b.

Ickham
The Early Mill

estimated, although it was probably not much more than 2.0 m.

We can be confident that the wheel was undershot, because the general levels of this estuarine landscape and the nearby later mill structures, negate the possibility of a hydraulic head sufficient for an overshot wheel. The later mills, some 140 m upstream, were clearly impulse wheels (see below) running within a close-boarded revetted mill-stream floored with planks, and it is therefore reasonable to assume that the earlier mill was also powered by an impulse wheel. The early mill wheel would have had radial floats and was served by a relatively high volume flow at low velocity. In the absence of figures for the head-race gradient and section, the water velocity cannot be calculated, but a float area of say, 0.56 x 0.56 m only requires a head-race velocity of just over 2.0 m/s to generate one horsepower. With the wheel revolving at a speed of approximately 10-12 rpm, we can conclude that the MR was significantly greater than

Fig. 30.

Ickham Early Mill
Artist's view

unity. An artist's view of the reconstructed machinery is given in Fig.29. A detailed examination of the foundation has revealed that probably not more than a few decades after the mill was built, the structure supporting the machinery and millstone decayed, settled and moved causing the introduction of new external support posts. About this time the mill was extended, but the new south-east wall suffered from excessive ground pressure that the miller attempted to overcome by creating an internal revetment and back-filling inside. An artist's external view of the *Early Mill* is given in Fig. 30.

11. Ickham, Kent, England. [Later Mills]

The later structure embodies the remains of a 15 m long section of a timber-lined mill-race, supported by transverse ground-plates with earth-fast posts for revetment and water-side structures. Structural analysis shows that two building phases can be identified. In *Phase One*, a water-mill existed at the downstream (north-east) end of this feature, where the mill-race was 1.36 m wide supported on transverse ground plates with planked bed and side-walls attached to earth-fast revetment posts. The water-wheel is thought to have been approximately 2.4 m diameter, and the width, which we can be more certain of, 1.1 m. (See Fig. 31.) Unfortunately no levels were recorded for the water-course, but this was clearly an undershot wheel with radial floats – probably not shrouded - and driven solely by impulse. The side posts, which are of irregular section, are paired on opposite banks, and the ground-plates that extend beyond the walls of the race do not have morticed ends. With no obvious evidence of joints, they were probably buried under the boarded side-walls and held by the posts. On the north-west bank there is a group of earth-fast posts whose minor axes are parallel and their proximity to each other indicate a load-bearing function. Their position suggests that the mill-side wheel-shaft bearing, gears and millstones were probably on the north-west bank of the water-course. On the south-east bank evidence of the larger posts necessary for supporting the water-side wheel-shaft bearing has disappeared.

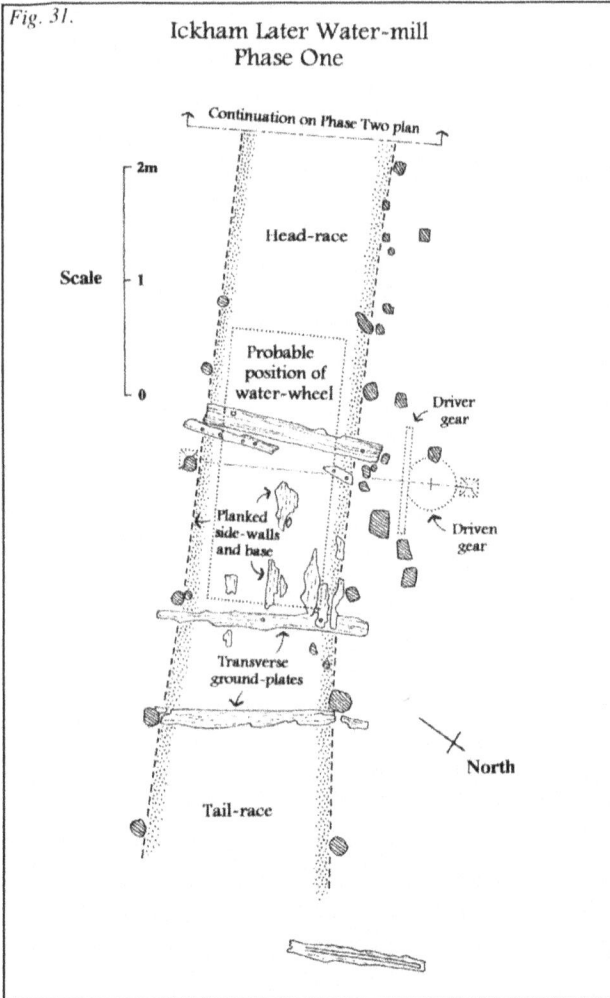

Fig. 31.

Ickham Later Water-mill
Phase One

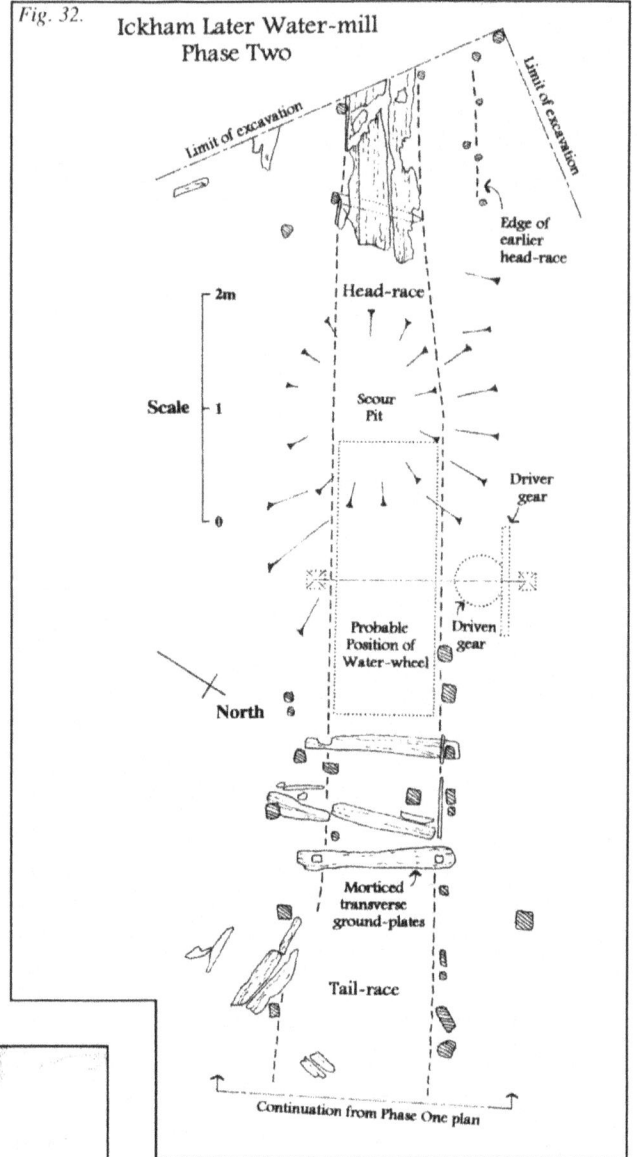

Fig. 32.

Ickham Later Water-mill
Phase Two

Ickham Later Mill – Phase Two – Artist's reconstruction

In over a century of operation in an unstable estuarine landscape, the structure of the mill, especially the water-side fabric, would have required maintenance and replacement. We can also imagine that the alluvial deposits in the tail-race would have required an increasing amount of labour as the years passed to maintain flow and avoid back-water under the wheel. In these circumstances, the favoured area to re-build and maintain operation was upstream, where fresh ground and probably a higher water-table existed. In *Phase Two* of the building, a new mill was built 7.5 m upstream from the earlier mill where the water-course was narrowed to 1.0 m wide and supported by transverse ground-plates with vertical posts morticed into the ends of the plates. (See Fig. 32.) It appears that the axis of the head-race for this mill was re-aligned some 7° from the original mill-race, the north-west edge of the earlier mill-race was abandoned and a narrower head-race created. The evidence suggests that this new head-race expanded in width as it approached the mill, an unusual arrangement. In this region the head-race was boarded on the bottom and the sides, and the depth of water would be proportionally lessened as the width of the race increased in the direction of flow. The diameter of the wheel is suggested as *c.*2.4 m and the width as 0.9 m. One significant feature of the *Phase Two* structure, is that it has a greater incidence of regular sectioned posts, was less decayed, and the general workmanship was superior to that of *Phase One.*

At the north-east end of the mill-race there are the remains of numerous posts close to the walls of the race, and, significantly, two that stand within the race itself. Clearly not for water control or a debris grille, they suggest that part of the structure existed here over the mill-race. The probable position for the water-wheel is shown upstream nearer to the boarded section of the head-race, although unfortunately, all of the structural support posts for the wheel, machinery, and the mill itself, have disappeared. In this area the archaeologists found a 'scour-pit', presumably created by the continuing flow of the water following the abandonment of power generation on the site. Once again no levels were recorded but one imagines that the mill-race serving both of these mill sites would have been graded to provide an approaching velocity. Both of the later water-wheels, which would have had radial un-shrouded floats, can be seen as low-velocity impulse wheels having relatively high volume flows. Unfortunately it is not possible to produce a meaningful hydraulic analysis of these mills, but both of the later wheels appear to have been slightly more powerful than the earlier water-wheel. An artist's impression of the later mill, Phase two, is shown in Fig. 33.

All of the coins from the later structure fall into the period A.D. 260-402 and the ceramic evidence, in conjunction with that of the small finds, indicates a demise of the structures at A.D. *c.*370-400. Unfortunately, although a great number of artifacts were found in association with the later structure, they were not recorded with sufficient accuracy to allow a separate analysis to explore the dating of the upstream and downstream water-mills.

The remains of twelve millstones were apparently all found in the vicinity of the two later mills. They range from 72-107 cm in diameter, with an average diameter of 84 cm. The majority is from 72-88 cm in diameter. Ten of the millstones found on the site had evidence of furrows suggesting that it was normal practice to dress the stones. On most of these stones the furrows could be seen arranged in harps[178] but the variations in design and the presence of negative lead[179] on some harps tells us that their knowledge of millstone dressing was still developing. The millstone fragments show a considerable incidence of degradation following their abandonment as rotary corn-milling stones. Many of them, especially those made of millstone grit, showed that they were subsequently used as saddle querns and whetstones. Amongst the artifacts a fairly large iron hammer-head was found, that displayed unusual mechanical deformation on one face. Having regard to the iron waste material and slag found on this site, we should not lose sight of the possibility that a water-powered forge-mill may have existed here.

12. Chesters Bridge, England[180].

In 1860, Clayton, excavating the eastern abutment of the Roman bridge just south of Chollerford Bridge, near Chesters fort, discovered a mill-race and millstones associated with the tower[181]. (See Fig. 34.) During this and other work on the site in the 1860's the evidence was not identified as a possible water-mill, even though several millstones were found[182]. At *Chesters Bridge* the generation of water-power was facilitated by a stone-lined water-course passing through the base of a tower (See Fig.35.) The source of this water would have been the River North Tyne, which now flows some 25 m away to the west. The width of the water-course varies throughout its length from 1.85 m to 1.93 m

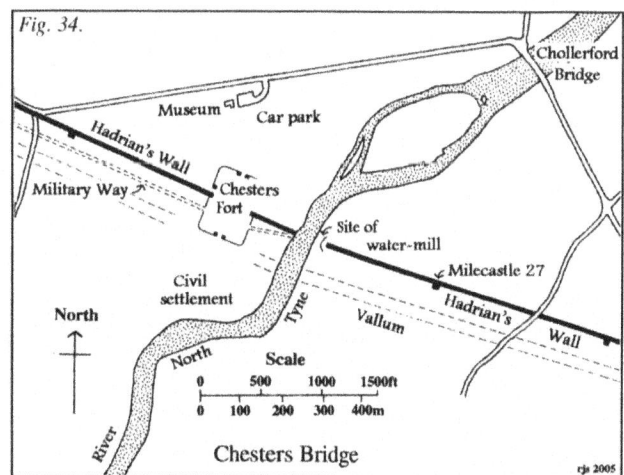

Fig. 34.

Chesters Bridge

---

178 The modern term for the circular sectors where the furrows are all parallel to each other. Strictly the shape is a 'circular ring sector' allowing that the eye of the stone creates an inner radius.

179 The leading furrow in a harp should be tangential to an imaginary circle around the eye of the stone. The radius of this circle is the 'lead' or 'draft'. The main reason for this is to ensure that the scissor movement of crossing and converging furrows induces the grain and meal towards the rim or 'skirt' of the stones. See Appendix 2 'Roman Millstone Dress'.

180 This is a summary of a report published by the writer; see Spain, 1984a, 103-105.

181 Clayton 1861, 80-85.

182 Archaeologia Aeliana 1861, 85; 1865, 86; Bruce 1867, 148.

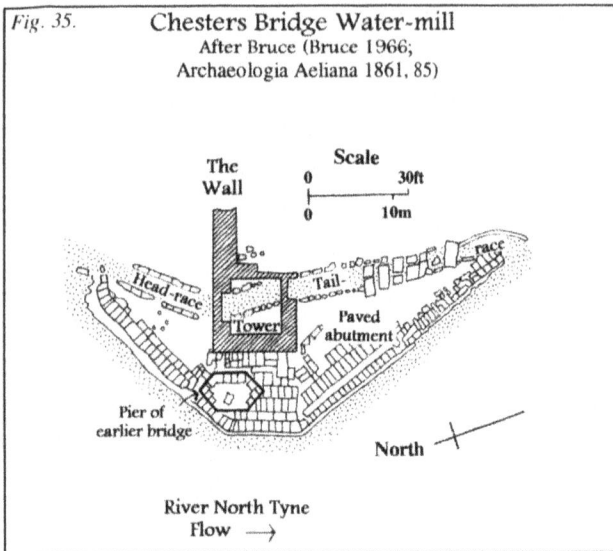

Fig. 35. Chesters Bridge Water-mill
After Bruce (Bruce 1966;
Archaeologia Aeliana 1861, 85)

interesting point of the partial blockage is that it was so constructed as to leave a clearway of 0.97 m wide by 0.53 m high, with the stones arranged to leave a neat rectangular hole low in the watercourse. Of greater significance is the position of this aperture against the east wall of the head-race, which makes the axis of the water through the mill more parallel to the walls. Such an arrangement would have improved the flow conditions through the tower and the application of water to the undershot wheel. It is therefore suggested that the partial blockage of the head-race through the north tower wall existed during the working life of the mill, perhaps installed soon after the building of the mill. The size of the wheel can be roughly estimated. If we are influenced by the aperture in the north wall and allowing that the skew axis of the water reduces the effective width of application to the wheel, we could expect a wheel from 0.6 m to 0.9 m wide and a diameter of say, 3.0 or 3.6 m at the most. Several millstones were found on this site confirming that the mill was used for corn-milling.

just before it passes into the tower, to 1.65 m through the mill and the tail-race[183]. Apparently it is not possible to determine the level of the original bottom of the course although the depth of the sides over the stone courses is approximately 0.84 m. A survey by Simpson showed the course to be almost level over its length of 39.6 m although the bottom of the walls indicated a drop of 11.5 cm[184]. This undershot wheel generated power solely by impulse, from a low-velocity large flow-rate river supply. The velocity and flow rate were determined probably less by the gradient of the mill-race bed and more by the bifurcation upstream, however this was achieved. The reduction in width of the mill-race where it passed through the mill would have caused an increase in velocity, but this by itself does not warrant the classification of an accelerated headrace. An exact dating for the working of the mill is difficult to suggest. It appears to have been built when the abutment for a second bridge was extended southwards[185].

Although clearly within the Roman period, for the Military Way passed over the tail-race, the entry of the head-race through the mill wall is partially blocked by stones, suggesting a crude earlier attempt to reduce water flow or an abandonment of water-power during the Late Roman period. Richmond[186] and Moritz[187] consider the mill to have been operational during the 3rd c. A.D. but the abandonment theory must be questioned. An important feature of the plan is the axis of the watercourse through the lower tower that is skewed and not parallel with the north-south mill walls. Why did they build it thus? Apparently the watercourse does not pre-date the tower structure. The

13. Willowford Bridge, England.

During 1923 and 1924, Shaw working on the Roman bridge over the River Irthing at *Willowford*, uncovered evidence of another probable water-mill, the third associated with Hadrian's Wall[188]. This water-mill is thought to have been constructed during the 3rd c. A.D. On the east bank three stone-lined watercourses were found between

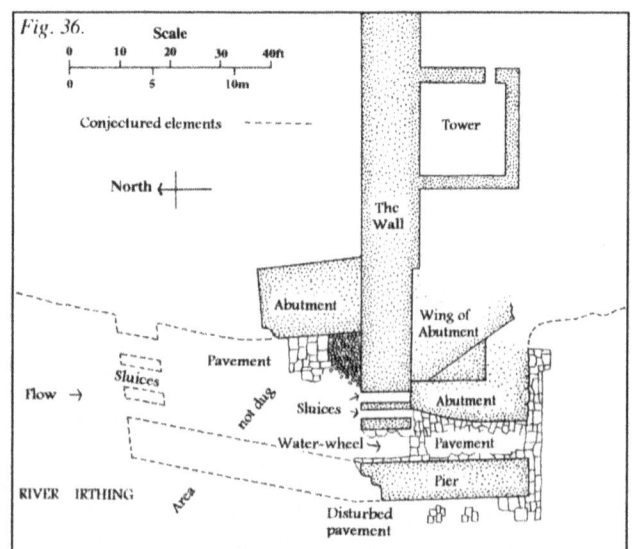

Fig. 36.

183 The writer is indebted to Mr. M.J.Fuller for the detailed site measurements of the mill and its watercourses.
184 Simpson 1976.
185 Bruce 1986, 81-2.
186 Richmond 1947, 166.
187 Moritz 1958, 136.
188 Shaw 1926.

abutments and the eastern-most bridge pier. (See Fig. 36.) A 1.7 m wide channel has been interpreted as a water-wheel emplacement and the two narrower parallel channels as sluices. The finding of millstone fragments strengthened the suggestion that a water-mill operated here[189]. But this interpretation of the *Willowford* evidence is not without problems and needs further thought.

The sluices, one or both, acting as a bypass, would have had a negligible effect in relieving the water pressure and flow to the wheel because their position and face area on the whole of the fabric normal to the river flow is insignificant. Furthermore, as Shaw noted, the lower courses of the wall would have been in danger of being undermined in times of flood[190]. To effect control over the volume of water approaching the water-mill and to provide a measure of protection, building fabric had to be extended from the pier upstream northwards to create a bifurcation. This would have been terminated at a convenient point upstream where sluice gates could be positioned and operated to create a separate water channel and head-race for the mill wheel. It is unfortunate that this area north of the pier was not dug by Shaw, however his work gives us a few tentative clues. These are (i) the pavement appeared to extend northwards upstream from the sluices, (ii) the north end of the pier was much disturbed and it was not possible to confirm the original upstream profile, (iii) large stones were found with checks on one surface like those covering the sluices, suggesting that the sluices had been more extensive at some previous period.

Shaw's plan of the bridge abutments and piers clearly shows several phases of work but how they relate to water-power generation is perplexing. The duplication of abutments and their positions suggests defensive developments in response to river movement and erosion. The extensive underwater pavements support this theory and strengthen the notion of the stone-lined channels being used for power generation and water control. But what are we to make of the south-west abutment, clearly a later structure that blocks the end of the eastern channel? Perhaps the only meaningful conclusion that we can draw from this is that this water-wheel site operated for some time and then was improved with substantial structural work.

Shaw found a pit or depression at least 1.5 m deep in the suggested wheel position, filled with cobble and loose gravel. This was clearly not a wheel-pit for such an

arrangement was impracticable and inefficient, so that we must conclude that the cavity was created by natural forces of erosion triggered perhaps by stone robbing. The mill structure would have spanned between the pier and the abutment and might have carried a footbridge above as a continuation of the rampart walk on the Wall. Allowing for underside clearance, a 2.7 m diameter wheel is suggested, which conveniently fits the length of the channel so that the mill building would enclose it. The driver gear would have been mounted on the wheel-shaft close to either the pier or the east face of the wheel channel. To obtain a satisfactory millstone speed the driver gear would have been fairly large to create a high MR because of the low velocity of the river. We can be certain of the type of application at *Willowford*. It was obviously a 'river' wheel of low velocity with the power generated solely by impulse, from a relatively large flow rate acting on radial floats.

14. Janiculum Hill, Rome, Italy.

During 1990 and 1991 excavations undertaken by Bell[191] confirmed the existence of several Roman water-mills, that had been seen and sketched by Lanciani[192] in 1886. The discovery revealed two parallel mill-races, one either side of the Aqua Traiana aqueduct, and bearing blocks and a gear-pit confirming the position of two water-wheels in the northern mill-race. Both mill-races were 1.7 m wide, paved and had walls coated with hydraulic plaster. (See Fig. 37.) The width of the wheels was probably close to 1.5 m. In the north mill-race, where the gradient of the bed was calculated to be 1 in 50, Bell identified the position of a gear-pit, and at a distance of 2.6 m upstream, a marble bearing block for another water-wheel. The diameter of the wheel suggested by the height of the bearing above the mill-race floor was c.2.30 m. In the south mill-race Bell found the level of the floor of the gear-pit was 1.0 m higher than its northern counterpart, and he therefore thought that the floor of the south mill-race was also higher, and was perhaps served by the Alsietina aqueduct. Wilson's excavations over two seasons in 1998 and 1999 at the west end of the mill complex, revealed further evidence which proved that the south mill-race was served from the Aqua Traiana[193]. With this conclusion he demonstrated that the

189 Shaw 1926, 485.
190 Shaw 1926, 469.
191 Bell 1994.
192 Lanciani 1910; 1891(a); 1891(b).
193 Wilson 2000.

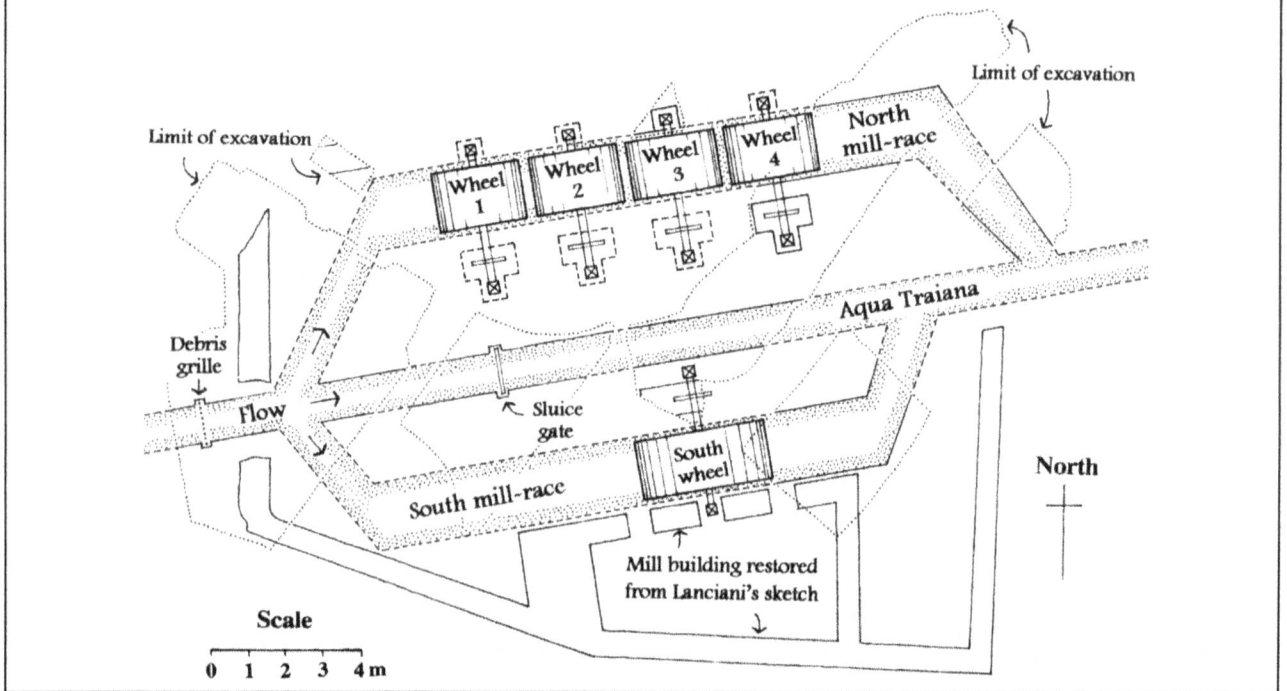

Fig. 37.

Janiculum Hill Water-mills
After Wilson (Wilson 2000, Figs. 4 and 5)
Bell (Bell 1994, Fig. 2) and
Lanciani (Lanciani 1910, sheet 27)

south water-wheel was larger, probably between 3.20 and 3.80 m diameter. The excavations also showed that there was room for only one wheel in the south mill-race, whereas in the north mill-race, at least three and probably four water-wheels existed, working in series. The water-mill complex was apparently built some time after A.D. 200 and abandoned A.D.*c*.400.

The gradient of the southern mill-race is unknown although Wilson observed that the mill-race floors lay at approximately the same level[194]. The level of water that prevailed in the southern mill-race was probably similar to that in the north race, but without more information concerning the levels of its bed we cannot advance our hydraulic analysis. We must not be misled by the diameter of the southern wheel. Its greater diameter does not necessarily mean greater power. On a bucket wheel this would follow but for an impulse wheel different conditions prevail concerning potential power[195]. Part Three Section 4 below addresses this phenomenon. The width of the south race at 1.7 m is the same as the north race, so that if the depth and velocity of water were the same, the potential power of the south wheel would be the same as that of the

upstream wheel in the north race.

The remains of a sluice-gate were found in the Aqua Traiana channel between the off-takes and the returns of the mill-races, which would have been closed to force water into both channels simultaneously. With this control arrangement the water flow into each channel would have been similar providing the gradients and the hydraulic resistances were the same. But the operational speeds of the wheels are imponderable. When we examine the series of water-wheels in the north race, the hydraulic conditions are unusual, indeed fascinating. As Wilson observes, the close setting of the wheels means that a wheel downstream of another is adversely affected by its turbulence[196]. But the hydraulic changes are not due solely to turbulence[197]. As the water meets a series of identical sized wheels whose floats are moving at a slower speed than the water, the average water velocity decreases. Furthermore, if the quantity of water flowing (Q) is a constant throughout the series – which it must be because there are no additions or subtractions to the flow – the depth of water must increase as, the velocity decreases. In fact the one is inversely proportional to the other. As the water moves downstream

194 Wilson 2000, 224.
195 The power resulting from a force of x kg on a wheel of y m diameter is the same if applied to a wheel twice the diameter because HP is proportional to the product of speed and torque. The increase in torque is balanced by the decrease in speed where the velocity of the centre of pressure is constant. This phenomenon is discussed in more detail in Part Three below.
196 Wilson 2000, 236.
197 Their proximity to each other means that the water issuing from one with splashing, eddies and surges, does not have time to regain laminar conditions before striking the floats of the following wheel. Such conditions and the resulting energy losses are beyond theoretical resolution. Nonetheless, we can learn something from a simplified approach to the physical properties.

from one wheel to another, two changes occur in the dynamics; [1] as the water velocity slows and its depth increases, the centre of pressure on the immersed floats rises and thereby the radius of the torque decreases, and [2] the rotational speed of successive wheels decreases because of the reduced water velocity acting in conjunction with a reduced radius of torque.

With the *Janiculum* evidence, we have two facts that influence our hydraulic analysis of the north channel, the bed gradient of 2%, and the lime incrustations on both walls of the north channel downstream of wheel 4, which Bell interpreted as the tail-race water at its greatest volume when *c*.0.50 m deep[198]. With some hesitation, the writer has undertaken a sequence of theoretical calculations that starts with the tail-race depth of 0.5 m and progresses upstream determining the changes in water depth due to float velocities 0.425 of the approaching water[199]. When the headrace of Wheel 1 is reached, the depth of water and bed gradient allows the application of Manning's formula to determine velocity, and thereby Q, the total flow rate. The following theoretical physical data is the result.

Table J – North mill-race – velocities and depths. Q = 10.5 ft³/s [0.3 m³/s]

Velocity (ft/s)	Depth (ft)
7.7	0.245
Wheel One	
5.79	0.328
Wheel Two	
3.76	0.50
Wheel Three	
2.18	0.869
Wheel Four	
1.16	1.64 [0.5 m]

Under these conditions, the depth of water entering Wheel 1 is only 0.245 ft (7.5 cm), barely enough to touch the floats, and Wheel 4, revolves at 3.6 rpm and generates less than one tenth of a horse-power! Clearly this flow rate and energy taken by the wheels does not support working conditions. If we now rework the calculation sequence, starting at the same water depth of 0.5 m (1.64 ft) in the tail-race of Wheel 4, but allowing the wheels to revolve at a velocity of 0.7 of the approaching water, the results are as follows.

Table K – North mill-race – velocities and depths. Q = 34.17 ft³/s [0.97 m³/s]

Velocity (ft/s)	Depth (ft)
11.96	0.512
Wheel One	
7.7	0.797
Wheel Two	
6.23	0.98
Wheel Three	
4.69	1.305
Wheel Four	
3.73	1.64 [0.5 m]

Both the depth and the velocity increase substantially through the series of wheels and the flow rate increases more than threefold. With these conditions, Wheel 1 generates 3.2 hp and revolves at 24.8 rpm, and Wheel 4, 0.49 hp revolving at 11.05 rpm. Remembering that the south mill-race would be taking another similar volume of water – though whether they could modulate the flow between the two channels we do not know – this flow rate (0.97 m³/s) for the north channel may be slightly excessive for the Traiana aqueduct.

This analysis is intended to demonstrate the power generation relationship between successive wheels in series. As we have seen, the calculation sequence is sensitive to the flow rate adopted[200], and the exercise should be seen as illustrating the relative performance of the wheels rather than their absolute power values. This result, is of course, purely hypothetical produced by the conditions that we have set, but it illustrates the range of possibilities for those conditions. It also demonstrates the sensitivity of the wheels interacting with each other, but how the operators handled this is debatable.

In the gear-pits Bell found fragments of basalt millstones *c*.0.75 m diameter[201]. If we assume a half-life thickness of 0.152 m (0.5 ft.) the top-stone would weigh 134 kg (296 lbs) and would absorb 1.0 hp when revolving at 61.5 rpm. Bell has shown, from his excavations of the gear-pits in both mill-races, that the driven gear would have been much smaller than the pit-gear (driver) due to the narrow confines of the pit[202]. He illustrates a lantern gear, which it probably was, with an MR of approximately 4 to 1. The detail does not matter, the critical feature is that this evidence suggests

198 Bell 1994, 78.
199 Allowances are made for the side and underside clearances of the floats, where water would be moving at a velocity similar to the approaching water.
200 And to a lesser extent, the 'leakage' flows allowed around the sides and below the wheels.
201 Bell 1994, 83.
202 Bell 1994, 85, Fig 14.

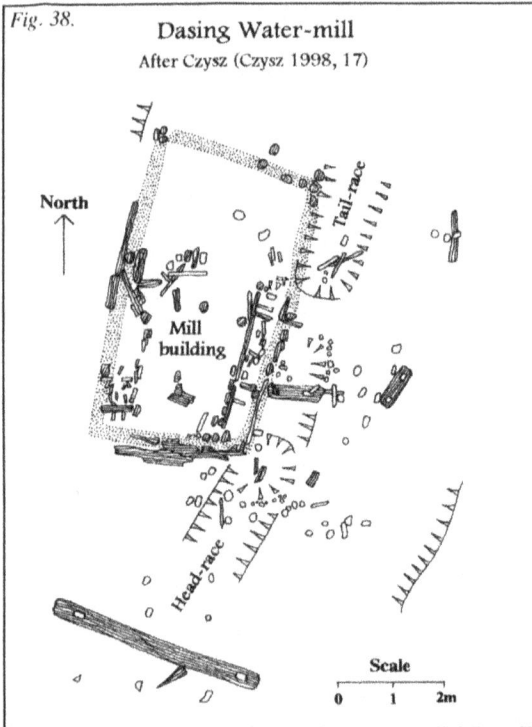

Fig. 38.
Dasing Water-mill
After Czysz (Czysz 1998, 17)

North

Tail-race

Mill building

Head-race

Scale
0   1   2m

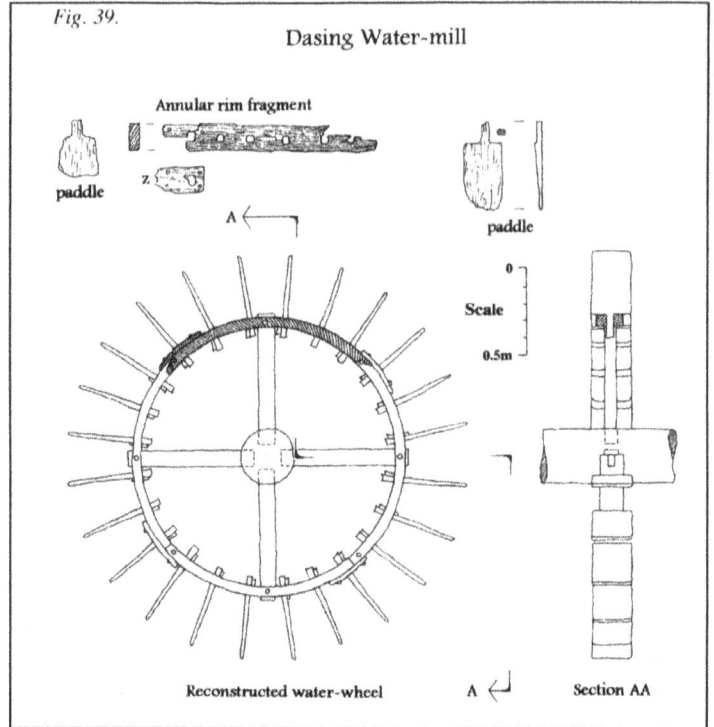

Fig. 39.
Dasing Water-mill

Annular rim fragment

paddle

z

A

paddle

Scale

0.5m

Reconstructed water-wheel   A   Section AA

that the millstones rotated faster than the water-wheels. The above wheel series analysis demonstrates that the generated power would have varied from wheel to wheel, suggesting that the MR also varied from mill to mill.

15. Dasing, Bavaria, Germany.

A Roman water-mill surely existed at Dasing, where lava millstone fragments and a group of earth-fast posts, dated by dendrochronology to A.D. 103-112, were found beside an ancient watercourse[203]. The dating makes this site one of the earliest Roman water-mills found to date but unfortunately the evidence was either very disturbed or limited, for no detailed records exist, and it is not possible to advance the examination of the hydraulic arrangements. However, this case study concerns another water-mill found close by that is Merovingian and not Roman. The reason why this is included in this collection of evidence is that it provides a parallel to several other Roman water-mills and gives us a rare insight into impulse wheel design. Later, we shall see that it is an exemplar of a design that was present in the northern provinces from the Early Empire through Late Antiquity.

203 Czysz 1994; Czysz 1998, 11-14.

The remains of this Merovingian water-mill shows that it had a rectangular floor plan with earth-fast posts and truss frame under a thatched roof. (See Fig. 38.) The mill-race beside the mill produced evidence of at least two ground-plates with through mortices. One was found apparently *in situ* very close to where the wheel operated, showing that it was an under-shot arrangement. The width inside the mortices was approximately 45 cm. But by far the most valuable and unique evidence from the site was the remains of the water-wheel's annular rim and several wooden paddles. The curved fragment of the rim pierced with through mortices, together with the remains of at least two paddles, shows that the wheel was probably close to 2.33 m in diameter with 24 radial paddles. (See Fig. 39.) The paddle evidence indicates that they were c.22.5 cm wide and 37 cm long (832.5 cm^2) and were probably wedged into the rim from inside. The wheel's annular rim was made up of four segments, half-lapped and pegged together and strengthened by a plate nailed over the joints on the outer surface. (See z on Fig. 39.) Four radial arms carried the wheel that were probably morticed into the wheel-shaft.

The reconstructed section shows the hursting supported on ground-plates and separated from the rather light-weight building frame. (See Fig. 40.) This foundation arrangement for supporting the heavy loads of the millstone platform can be seen as a logical and practical development for an

40

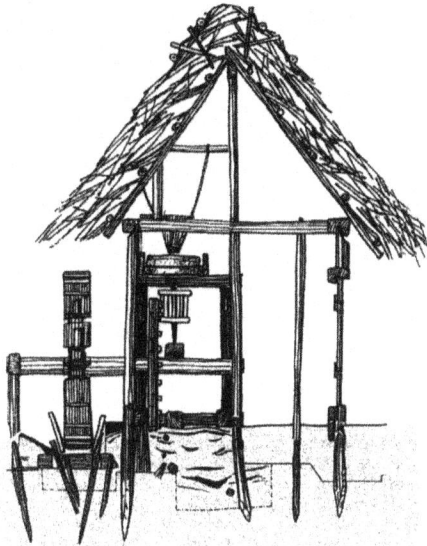

Fig. 40.

Dasing Water-mill
Artist's reconstruction
After Czysz (Czysz 1998, 21)

improved structural design. Although the gear ratio illustrated is realistic, the writer favours the driver gear on the 'land-side' of the lantern gear rather than the 'water-side', to improve access and maintenance. The arrangement of the wheel-trough is interesting. During the excavation the *in situ* ground-plate close to the wheel position was found with stakes or posts still in position passing through the mortices[204]. These stakes were tilted away from each other that have been interpreted as implying inclined supports for the side-wall planks of the head-race trough. The section in Fig. 40 shows this clearly. This would explain why the distance between the mortices in the ground-plate (45 cm) is considerably greater than the width of the paddles (*c*.22.5 cm). Whilst this seems to be a realistic interpretation of the evidence, the inclined flanks of the trough create a trapezoidal section and reduce the efficiency of application because a proportion of the water escapes the paddles. The deeper the water, the greater the proportion escaping the paddles. If this design of inclined trough walls existed upstream of the wheel, the 16° deflection in the axis of the head-race at the south-east corner of the mill would have caused agitation and surging conditions at the wheel, especially with a fast flow. The site drawing does not show the ground levels of the mill-race and so we have no idea of the gradient of the approaching head-race. Although the millstones were small (50-60 cm in

204 Czysz 1998, 11 (photograph).
205 Volpert 1997.
206 Volpert 1997, 246, Abb. 4.
207 Volpert 1997, 248, Abb. 5.

diameter) it is likely that this was an accelerated head-race. To drive the 56 cm diameter top stone found at the site at 90 rpm would require an impact velocity on the paddles - assuming that the full face area was used – of *c*.2.9 m/s.

16. München-Perlach, Bavaria, Germany.

At München-Perlach an earth-fast wooden structure beside a watercourse, where numerous millstone fragments were found, has been confidently identified as a Roman water-mill[205]. A plan of the post-holes shows a square shaped building on the west bank of a 3-4 m wide stream[206]. (See Fig. 41.) The longitudinal section of the stream revealed a distinct shoulder and profile beside the mill building that marks the position of where the water-wheel operated. The slope of the bed of the stream, both head-race and tail-race sections, suggests that a good flow velocity existed[207]. Although two cross-sections were cut on the mill-stream, including one just three metres downstream of the wheel, no evidence of revetment or a boarded race were found. The archaeological horizons were apparently truncated below the Roman ground surface by perhaps 0.5 m, as indicated by Volpert's section[208]. At least two of the post-holes of the water-side wall of the mill were found in

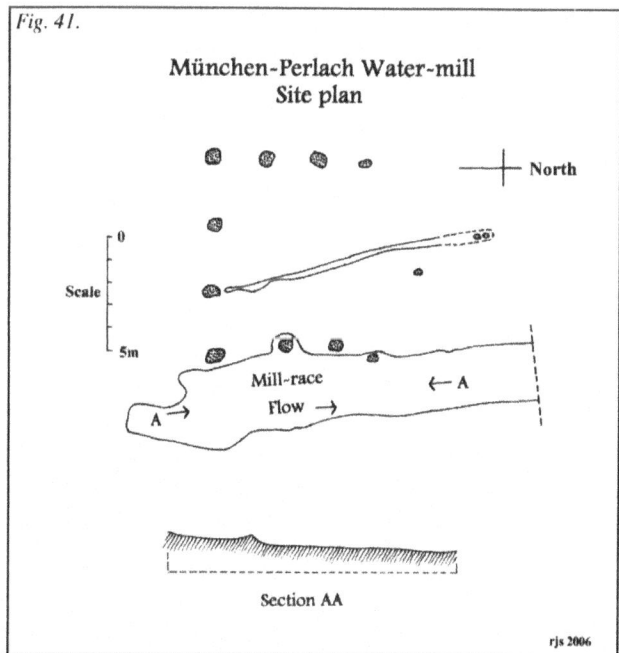

Fig. 41.

München-Perlach Water-mill
Site plan

North

Scale

0

5m

Mill-race
Flow →

← A

A →

Section AA

rjs 2006

41

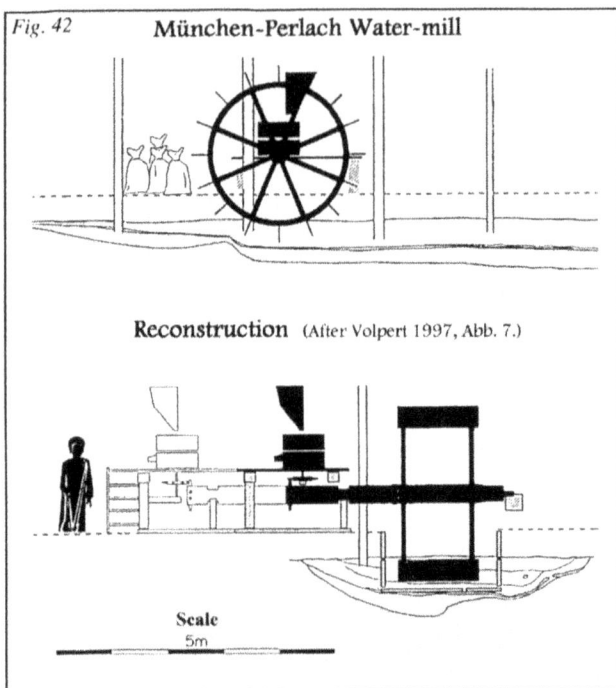

Fig. 42 München-Perlach Water-mill

Reconstruction (After Volpert 1997, Abb. 7.)

Scale
5m

the mill-race that suggests that if the race was boarded, traces of the supporting posts should have been discovered. None were found, so that Volpert's section of his reconstruction of the mill showing the wheel operating in a boarded race with planked walls and base is supposition, and should be treated with caution. The wheel may therefore have worked within the mill-race without revetment or wooden channeling. This supports the idea that the mill-race was not man-made but a palaeochannel.

Numerous fragments of millstones were found at the site and the diameters of four of them have been determined, ranging from 0.60-0.895 m diameter. At least three of these stones were top stones, and possibly the fourth, that shows furrows. The inclination of their grinding faces varies greatly from fairly steep to almost flat. This variation in millstone size and shape suggests that different milling practices existed during the life of the mill.

In his reconstruction Volpert suggests that the water-wheel had to be a minimum of 2.3 m diameter and his drawing shows an undershot wheel with radial arms and floats, 3.14 m diameter and 1.45 m wide. (See Fig. 42.) He also indicates a duplex drive, where an optional arrangement of an extended wheel-shaft powers a second set of millstones and gearing. Recently, several Late Roman duplex-drive water-mills have been discovered in Israel apparently driving two pairs of small Pompeian-style stones (See site

208 Volpert 1997, 248, Abb. 5.

no. 25 below.) and at *Fullerton* the possibility of a wheel driving two pairs of millstones is briefly discussed, but on balance is considered unlikely. (See site no. 6 above.) The mechanical ratio shown on the drawings, approximately 1 : 1, is totally unrealistic, for the millstones would need to rotate much faster than the water-wheel. According to the ceramic evidence the occupation of the site, and presumably the operation of the water-mill, commenced at the end of the 2nd. c. A.D. The end date is more difficult to ascertain, but none of the finds date beyond mid. 4th. c. A.D.

17. Oderzo, near Venice, Italy.

During 1986 and 1989 an emergency excavation revealed an ancient river bed and Roman structures, which have been identified as a quay and an adjacent revetted watercourse[209]. The watercourse was separated from an adjacent river by a long narrow artificial island which created a bifurcation upstream. In an earlier phase the diverted water apparently created a larger area of water bounded by substantial revetted embankments of oak posts and beams identified as a quay. Later, the quayside was expanded and revetted walls of earth-fast posts and planks, which converged further downstream, extended the channel parallel to the river. (See Fig. 43.) Where this channel narrowed to a width of 1.5 m, near the southern limits of the excavation, the bed of the channel was built up to reduce the water depth, and on top was laid a planked floor 4.80 m long. Two layers of floor planks were found, but the top layer was shorter and its downstream end had been elevated by a transverse beam inserted beneath, resting on top of the earlier floor. In this region the ends of the wall planks were morticed into vertical grooves of the wall-posts. In a final stage of work, the width of the watercourse was made parallel at c.1.50 m for a distance of at least 16 m upstream of the feature described above. These features have been identified as the head-race for a Roman watermill dated 2nd c. A.D. The mill, which was positioned on the very edge of the excavation, yielded little evidence apart from some foundations supporting a small platform, probably part of the mill building. An un-scaled reconstruction of the wheel arrangement shows the water entering an under-shot wheel

42

down a 30° slope. The drawing, although crude, is a reasonable interpretation of the evidence, and we can be confident that the depiction of an accelerated race serving a radial float wheel is realistic. An inclined wooden trough would have been used to deliver water into the wheel, which probably had a width of *c*.1.40 m.

The outstanding feature of this water-mill is the effort taken to create an accelerated head-race. The nearby river was in ancient times, and still is, fairly wide, and the creation of the adjacent quay and dock area suggests low velocity slow running navigable waters. In this situation, where the mill builders could not readily obtain a head of water without creating a very long bifurcation upstream, they improved potential power by increasing velocity. We do not know the length of the tail-race, but it is possible that it travelled some distance to obtain an adequate fall in level from the head of water at the wheel. The convergence of the head-

race walls in conjunction with the reduction in the depth immediately approaching the wheel would have greatly accelerated the flow and provided ample power. Control of the water must have been provided upstream at the bifurcation, for no evidence of a bypass was found near the mill. This would have been rather difficult to achieve while the quay was operational and prior to the head-race being made a narrower parallel channel.

18. Haltwhistle Burn Head, Northumberland, England.

In contrast to the Continental sites, the Britannia water-mills have produced little evidence to support a comprehensive hydro-mechanical analysis, with one exception, the 3rd c. A.D. Roman site at *Haltwhistle Burn Head*, close to Hadrian's Wall. The site was discovered and excavated by Simpson in 1907/8 but not fully published until 1976[210]. His interpretation of the remains was masterly, surely a reflection of his engineering training, a combination of disciplines rare among archaeologists.

The mill-race was cut across a bend in the Haltwhistle Burn River beneath a modern sheep-washing pen, with the head-race gradient increasing over its length of 17.5 m as it approached the wheel position. The later part of its bed was cut out of solid rock. (See Fig. 44.) This was probably no

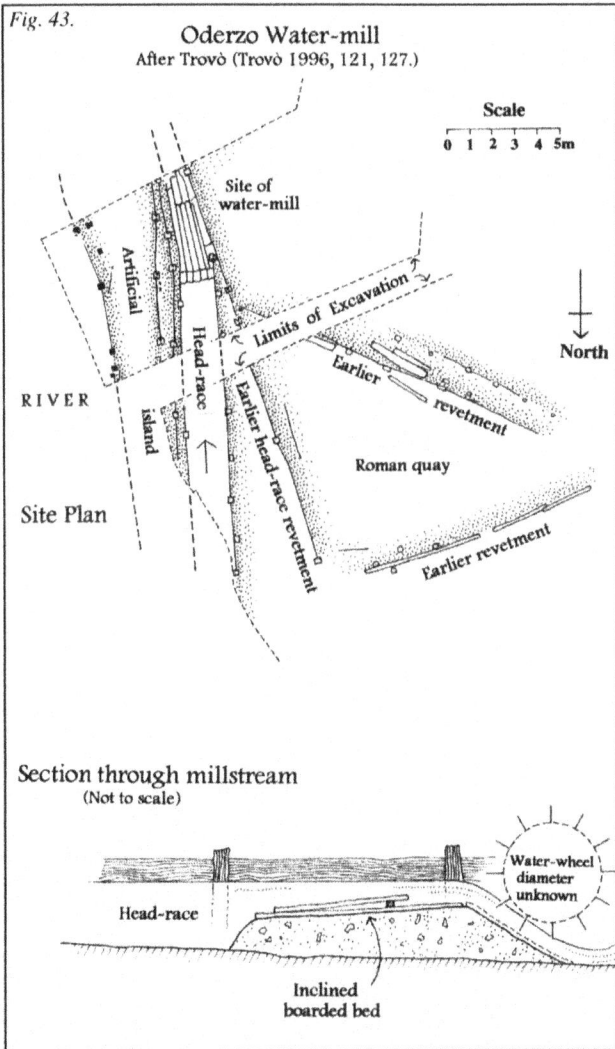

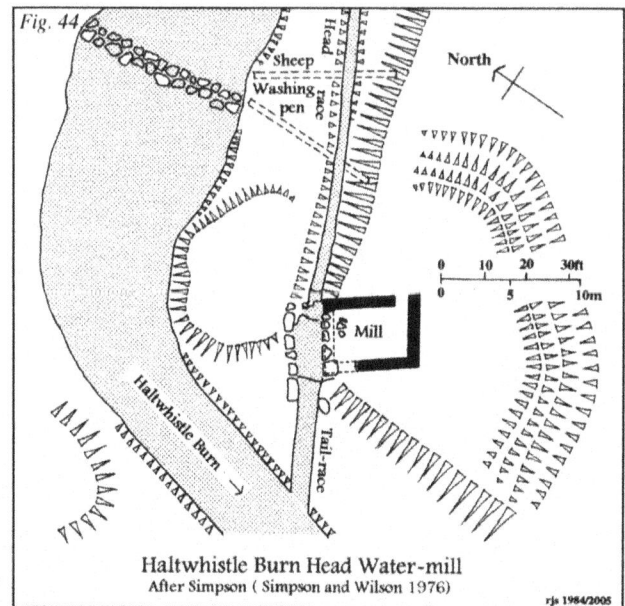

Fig. 43.

Oderzo Water-mill
After Trovò (Trovò 1996, 121, 127.)

Scale
0 1 2 3 4 5m

Site of water-mill

Limits of Excavation

North

Artificial

Head-race

island

RIVER

Earlier

revetment

Earlier head-race revetment

Roman quay

Site Plan

Earlier revetment

Section through millstream
(Not to scale)

Head-race

Water-wheel diameter unknown

Inclined boarded bed

Fig. 44

Sheep Washing pen

Head race

North

Mill

Haltwhistle Burn →

Tail-race

0 10 20 30ft
0 5 10m

Haltwhistle Burn Head Water-mill
After Simpson (Simpson and Wilson 1976)

rjs 1984/2005

209 Trovò 1996.
210 Simpson published a very brief note of his discovery in Proc. Soc. Newcastle-upon-Tyne, 3, iv, 167, Discoveries per Lineam Valli. The writer is indebted to Dr.Grace Simpson for the information she kindly provided from her father's site note books prior to publication. Simpson 1976.

accident of siting for the scouring velocities that existed in the race necessitated revetment of the head-race banks for most of its length. For the last two metres the water was carried to the wheel by an inclined wooden trough, some remains of which Simpson found in the bottom of the watercourse beside the mill. The wheel-pit, with ample clearance for maintenance of the wheel and land-side bearing, was cut out of solid rock as low as possible without causing tail-water under the wheel. Enough of the mill building was found, including walls of 3-5 courses *in situ* above a footing course, to allow a reconstruction of the wheel-shaft position and thereby the wheel diameter, which was *c*.3.6 m. (See Fig. 45.)

The detailed and well-recorded excavation of the head-race has made possible a hydraulic analysis[211] that shows that it was constructed to give the water progressively faster velocity as it approached the wheel. (See Fig. 46 and Table L.) The dimensions of the wooden trough confirm the width of the wheel as 0.35 m but more important, it indicates that the builder took pains to control the application of water to the wheel.

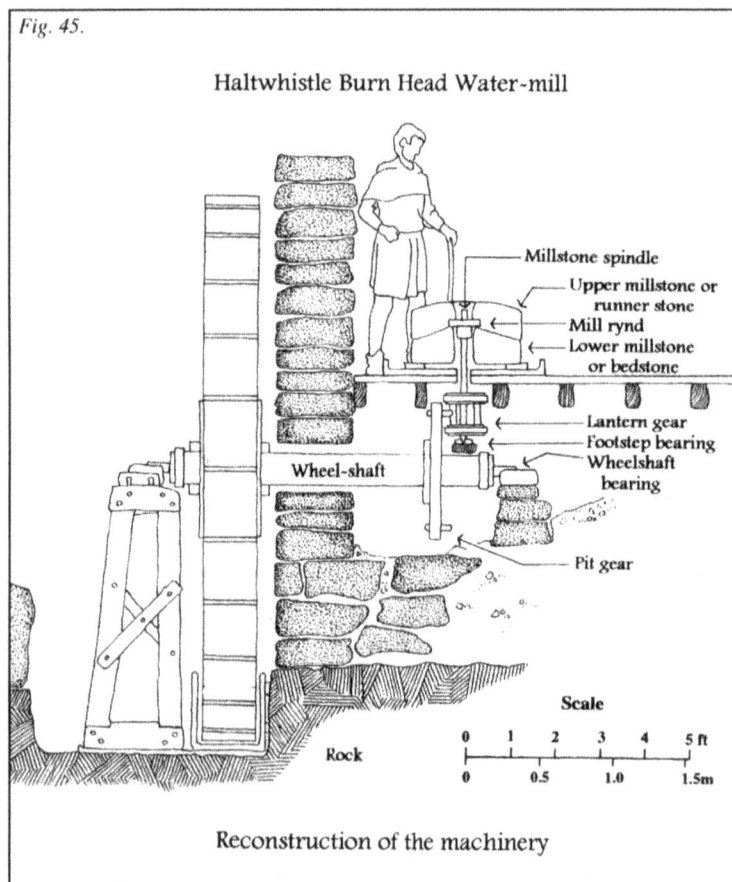

Fig. 45.

Haltwhistle Burn Head Water-mill

Millstone spindle
Upper millstone or runner stone
Mill rynd
Lower millstone or bedstone

Lantern gear
Footstep bearing
Wheelshaft bearing

Wheel-shaft

Pit gear

Scale

| 0 | 1 | 2 | 3 | 4 | 5 ft |
Rock
| 0 | 0.5 | 1.0 | 1.5 m |

Reconstruction of the machinery

Table L - Physical properties of head-race

Section of course	Horizontal length (m)	Gradient of bed	Material	
			Bed	Sides
A to B	11.4	0.0311	Sand and gravel	Possible bratticing
B to C	3.96	0.0612	Smooth rock	Stones with bratticing
C to D	2.14	0.351	Un-planed timber	

In the hydraulic analysis, where it is assumed that the depth of water entering the wheel was 0.2 m, the sequence of calculations shows that the final impact velocity is 15.16 ft/s (4.62 m/s) with a flow volume of 13.9 ft^3/s (0.4 m^3/s). At this velocity the total kinetic energy available is 5.63 hp. There are now two different approaches to determine the power generated by the wheel. The simplest way is to assume an overall efficiency for the wheel and multiply it by the kinetic energy. If we assume a wheel efficiency of 30%, allowing for friction of the bearings, leaks, splashing etc, the maximum wheel-shaft power would be 0.30 x 5.63 = 1.69 hp. The second alternative method is to establish the force acting on the wheel and convert this to a torque and enter this figure into the basic horsepower formula. Using this method[212] results in a power of 2.37 hp. From this we must subtract an amount for wheel-shaft friction, leaks, splashing etc, and we are advised that a figure of 30% should be allowed for this[213]. The theoretical power available from the wheel-shaft is therefore 2.37 x 0.70 = 1.66 hp. that compares favourably with the kinetic energy method. Finally, we must subtract an allowance for the footstep bearing and gear friction (6%) leaving a balance of 1.51 hp for the millstones.

The flow rate that creates this power provides for a 'full' wheel, enough water to submerge the floats as they pass through the trough. A lesser flow would, of course, produce less power, but if a greater flow were allowed in the head-race, it is likely that no discernible increase in power would occur. Indeed it is possible that a slight

211 Much of the following analysis comes from an un-published hydro-mechanical analysis of Haltwhistle Burn Head Mill by the writer dated April 1976. Spain 1976.
212 Using a wheel speed of 11.36 rpm that is determined by a mean float velocity equal to 0.425 of the water velocity.
213 'Industrial Archaeology of Watermills and Waterpower', Project Technology Handbook, 11, 1975, 57.

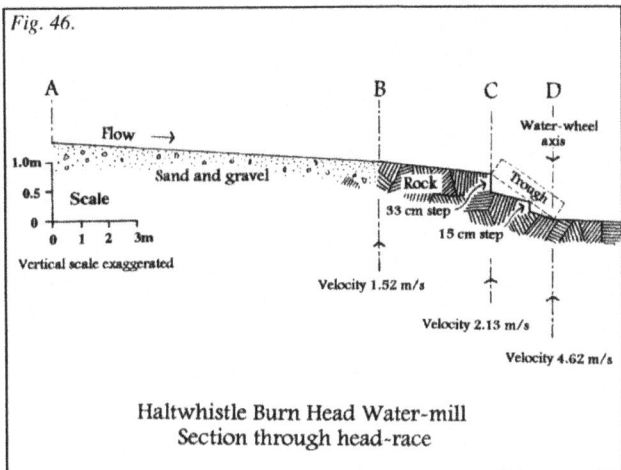

Fig. 46.

Haltwhistle Burn Head Water-mill
Section through head-race

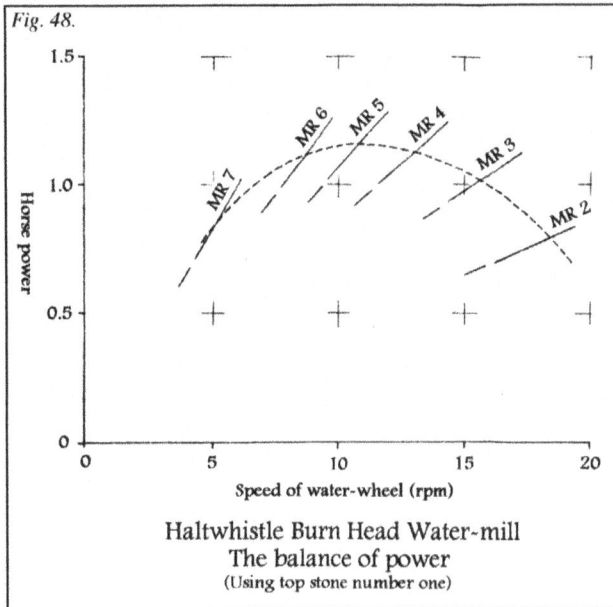

Fig. 48.

Haltwhistle Burn Head Water-mill
The balance of power
(Using top stone number one)

decrease might occur due to increased turbulence and back pressure on the floats. But we can be fairly confident that with the arrangement of the mill-race there would have been no difficulty in diverting ample water from the nearby Burn. (See Fig. 47.)

The remains of several millstones were found varying from 0.63 – 0.97 m diameter. Amongst the fragments of six different upper millstones discovered the largest, 30 ins. (0.76 m) in diameter and 6 ins. (0.152 m) thick at the rim, would have weighed 364 lbs (165.5 kg) when complete[214]. If we adopt the coefficient of friction of 0.351 in absence of other information to guide us, the power needed to drive this stone at 60 rpm is 1.22 hp. Knowing this and the power available from the waterwheel, our final enquiry is to see if we can shed light upon the gear ratios by looking at the balance of power that existed at different speeds. If the power generated by the water-wheel is directly related to the efficiency of application, then this can be represented on a power/wheel speed graph. On this graph the maximum

power of 1.51 hp available to the millstones occurs at a wheel speed of 11.36 rpm. Onto this we can now superimpose the power needed for the millstones at different gear ratios. (See Fig. 48.) For any MR a balance of power exists where the lines intersect. We are reminded that the millstone power lines relate to the heaviest section top stone found. As a top stone ages and becomes thinner and lighter, the power needed reduces, and with a fixed MR the water-wheel speeds up. The balance of power will 'track' down the generated power curve. This tells us that when a new heavy top stone was installed, if it was combined with an MR that utilized the maximum power i.e, 1.51 hp, it would speed up during its life and continue to optimize the power. If a stone was introduced with the wrong combination of millstone weight and MR, then as it became lighter it would reach a limit in speed; it could only rotate

Fig. 47.

Haltwhistle Burn Head Water-mill
Artist's view – section through millstream

Fig. 49.

Haltwhistle Burn Head Water-mill
Artist's view from downstream

214 Measuring a radial section and using Pappus or Gildinus theorem to determine its volume, and a density of 160 lbs/ft³ for upper limestone millstone grit. The writer is grateful to the Institute of Geological Sciences, London for providing information concerning stone densities.

faster if a higher MR was installed. If the top stones varied greatly in weight when new, and they all used the same MR, then some of them would not obtain the full power potential in their life cycles. If the miller was wise to this, he would have taken one of two actions to optimize output, either have all the new top stones made roughly the same weight and diameter, or, employ different MR's for different stones, most likely by changing the smaller driven gear.

Using the production/power ratio of 117 lbs/hp.hr (53.2 kg/hp.hr) and the net power available for millstone work of 1.51 hp, the daily output, assuming a ten hour working day and optimum production would be 1767 lbs. (803 kg.) Assuming that 90% of the product was for human consumption with a daily rate of 900 g/person, and allowing for a six day working week, this watermill could have supported 690 people[215]. (See Fig. 49.)

19. Martres-de-Veyre, Puy de Dome, France.

This Gallo-Roman site was discovered in 1966 and published by Romeuf twelve years later[216]. The numerous artifacts found at the site indicated that this mill was built and operated for a relatively short period during the late 2nd c. A.D. Fig. 50 is a facsimile of the published plan, and shows the position of the water-wheel A and the gear-pit B. The longitudinal section has been generated using the levels provided in conjunction with Romeuf's section that depicts a 1.85 m diameter water-wheel positioned with its underside touching the bed of the wheel-pit[217]. The writer considers that this is an impractical position for a working wheel and has re-examined the evidence to clarify its probable size and level.

Let us first consider the level of the water-wheel. Although the site levels show a drop of 5 cm in the tail-race a short distance from the wheel, four metres away the bed of the canal is 0.14 m above the wheel-pit bed. As the canal appears to be transporting water past the point where the tail-race enters it, we have to assume that there would have been a depth of water at the junction. Even if the depth was as little as 0.2 m, this would create a depth of water in the wheel-pit of 0.34 m. The canal is recorded as varying from

2.0 to 2.5 m wide, dug 1.0 m deep into the ground, and constructed with basalt walls 0.8 m thick. Unfortunately there is no indication of what depth of water flowed in the canal, but it is reasonable to assume that the miller would not have operated his wheel standing in backwater, that is, with the bottom of the wheel immersed.

In Romeuf's longitudinal section of the mill-race the wheel-pit is shown with a curved breast which we presume represents the two concave depressions a and b. The wheel-pit would have been lined to prevent erosion and preserve its shape but it is unclear from the drawing or the text whether or not it was stone or wood-lined. No matter, whatever the lining, it has disappeared and we must therefore accept that the surfaces found and delineated would have suffered damage by natural forces and perhaps stone-robbing following the abandonment of water-power generation at this site. The deep curved wheel-pit as shown by Romeuf should therefore be viewed with caution. When we position the bottom of the wheel at least 0.2 m above the bed of the canal, the curved breast of the wheel-pit becomes less significant. Nevertheless, the distinct steep step below the wheel tells us that a curved breast may have existed, but it is equally likely that the wheel operated within a steep wooden trough. Whatever the arrangement, this wheel had the advantage of receiving water of a considerable velocity at its face, as is shown by the declination of area E. Assuming that the wheel stood above the water level in the canal, and allowing for the gradient and level of the approaching head-race, it is very likely that this wheel had radial floats and generated power by impulse. The hydraulic head of the wheel was close to 1.5 m.

Within the wheel-pit the parallel flank walls were probably stone-lined. Certainly on the south side, the foundations of the mill-wall would have formed the pit wall, and on the opposite side, depression c is probably the platform for the stone side wall and wheel-shaft bearing. A few stones of this wall remained in situ at d but others had fallen over or had been robbed out. As Romeuf intimated, the width of the water-wheel would have been slightly smaller than the width of the wheel-pit of 0.7 m, say 0.6 m. Its diameter is far more difficult to ascertain. According to the scale of Romeuf's section drawing, the wheel is 1.85 m diameter, but the text suggests a diameter of between 1.6 and 1.8 m. Whilst the axis of the wheel-shaft is readily identifiable on the plan, its vertical position is unknown, somewhere above

215 See Part Three, Mill Production, below.
216 Romeuf 1978.
217 Romeuf 1978, 27.

the extant levels found in the excavation. On the longitudinal section, neither the walls nor floor of the gear-pit nor the canal bed help us to determine the level of the shaft and thereby the diameter of the wheel. In conclusion the writer favours a slightly larger wheel at between 1.8 and 2.0 m diameter, but must admit to a degree of guesswork.

The source of water for the mill is believed to be the La Monne stream approximately 2.5 km from the site but no mill-race has been found. In area *E* no stone walls, cement

or post-holes were found and Romeuf concluded that the head-race ran down the man-made slope towards the wheel[218] as an open earth channel. Such an arrangement would not have endured, for the water accelerating down the decline would have scoured the earth away. The head-race could have been carried in a channel of dressed stones with a cement lining on the water faces. But we have evidence, albeit circumstantial, that an alternative construction probably existed. In area *E* a considerable number of iron nails were found[219], which the writer considers as indicating the likely existence of a wooden head-race perhaps supported by transverse ground-plates, which would agree with the absence of post-holes. Such a wooden head-race, having a declination of 6.5° for a distance of 4 m approaching the wheel would have generated an impact velocity in the order of 3.0 m/s.

Feature *C* is enigmatic, and there are two possible explanations that we can explore. Area *C* is a concave depression whose longitudinal axis is parallel to the mill-race that we have already identified. It occupies the same position as area *A* (wheel-pit and tail-race) relative to area *E*; that is, it enjoys a similar hydraulic head (1.2 – 0.14 = 1.06 m) at the bottom of the man-made watercourse *E*. On plan, area *C* appears to be a duplication of area *A*, creating a parallel watercourse of similar dimensions and fed by an accelerated flow. The first explanation for this feature is that it could be simply a bypass channel for the mill, where the water, excess to the mill's requirements, was diverted. Such a channel would allow the water-wheel to be stopped, by diverting all of the water using a sluice-gate immediately upstream of the top edge of *E*. Our interpretation of the iron nail evidence in area *E* can be repeated for the race serving as a bypass; a wooden structure parallel to the mill head-race. But if a bypass was intended, why create such a wide excavation of *E* parallel to the mill-race? And why was

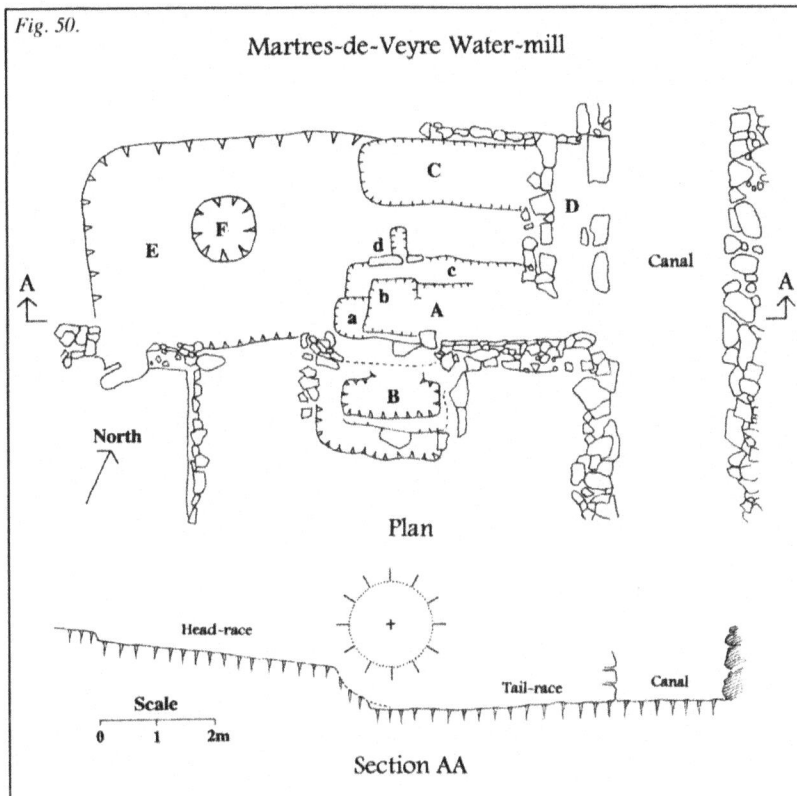

Fig. 50.

Martres-de-Veyre Water-mill

Plan

Section AA

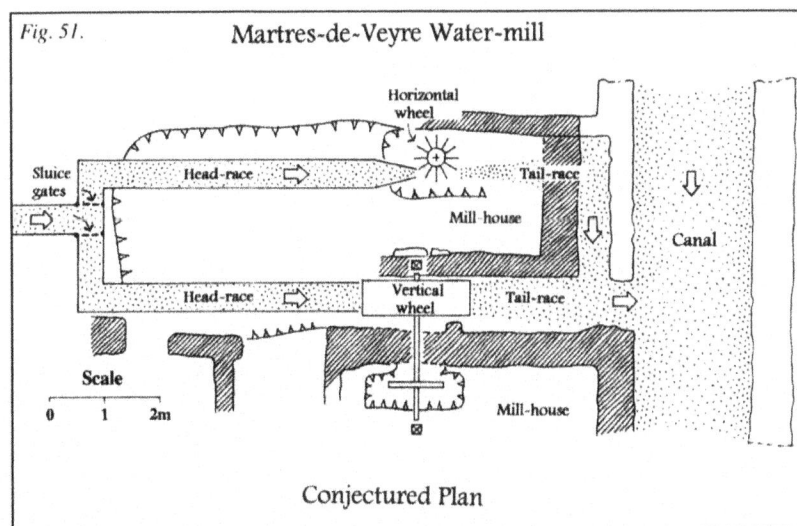

Fig. 51.

Martres-de-Veyre Water-mill

Conjectured Plan

218 Romeuf 1978, 31.
219 Romeuf 1978, 36.

area *C* dug? The bypass channel could have remained at the level of the original ground above *E* and carried along eastwards towards the canal. This brings us to the second possible explanation for area *C*.

Pivotal to this alternative explanation is the evidence of a great abundance of iron nails found in area *C*[220]. A similar collection, described as a '*great number of nails of all sizes*', was found in the wheel-pit, area *A*, beyond doubt primarily the remains of the wooden water-wheel. The evidence suggests that some structure existed in area *C*, but what was it? It was not a vertical water-wheel, because there is no evidence of a gear-pit or related structure that would have existed on the north side of area *C*. The writer therefore proposes that the second alternative, is that a horizontal water-wheel may have operated in area *C*.

In addition to the circumstantial evidence of a hydraulic head and the remaining nails, we should note that horizontal wheels required much less building structure to house the machine. With a single rotating mass comprising the top millstone and water-wheel mounted on the vertical millstone spindle, the foundations for such a mill were limited to the mill floor and the footstep bearing. This bearing, underneath the bottom of the spindle, whether made of iron or stone, would have required a very small area. In other words the 'foot-print' of such a mill is very simple – an outline of stone (or wooden) walls astride a watercourse. There is another interesting feature relating to the gear-less more simple horizontal mill. The water is applied to the wheel as a high velocity stream or jet, concentrated upon the radial blades. To stop the wheel and cease work, the water jet is diverted either by re-directing the nozzle or, by simply deflecting the stream immediately in front of the nozzle away from the wheel. At *Martres-de-Veyre*, water flowing towards area *C* could therefore have acted as a bypass for the vertical water-wheel and, at the same time, driven a horizontal wheel.

But although we have arrived at a possible solution for area *C*, the function of area *D* is unclear. Romeuf believed that a sluice-gate existed in area *D* controlling the water to the vertical water-wheel somehow by modulating the flow in channel *C*. The reason for this rather odd interpretation is that no structural remains that might have suggested the presence of a sluice-gate, were found upstream of area *A*.

Such a conclusion ignores the possibility of erosion or stone-robbing following abandonment. The suggestion of a sluice-gate downstream of the wheel for controlling its operation is illogical; the gate would act as a dam and flood the wheel and probably the gear-pit as well, because of the hydraulic head of 1.2 m above the wheel-pit bed. With area *D* being lower than area *C*, this would be the obvious channel for the tail-race from the proposed horizontal wheel in *C*. The substantial wall between *C* and *D*, suggests that this was the foundation for the east wall of the horizontal-wheeled mill-house. If so, its tail-race had to pass over the stones into channel *D*. Fig. 51 shows the suggested plans of the two mills. The 'scour-pit' recorded on the site plan in area *E* was probably created when the site was abandoned but water still flowed after the wooden mill-races decayed[221]. This suggests a central position for the mill-stream serving the two parallel races.

Fragments belonging to at least eleven different lava millstones were found, including six bottom stones (*metae*) and five top stones (*catilli*)[222]. Their diameters varied from 0.48-0.92 m and their thickness from 0.09-0.33 m. Diameters close to 0.5 m are rare for millstones and are more likely to be querns. Although only two top stones could be assembled from the fragments, it showed that they were under-driven by the millstone spindles projecting through the stones, splitting into two and turning down to engage with two diametrically opposed cavities in the top surface of the top stone. This design of drive has also been found at other Early Roman mill sites and runs counter to the theory that the gap between millstones was adjustable for controlling the quality and reduction of the meal. With the engagement provided by down-turned tangs in unleaded cavities, the whole weight of the top stone bears upon the meal, and continues to do so as it wears thinner and lighter. Although the length of the gear-pit at 1.7 m is unusually long, Romeuf's suggested diameter for the driver gear of 1.0-1.1 m is probably realistic. The variation in the diameter of the millstones combined with the uncertainty of the size of the water-wheel, makes further hydro-mechanical analysis rather fruitless, but the accelerated head-race is a strong indication that this vertical water-wheel was relatively fast.

220 Romeuf 1978, 36.
221 A similar 'scour-pit' was found at the Ickham (Later) mill site, undoubtedly caused by flowing water following the cessation of water power generation.
222 Romeuf 1978, 32, 33.

20. Hagendorn, Switzerland.

This site was unearthed in 1944/45 by Joseph Speck who identified the wood and millstone fragments as belonging to a water-mill[223]. Dating of the artifacts suggest that it was built in the last quarter of the 2nd c. A.D. but did not survive into the third century. The remains of numerous earth-fast posts, some dislocated ground-plates and planks were found together with 25 fragments of wood identified as parts of water-wheels. Analysis and reconstruction of these fragments has indicated that they relate to at least three different wheels having radial paddles with tapered shanks morticed into wooden wheel-shafts. The paddles show that two of the wheels (nos.1 and 2) were shrouded and all three had sole boards with end tenons morticed into the paddles. (See Fig. 52.) The sizes of the wheels have been ascertained as (no.1) 2.15 m diameter by 0.23 m wide; (no.2) 2.30 m x 0.23 m and (no.3) 2.20 m x 0.23 m, but the dimensions should be treated with caution. Although the dimensions of the paddles and thus the widths are accurate, only one of the paddle types, for wheel 1, was complete in its length[224]. Nonetheless, the reconstructions are convincing. On both of the shrouded wheels the paddles project beyond the outer rim of the shroud. Gähwiler and Speck's reconstruction of Wheel 1, using the dimensions of the radial paddle and sole board, and allowing for a 39 cm diameter wheel-shaft, suggest that it had 25 paddles. A most interesting fragment of a 39 cm diameter oak wheel-shaft was found that was morticed to receive 27 radial wooden cogs, analysed as being made of fruit-wood. A reconstruction depicts this driver gear as being overhung, for the shaft was reduced in diameter a short distance from the end to act as a bearing, a most unusual arrangement. Evidence of this form of Roman wheel-shaft bearing and overhung gear is currently unique. Among the remains was also found a curved wooden trough[225] measuring 2.5 m long x 0.28 m high x 0.46 m wide, which the writer suggests was probably related to wheel number 3, which was un-shrouded[226].

On the assumption that a millstone requires to rotate at least as fast as a rotary quern, the MR has to be greater than unity, so that the millstone is 'geared up' and rotates faster than the water-wheel. Even with the faster impulse wheels, a minimum MR of three or four to one is needed to move the top-stone at a reasonable practical speed. With the design of the *Hagendorn* driver gear beyond doubt, we can identify a problem in arranging a speeding up of the millstones. The

design of the radial-cogged driver gear tells us that it has to engage with a similar shaped horizontal gear mounted on the vertical millstone spindle. To install a smaller diameter driven gear requires the axis of the millstone spindle to be as close as possible to the vertical plane of the driver gear. This is achieved by positioning the bridge-tree as close as possible to the end of the wheel-shaft, as Gähwiler and Speck have illustrated[227]. (See Fig. 53.) This is surely the reason why the driver gear is overhung, for if the end of the shaft had been supported by an iron journal, it would have pushed the axis of the millstone spindle away from the driver gear, or, the bridge-tree would have to pass above the journal. Either alternative makes the gear engagement more difficult to arrange. Thus we can conclude, the adoption of

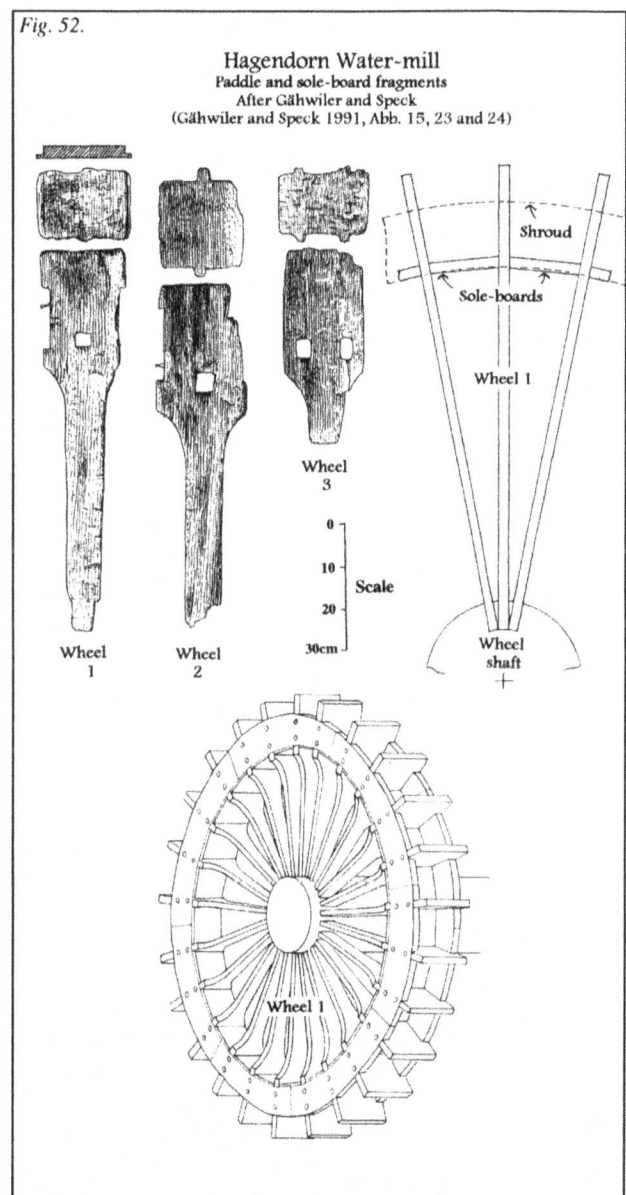

Fig. 52.

Hagendorn Water-mill
Paddle and sole-board fragments
After Gähwiler and Speck
(Gähwiler and Speck 1991, Abb. 15, 23 and 24)

---

223 Gähwiler and Speck 1991.
224 Gähwiler and Speck 1991, 47, Abb. 15. The text provides no clue as to how the diameters of wheels 2 and 3 were determined.
225 Gähwiler and Speck 1991, 51-52.
226 It would be interesting to see if dating the different wheels and the trough might tell us if the un-shrouded wheel and trough post-dated the other two wheels thus indicating a design development.
227 Gähwiler and Speck 1991, Abb. 47, 48.

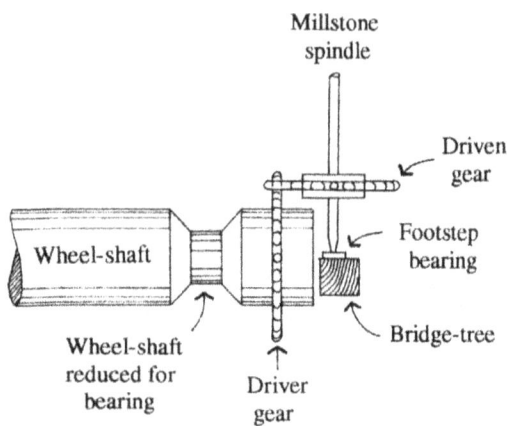

Fig. 53.

Hagendorn Water-mill
Gear positions

Millstone spindle

Driven gear

Footstep bearing

Wheel-shaft

Bridge-tree

Wheel-shaft reduced for bearing

Driver gear

radial cogs morticed into the wheel-shaft brought with it the disadvantages of a gear ratio close to unity and a wheel-shaft bearing involving two wooden friction surfaces.

The remains of several millstones were found, including a 0.75 m diameter top stone weighing 58 kg, and a quarter of a thick bedstone 0.90 m diameter, estimated to have weighed 200 kg when complete. The section of the larger and heavier stone suggests that this may have been a top stone because of its concave underside, unusual for a bed-stone. Moreover, the slope of the concavity is close to that of the surviving top-stone's grinding face[228]. The different diameters suggest that a range of sizes were used.

Unfortunately the hydraulic head approaching the wheel is

Fig. 54.

Hagendorn Water-mill
After Bisig (Gähwiler and Speck 1991, Abb. 51)

unknown. Although Gähwiler and Speck consider alternative hydraulic arrangements they conclude that a high velocity steeply inclined head-race probably served the wheels. They point out that this design has featured in the Northern Alpine watermill tradition for many centuries[229]. The writer considers that there are four features that support the notion of an accelerated high velocity headrace; *first*, the curved wheel-trough; *second*, the shrouded rim – rather unnecessary and ineffective for a low velocity undershot wheel; *third*, the face area of the paddles (wheel 1, 0.23 m x 0.20 m) would be too small for developing power at low velocity, and *fourth*, the relatively small diameter driver gear that suggests, seeing that it must have engaged a similar spur gear with radial cogs, a very low MR. This shows that to obtain reasonable stone speeds, a high velocity water-wheel was needed. The authors depict what is virtually an MR of 1 to 1[230], and if this were close to reality, the top stone would revolve at the speed of the water-wheel. Having regard to the face area of the paddles, it is reasonable to assume that the head of water for the water-wheel was probably in the order of two or three metres. Nonetheless, with this hydraulic head and gear ratio the top millstone would have revolved unusually slowly, at approximately 20 rpm. Figure 54 is an artist's view of the mill. A one-fifth scale reconstructed model of this mill has been made and is exhibited complete with water-wheel, driver gear (27 cogs), driven gear (25 cogs), bridge-tree, pair of millstones and spindle[231].

Because only one water-course some 2.5 to 3.0 m wide was found at the site close to all the artifacts, the writer considers it likely that all of the wheels were variations in design relating to a single mill site. Such changes could well occur during the four or five decades of operation. It is interesting that Gähwiler and Speck consider that Wheel 3 may have developed last, and having regard to the curved trough found, the writer is also inclined to this view. An alternative arrangement is for two, or less likely three, of the wheels to have coexisted in close proximity to each other, but to have received the water in parallel to each other. An illustration of a modern Alpine mill with this arrangement is shown by Gähwiler and Speck[232].

228 Gähwiler and Speck 1991, 50.
229 Gähwiler and Speck 1991, Figs. 28, 32, 33, 34 and 51.
230 Gähwiler and Speck 1991, 70, Fig. 47.
231 Gähwiler and Speck 1991, Abb. 46, 47 and 48. The model is in the Kantonalen Museum für Urgeschichte in Zug, Switzerland.
232 Gähwiler and Speck 1991, 60, Abb. 32.

50

21. Saint-Doulchard, France.

At this site several structures were found including what is believed to have been a water-mill, in use during the first half of the 1st c. A.D[233], which, if proved, would make this mill one of the oldest found. The layout of the mill is unclear but included among the finds were two wooden paddles. (See Fig. 55.) Looking first to paddle A, although it is spade-shaped, it is clearly not intended for working the soil for the shoulders are unshod and unworn, and the cutting edge is blunt-ended. The archaeologists report does not confirm the absence or presence of evidence in the edges of the paddle that would indicate the existence of shrouds. We have therefore to assume, giving them the benefit of doubt, that no fixings were evident. The face area of the paddle is small at 160 cm^2 and clearly not related to a bucket wheel, so that we must think in terms of a wheel driven by impulse having a fairly high impact velocity. For effective power generation the open paddles would have to be moving within a close-fitting trough, preferably curved, to contain the fast moving water[234].

Paddle B has a puzzling and intriguing shape. The first impression is that its shape may be the result of decay, wear or breakage, but it clearly has symmetry about the axis of its shaft. A small break has been identified suggesting that the examiners have confirmed and accepted its shape as being original. We therefore have a leaf-shaped paddle, distinctly different from the rectilinear-shaped paddle A. What does this tell us? We should take some confidence in the fact that these two different shaped paddles were found at the same site. If paddle B only had been found, we might have included in our options, albeit briefly, that it was a propulsion or steering oar for a boat. However, because paddle B was discovered in close proximity to A, we have to consider that it could be an alternative form of the same type of artefact. We have proposed that paddle A, because of its shape, worked in conjunction and close proximity with other fixed elements of the machine to effect power generation. This cannot be proposed for paddle B, for its shape tells us that it did not rotate within any form of trough or enclosure. Its design is impractical for such an arrangement. And so we appear to have evidence of two different impulse wheels, one enclosed within a trough, and one open. But the face area of paddle B at 103 cm^2 (16 in^2) is much smaller than paddle A. Compared with the three *Hagendorn* paddles that were just over 400 cm^2, this makes

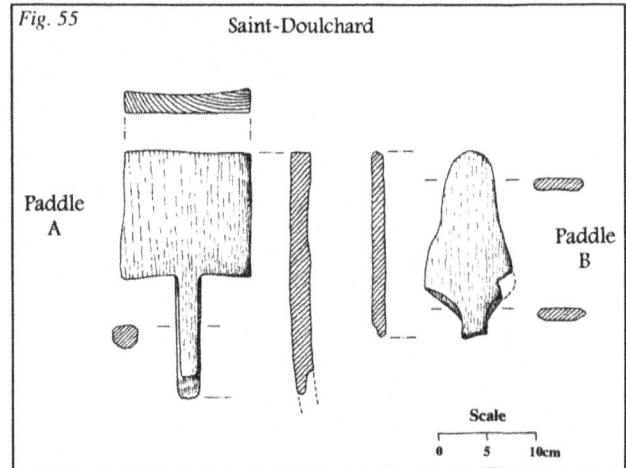

Fig. 55   Saint-Doulchard

Paddle A   Paddle B

Scale

0   5   10cm

B an unusually small paddle. If we assume that all of its area was subject to water pressure, it would require an impact velocity close to 4 m/s (13.1 ft/s) to generate 1.0 hp[235].

The smallness of paddle B must place it on the limit of effective power generation to drive a millstone. Its round shape suggests that a similar sectioned jet of water may have impinged on it. Its face area brings to mind the early Irish and Anglo-Saxon horizontal water-wheels[236], but a feature of those is that all the paddles are not only somewhat larger than paddle B, but they are either hollowed, spoon shaped, or flat faced and inclined so that the sloping water jet strikes normal to their face. Paddle B shows no evidence of these features. The design of these early paddles suggests that we should view paddle B as a dubious power generator. If evidence of small millstones had been found, it would have improved our confidence, but none were found. We need to ask ourselves, could the wheel arrangement and the environs of the mill provide an accelerated headrace to achieve this impact velocity? If not, we have to revise our thoughts radically on the power potential of this site and our interpretation of the wheel paddles.

22. The Baths of Caracalla, Rome. [Later Mills]

The two earlier water-mills that existed within the subterranean chambers below the Baths, driven by bucket wheels (See site no. 4 above), were replaced by two

---

233 Rialland 1989; Champagne, *et. al.* 1997.
234 Curved troughs have been found at Hagendorn and at La Bourse, Marseille. Guéry and Hallier 1987.
235 This would power a top-stone having a diameter of 0.75 m and a half-life thickness of 0.152 m (0.5 ft), which would absorb 1.0 hp when revolving at 61.5 rpm. Depending on the number of paddles and the wheel diameter, the axis of the water jet may not be always normal to the face. An allowance has been made in these calculations for this.
236 Watts 2002, 63-82.

new identical accelerated head-race overshot wheels, built into the south-east half of the chamber, around or shortly after mid. 3rd c. A.D. The reasons for the building of the new mills are unclear. Wikander implies that they were rebuilt following a fire, a suggestion that appears to be tenuously based on three charcoal-blackened finds of pottery amongst 119 sherds from the same area[237]. As suggested by Wikander it is quite possible that the conversion of some of the adjoining basement rooms into a large *Mithraeum*, and the reconstruction works of Emperor Aurelianus following a fire in the Baths, may have had an effect on the mills. But the writer is of the opinion that corn milling operations may not have been interrupted for very long, if at all, because (a) the pottery which has indicated a period of disuse all came from a very small area (0.6m²) of the whole site. The significance of this area and its relationship with the remainder of the structure has yet to be satisfactorily determined; (b) as far as we can tell, theoretically at least, the earlier Mill A (See Fig. 16 above) could have continued working as the later mills were being built; (c) the miller could maintain some, possibly most, of his normal production by keeping Mill A at work, otherwise; (d) why preserve the plan of Mill A? It could have been demolished and its valuable floor area given over to the new works; and (e) it seems extremely unlikely that a fire in the Baths above could have spread to this subterranean chamber with its continuous and plentiful supply of water.

The building fabric associated with these new wheels and their machinery has been thoroughly examined and reconstructed by Schiøler and Wikander[238]. The builders used approximately the same sized water-wheels as the earlier wheels but cleverly adopted a lapped wheel arrangement, which gave them a high utilization of space. (See Fig 56.) The common pit for the two new wheels was made deeper to provide a greater head of water onto the wheels, and each wheel was probably given an independent head-race from the old water inlet at the back of the chamber. The water was applied to the wheels using steeply-angled head-race troughs, and the remains of one of the well-worn wheel-shaft bearing stones tells us that the water was applied over the top of the wheel-shafts[239]. When the floor of the new common wheel-pit was lowered, the old tail-race in the south-east wall was abandoned and blocked. From one corner of the wheel-pit, a new tail-race drain was built and its important feature is that it was considerably smaller than the original drain serving the earlier wheels.

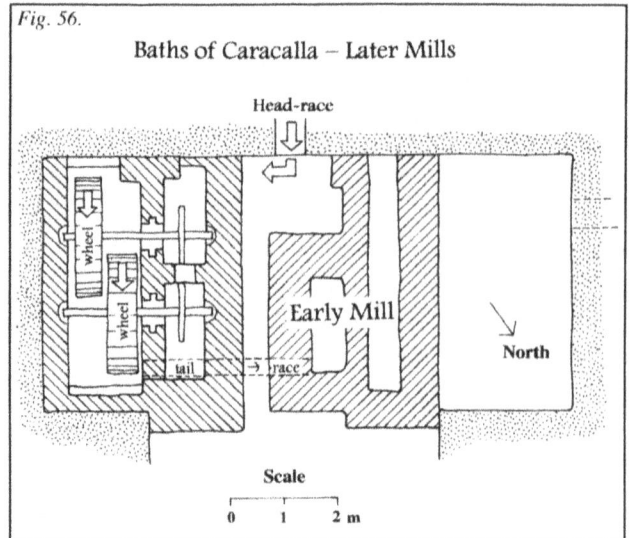

Fig. 56.

Baths of Caracalla – Later Mills

In the following analysis the writer has adopted Schiøler's proposed total flow rate of 0.1 m³/s through the mill chamber[240]. This flow rate, which is critical in the examination of these later wheels, is well founded, for the following reason. Although a slight fall was recorded on the tiled floor of the wheel-pit, both Schiøler's section[241] and the writer's site measurements suggest that the soffit of the new drain was at the same level as the underside of the water-wheels. Knowing that the operators could not have allowed the wheels to operate partially immersed in water – the drag effect would slow them down – we cannot allow in our calculations that the drain would operate fully flooded. If we assume the drain to be three-quarters flooded, with a flow rate of 0.1 m³/s, the average velocity would be 1.13 m/sec. Although we do not know the gradient of the drain, this flow rate is probably near the practical limit for an enclosed aqueduct of this size.

There are two obvious ways in which the flow of water to each wheel could have been controlled. On the back wall close to the water inlet, there appears to have been a sluice-gate controlling the flow to the water-wheels. There are iron stains on the deposits on the bottom of the emplacement and immediately below, presumably from the iron fittings on the gate. Schiøler and Wikander proposed a vertical division in the head-race downstream of the sluice-gate, to facilitate separate control of each wheel, and that seems a highly practical suggestion. Such an arrangement not only had the advantage of modulating the flow between the wheels, but also provided a bypass that allowed one wheel to receive the whole flow when the other wheel was inactive. But the most effective way to control a wheel

237 Schiøler and Wikander 1983, 55, 58-60, 62 item 9, 63.
238 Schiøler and Wikander 1983.
239 Schiøler's dynamic resolution is illuminating.
240 Schiøler 1986.
241 Schiøler and Wikander 1983, 52, Fig.7, section ZZ.

would be to hinge or pivot the top of the head-race trough, so that to take water off the wheel, the bottom end of the trough would be raised, shooting the water over and clear of the wheel[242]. The position and height of the wall in front of the northern wheel[243], suggests that this was introduced for just that purpose, to deflect water back down into the wheel-pit but still allow access for maintenance around the edge. A pivoted delivery trough also has the advantage in being adjustable to direct the very fast but shallow water stream to its optimum position for application, whether onto buckets or floats. Perhaps both methods of control existed, because the sluice-gate provided the distinct advantage of diverting all the water to either wheel – very desirable with a diminished supply – and the pivoted trough would probably be needed to adjust the impact of the jet when it doubled (or halved) in thickness. If the operators wanted both wheels idle they had either to pass the water clear over the wheels, or close the sluices and divert the water to the old or new drains. They might also have been able to divert the water before it entered the mill chamber. But these ruminations are minor compared with the major question facing us, were these water-wheels powered by impulse or weight? Schiøler's text does not shed light upon this question but his axonometric reconstruction[244], cleverly shows a wheel with sole boards and inclined (non-radial) straight floats. (See Fig. 57.) This design reflects power generation by both impulse and weight. Let us see what a hydraulic analysis reveals.

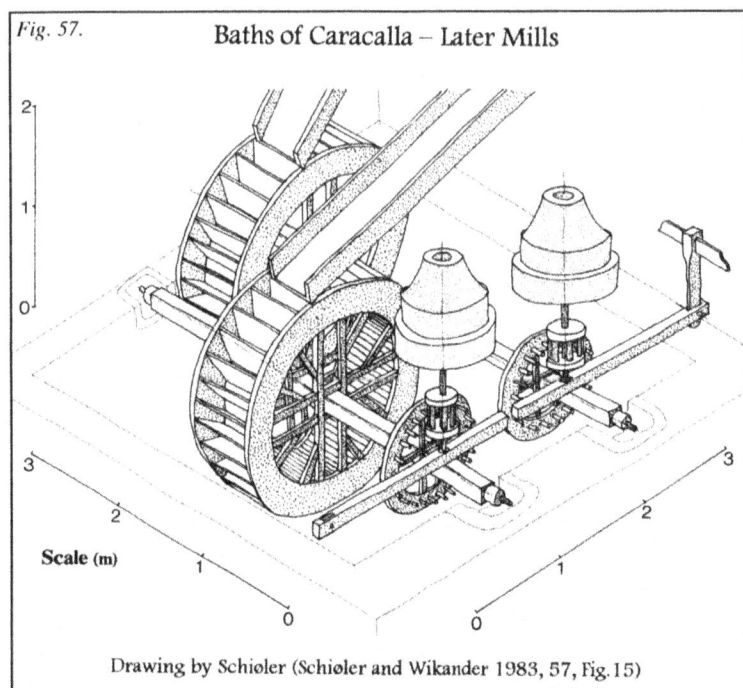

Fig. 57.

Baths of Caracalla – Later Mills

Scale (m)

Drawing by Schiøler (Schiøler and Wikander 1983, 57, Fig.15)

As a basis to this enquiry we need to assume that the flow rate to each wheel is 0.05 m³/s, which is one half of the total flowing through the chamber. Although we have accepted that the water control arrangement would probably have given the advantage of one wheel receiving the entire flow, it is considered that the existence of two duplicate wheels meant that simultaneous operation was the intention of the builders, and not standby or alternating operation. Critical evidence concerning the diameter of these water-wheels is provided by the grooves made by the rim of the north wheel rubbing against the wheel-pit wall. Allowing for the movement that had occurred in the wheel-shaft bearing, site measurement suggests that the wheels were close to 2.18 m diameter with a head of 1.04 m. This compares with Schiøler's conclusion that the diameter of the wheels lay somewhere between 1.95 and 2.10 m, but we should note that his intention was not to make detailed measurements and that nearly all his measurements were given as multiples of 5 cm[245]. The rubbing of the north wheel against the pit wall shows that the wheels operated with a minimum of clearance on the sides. Allowing for the fact that calcium deposits have tended to close in towards the wheel sides, site measurements show that the wheels, when last operating, were approximately 0.53 m wide.

Schiøler's reconstruction suggests that the head-race troughs had different slopes, the southern trough being much steeper than the northern. It is possible that both head-race troughs had the same declination and for this arrangement, the northern trough would have required a longer horizontal section. But the option is not important and in the following analysis the steeper trough with a slope of 46° from the horizontal, is examined. Calculations show that with a flow rate of 0.05 m³/s, the depth of water entering the top of the trough, where critical flow occurs[246], would be 9 cm, and the velocity 1.22 m/s. The velocity of impact, allowing for the resistance of the wooden trough and a free fall onto the wheel of a few centimetres, is 4.6 m/s. The average thickness of the water jet entering the wheel would be 2.4 cm.

Let us first consider how a wheel driven solely by weight of water behaves. Fig. 58 shows a design of wheel with 32 straight inclined floats

242 This water control method has been suggested for the Athenian Agora Mill. Spain 1987, Figs. 3 and 4. See Mill no. 23 below.
243 Schiøler and Wikander, 1983, Fig 2.
244 Schiøler and Wikander, 1983, 57, Fig 15.
245 Schiøler and Wikander, 1983, 51.
246 The gradients and sections upstream of this point do not affect the hydraulic conditions downstream.

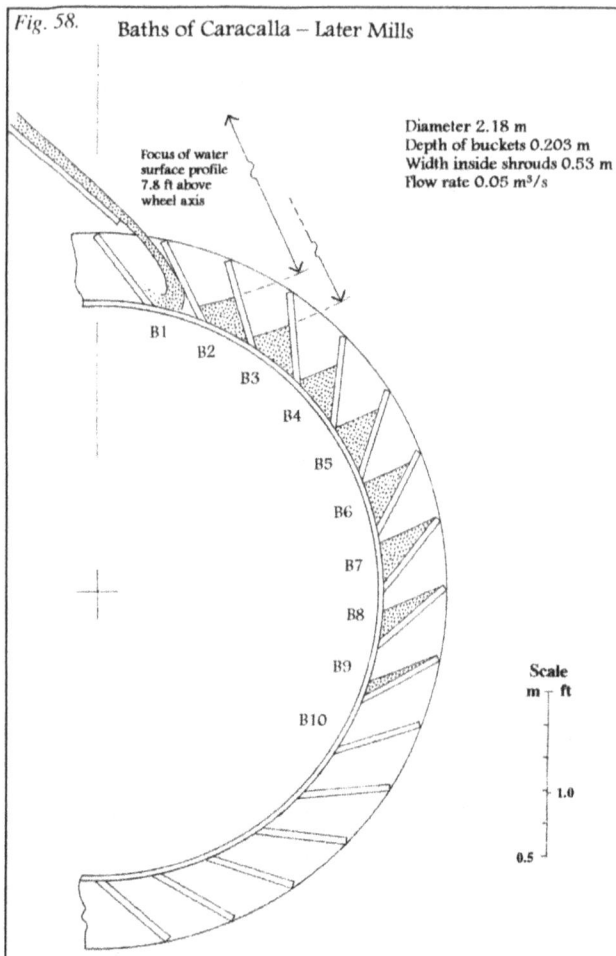

Fig. 58. Baths of Caracalla – Later Mills

Focus of water surface profile 7.8 ft above wheel axis

Diameter 2.18 m
Depth of buckets 0.203 m
Width inside shrouds 0.53 m
Flow rate 0.05 m³/s

Scale
m ┬ ft

1.0

0.5

with sole boards. This wheel would have a rim velocity of 6.5ft/s (1.98 m/s) and therefore revolve at 17.4 rpm. The buckets are shown loaded from a source with a flow rate of 0.05 m³/s allowing that 10% is lost to splashing. The effect of centrifugal force has been calculated and shown on the drawing, and causes a zero load from bucket number 10 and below. Table M shows the torque analysis.

Table M – Torque analysis of wheel allowing for centrifugal force. Flow rate 0.05 m³/s

Bucket no.	Load (lbs)	Moment (ft)	Torque (ft.lbs.)
2	10.75	1.29	13.9
3	10.75	1.8	19.4
4	10.75	2.23	24.0
5	10.75	2.58	27.7
6	10.75	2.83	30.4
7	10.75	2.98	32.0
8	9.3	2.98	27.7
9	7.3	2.88	21.0
		Total	196.1

The torque totals 196.1 ft.lbs that at 17.4 rpm generates 0.65 hp. We need to add to this the impulse effect of the water hitting the wheel at 4.6 m/s. The surfaces that this body of water impacts upon is a combination of shrouds and moving angled wooden surfaces and an agitated water surface. We cannot calculate the reaction of the impulse force in these changing conditions, but the maximum value, assuming a hard surface normal to the axis of flow, would generate 0.29 hp. If we make a rash assumption that one half of the power generated by impulse was lost to turbulence, eddies etc, then a very approximate figure, for the total power that this wheel would generate is 0.8 hp. Accuracy at this stage is not important, the general order of magnitude must guide us. The total potential KE for this flow and head is 2.362 hp, so that the theoretical efficiency of this wheel design is approximately 34%. If the balance of power were less than 0.8 hp, the wheel would revolve faster than the speed caused solely by weight, due to the impulse effect. But the losses caused by centrifugal force would be greater and fewer buckets would hold water.

Schiøler and Wikander have provided a valuable interpretation of both driver gears where they rubbed against the division wall between the gear-pits. Their iron-bound rims have scored deeply into the brickwork allowing us to determine their overall diameter of 112 cm[247]. Schiøler also identified some shallower scoring adjacent to the rim marks within the southern pit as wear made by the cogs. The interpretation of these marks is difficult due to the decay and the dust that pervades this underground chamber, but it is far more likely that we are seeing wear caused by the gear being in different positions or by different gears being installed during the extended life of these mills[248]. It is worth noting that the driver gear diameters of 112 cm coincide exactly with the *Agora* pit-gear of 111 cm, the only other archaeologically proven example. In all three machines the evidence of wear invites the suggestion that the miller used pit-gears as large as he could install, but two other factors influence our thoughts. First, with the driven gear taking the form of a lantern-gear, the minimum possible diameter that the driver gear could be to effectively engage and disengage the lantern, (allowing for the depth of the bridge-tree, clearances for the wheel-shaft, footstep bearing and lantern discs etc.) is 100 cm. Secondly, the wear in the south gear-pit wall was primarily caused by movement of the wheel-shaft journals, reacting to the thrust

247 Schiøler believes them to have been *c*.95 cm. Schiøler and Wikander 1983, 53-4, Fig. 10.
248 The miller would surely not tolerate the wooden cogs rubbing against the wall because they would rapidly wear away and weaken; moreover, unless the rim wears deep into the brickwork, the cogs cannot touch the wall.
249 Its pitch circle diameter is 12.95 cm.

of the water acting on the wheel. The support stones for the bridge-tree are still in place in both of these mills, and the limits of position can be measured, suggesting that the maximum diameter for the driven gear was c.46 cm. The minimum MR was therefore c.2.2 to 1.0 (i.e. 100 cm driver to 46 cm driven). The maximum MR using the six-staved Zugmantel gear as a model for the driven lantern gear[249] is c.8.0 to 1.0.

Several fragments of millstones were apparently found during the 1912 excavations[250], but these have not been located in spite of enquiries and searches[251]. These might have helped us in determining the balance of power, but our only guide is the single lava millstone built into the foundations of one of the walls. Its position tells us that it belongs to the earlier period of milling. However, if we assume that its diameter, 0.76 m, was typical also for the later period, we can calculate that it would weigh 320 lbs (145 kg) when its thickness was 0.152 m. For the weight and impulse-driven wheel generating 0.8 hp, if we allow 9% of the power for bearing and gearing friction, then a balance of 0.728 hp is available for the millstones. Using the 320 lb (145 kg) top stone, this power would result in a speed of 43 rpm and the MR would be 2.47 to 1.0.

If the wheel was driven solely by impulse, the optimum rim speed for maximum power would be 1.75 m/sec, and at this speed the power generated would be 0.25 hp. Allowing 9% for friction loses, a balance of 0.23 hp is available for the millstones. With the same weight top stone, this power would drive it at 14 rpm. Even if we allow for a lighter stone, the impulse wheel has insufficient power for reasonable performance, and so the conclusion appears to be that these later wheels used both weight and impulse, supporting Schiøler's design. In some ways our analysis confirming a relatively low stone speed is not surprising; with a reduced water flow we should have anticipated this. Although our assumptions concerning the reaction of a high velocity jet upon a bucket wheel invites criticisms and judgement[252], we cannot escape the conclusion that it is an imperfect arrangement. Nonetheless it endured because the heavy deposits of calcium carbonate tell us that. Why did their design for the new wheel change so radically? Was it prompted by technical development or a diminution in the water supply? The builders clearly chose not to install larger diameter wheels; indeed if they had, only one 3.22 m diameter bucket wheel could have been accommodated.

Perhaps two were installed to maintain the flexibility of operation that had existed in the earlier arrangement, possibly to provide different functions or treatments of grain. The mill is believed to have been abandoned in the 5th c. A.D. but may have continued until the Baths were definitely closed in A.D. 597.

The *Caracalla* evidence is intriguing and potentially valuable. In the last quarter of the 3rd c. A.D. the opportunity was taken to replace two bucket water-wheels with new wheels driven by accelerated head-races generating power from both impulse and weight. Almost identical sized wheels and pit-gears were installed, and to achieve this the floor of the wheel-pit was lowered, telling us that the builders were intent on accelerating the head-race, presumably to achieve higher wheel speeds. This assumption is supported by the site evidence that confirms the size of the pit-gears, which if engaging with 6-stave lantern-gears had the potential of driving the millstones at 140 rpm. But this new arrangement, according to our analysis, still incorporated power generation mainly by weight of water, and yet we appear to have earlier examples of fast wheels driven solely by impulse[253]. Why then was this hybrid wheel adopted? We might imagine that in Rome, the very latest developments in water-power technology would be to the fore, but we have no idea who might have influenced and overseen the changes.

23. Agora, Athens, Greece.

During the early 1930's excavations in the *Agora* of ancient Athens revealed a most interesting and important specimen of a Roman watermill, whose working life has been dated to A.D. 457-570. Parsons produced an unusual and stimulating interpretation of the evidence[254], skillfully comparing and illustrating his analysis and findings with the well-known text of Vitruvius[255]. The reconstruction of the mill, which sprang from his keen observations and understanding of the mechanical evidence within the building fabric, remains to this day a major contribution to our knowledge of Roman watermills.

In the *Agora* mill the diameter of the water-wheel can be

250 Ghislanzoni 1912, 325.
251 *Pers. comms*, Wikander to Spain, March 1988.
252 The relatively high velocity transfer differential questions the assumption of a 10% allowance for splashing etc, but it is balanced to some extent by the low volumetric efficiency of the wheel – see buckets 2 and. 3 in Fig. 58 - that illustrates containment. But the reaction of the jet on the wheel is another matter. In truth the dynamics and performance of this accelerated head-race acting on a bucket wheel are beyond theoretical resolution and can only be satisfactorily resolved by functional analysis using replication.
253 Hagendorn, Venafro, St. Doulchard and probably Lösnich.
254 Parsons 1936.
255 Vitruvius, Book 10, ch. 5, see The Ten Books on Architecture, M.H.Morgan, trans, 1960.

determined accurately at 3.24 m from the scoring which its rim made in the lime deposits on the wheel-pit wall. (See Fig. 59.) Its width was 0.49 m outside the shrouds. The wheel-pit, which was cut some 3 m deep into bedrock, was clearly made to allow the wheel to be set low in order to create a high head, allowing for an underside clearance of 0.6 m. The head-race approaches from the south and takes a straight course directly towards the wheel over the last 20 m. Unfortunately, although the foundation wall of the race can be seen, the remains of the water channel on the top disappear 13 m from the edge of the wheel-pit. However, southward of this point, upstream, the floor tiles of the race were found preserved which allowed Parsons to suggest that originally it delivered water at a height of c.1.4 m above the top of the wheel. According to the published section and plan of the head-race the bed actually lifted by 6.6 cm in 14.3 m before it took a straight line towards the wheel, where it then inclined downwards at a gradient of 0.009. We have no way of telling how this profile related to the gradients that existed during the mill's life. If the gradient of 0.009 continued to the wheel-pit, then the head of water was nearer 1.3 m than 1.4 m stated by Parsons[256]. (See Fig. 60.)

Parsons has assumed that the head-race was brought to the edge of the wheel-pit, (its south face) and then accelerated down onto the wheel by an inclined wooden chute. There is no archaeological evidence to tell us where the acceleration began, and it might have occurred earlier than Parsons has shown and been carried by a less steep trough. However, the velocity of application is insensitive to the inclination of the trough within broad limits, for it is the vertical head that has greater relevance. The assumption that the high end of the trough was positioned above the south face of the wheel-pit is entirely reasonable, this being the logical position for a change in material in the head-race. Wherever the change of gradient occurred, there is no doubt that a fast flow existed as confirmed by the shape of the lime deposits on the sides of the wheel-pit[257]. The following analysis has assumed a head of 1.4 m and a declination of the wooden trough of 37° from horizontal. (See Fig. 61.)

The question we must now ask ourselves is whether the water passed over the wheel-shaft or below it, and probably the best approach to this is to examine how the water was controlled onto the wheel. To achieve this the water had either to be diverted from the head-race through a bypass or deflected from the wheel itself. Fortunately, during 1959, further excavations some 45 m to the south beneath the *pronaos* of the south-east Temple, the pit of another water-

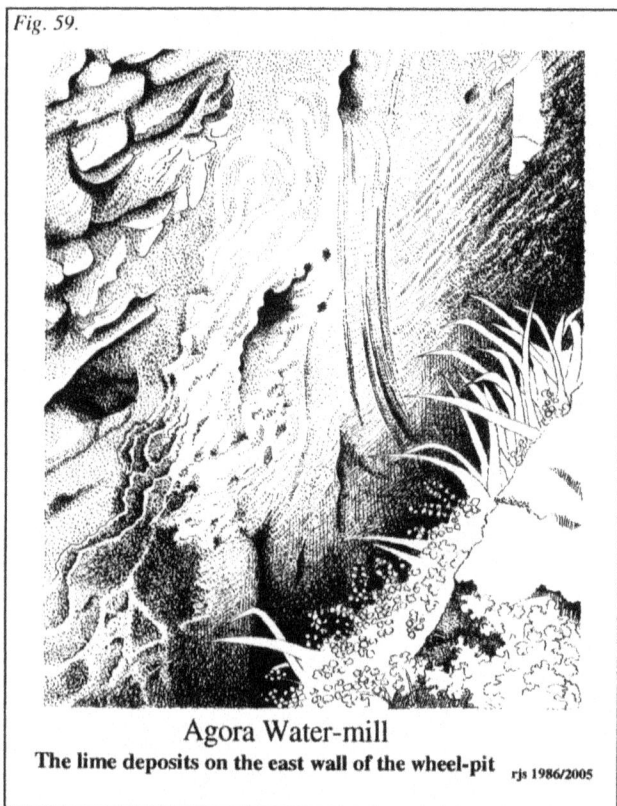

Fig. 59.

Agora Water-mill
The lime deposits on the east wall of the wheel-pit   rjs 1986/2005

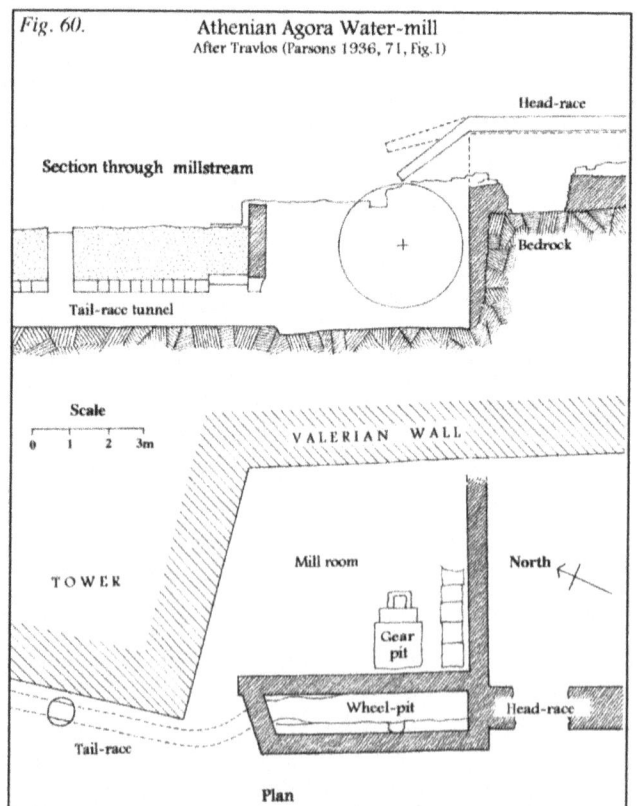

Fig. 60.   Athenian Agora Water-mill
After Travlos (Parsons 1936, 71, Fig.1)

Section through millstream

Head-race

Tail-race tunnel

Bedrock

Scale

0 1 2 3m

VALERIAN WALL

TOWER

Mill room

Gear pit

North

Tail-race

Wheel-pit

Head-race

Plan

256 See Parsons 1936, Fig 1, 71.
257 Personal observations made by the writer during 1986.

56

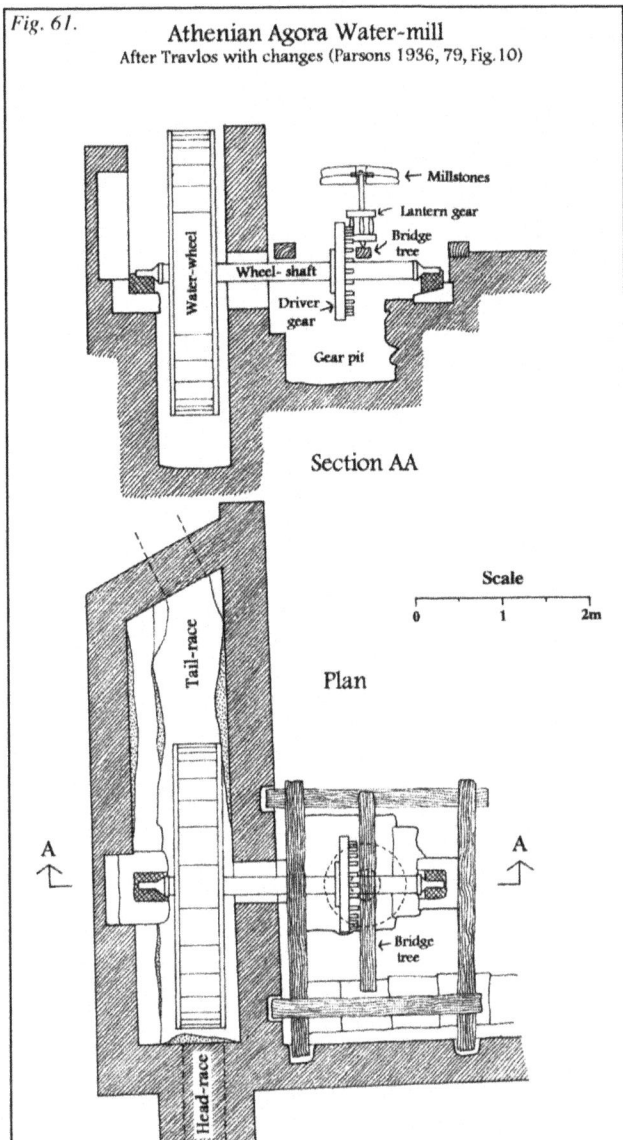

Fig. 61.

Athenian Agora Water-mill
After Travlos with changes (Parsons 1936, 79, Fig.10)

Section AA

Plan

Scale
0   1   2m

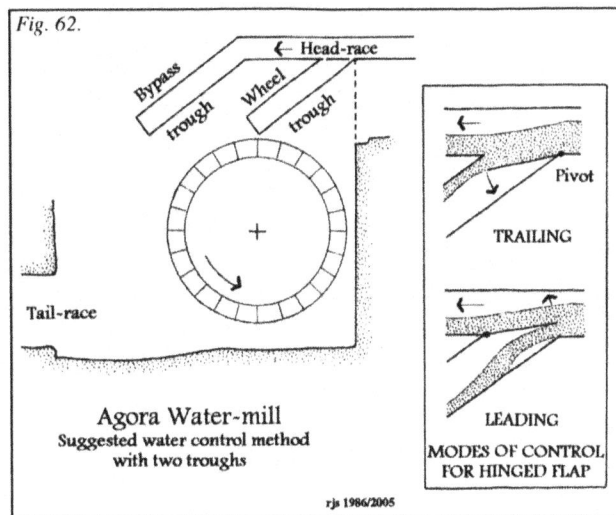

Fig. 62.

Agora Water-mill
Suggested water control method
with two troughs

TRAILING

LEADING

MODES OF CONTROL
FOR HINGED FLAP

rjs 1986/2005

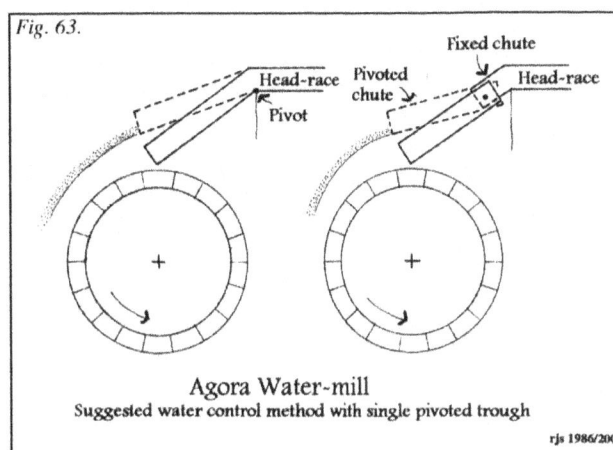

Fig. 63.

Agora Water-mill
Suggested water control method with single pivoted trough

rjs 1986/2005

mill was found[258], which showed that no bypass conduit or channel existed between the two mills. We therefore know that water control was effected within the mill itself, in the wheel-pit. Within the confines of the *Agora* wheel-pit, there are only two routes for the excess water, either between the wheel breast and the south wall of the chamber or, taken

over the wheel and discharged down towards the tail-race tunnel clear of the wheel. It is the opinion of the writer that the position of the wheel in conjunction with the deposition and shape of the calcium deposits indicates that the water was diverted over the wheel to effect control and disengagement of the wheel[259]. Of the alternative arrangements that can be visualized to effect this 'overshot' arrangement (See Figs, 62 and 63.) the writer favours a single trough pivoted on the edge of the wheel-pit that is consistent with the mineral deposits on the south wall, assuming they were made during

Table N – Flow and velocity variations

Depth of water in the head-race		Impact velocity		Flow rate		Head-race velocity	
(inches)	(m)	(ft/s)	(m/s)	(ft³/s)	(m³/s)	(ft/s)	(m/s)
15	0.381	19.46	5.93	10.9	0.309	6.34	1.93
12	0.305	19.0	5.79	7.8	0.221	5.67	1.73
9	0.229	18.44	5.62	5.1	0.144	4.95	1.51
6	0.152	13.93	4.24	2.8	0.079	4.07	1.24

258 Thompson 1960, 349.
259 For a more detailed examination of this see Spain 1987, 335-353.

the operational life of the mill.

Our next enquiry is to determine whether the wheel was powered by weight or impulse of water. A hydraulic analysis of this arrangement shows that the velocity of application is high. Table N gives the theoretical water impact velocities, at mean depth of the buckets or floats, for different depths of water in the head-race approaching the top of the trough. The calculations allow for a free fall from the end of the trough that averages 0.225m.

It can be seen that when the head-race is from 50-90% full the velocity of application is approximately 19 ft/s (5.79 m/s). A bucket wheel 3.24 m diameter would normally have a rim velocity of approximately 5.5 ft/s (1.68 m/s) and therefore revolve at *c*.10 rpm. However, with the velocity of the water 3.5 times that of the rim speed, extreme agitation and turbulence would occur within the buckets and an impulse effect would be generated. It is not possible to determine accurately by theory the resulting wheel speed or power generated in these conditions using buckets[260]. The writer considers that this wheel most likely generated power by impulse rather than weight, and probably had radial floats. (See Fig. 64.) Let us examine the performance of the wheel under two head-race flow conditions, having water depths of 12 inches (0.305 m) or 9 inches (0.229 m). With a 12 inch depth the flow rate is 7.8 ft³/s (0.221 m³/s) and the impact velocity generates a power of 2.05 hp at a wheel speed of 14.5 rpm. A 9 inch depth head-race has a flow rate of 5.1 ft³/s (0.144 m³/s) and generates 1.305 hp at a wheel speed of 14.1 rpm.

Parsons found that the iron hoop on the rim of the driver gear had scored the edge of the gear pit, and thereby determined its overall diameter as 1.11 m. His conclusions concerning the gear ratio of the mill (1.11 driver to 1.36 driven) rest solely on his interpretation of the marble slab below the east wheel-shaft bearing block as being the support for the millstone spindle bridge-tree[261]. The writer has proposed that an alternative arrangement existed, whereby the footstep bearing was supported on a bridge-tree that extended across the width of the platform frame (See Fig. 65.)[262] This would have provided a more practical method for adjusting the vertical movement of the millstone spindle by pivoting one end of the beam, and more important, allowed a gearing-up of the millstones.

The remains of six lava millstones were found on the site, varying in diameter from 0.716-0.824 m. Five of these

Agora Water-mill
The west bearing support stone

rjs 1986/2005

stones were top stones with an average diameter of 0.76 m, varying in thickness from 7.2 to 2.4 cm, clearly worn thin to the limits of their usefulness. Calculating the average weight of these stones[263], the horsepower required is 0.325 for a speed of 60 rpm. Clearly with top stones of this weight the mill is greatly over-powered, so that the miller could

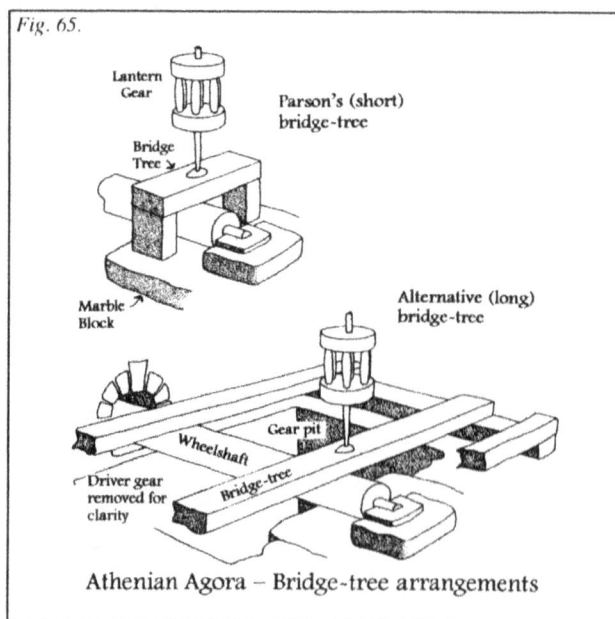

Athenian Agora – Bridge-tree arrangements

---

260 An analysis by drawing a reconstruction of the Agora wheel as a bucket wheel shows that its capacity at 10 rpm would be met by a head-race depth of nine inches (0.229 m). Its theoretical potential power works out at 2.77 hp allowing for the effects of centrifugal force, but as stated, the impact velocity is too great for this type of wheel.

261 Parsons 1936, 83.

262 Spain 1987, 348-50.

263 Using stones a, c and f in Parsons Fig 17. Stones b and e are remarkably thin and have such a regular and smooth section as to invite the suggestion that they may have been used as bottom stones.

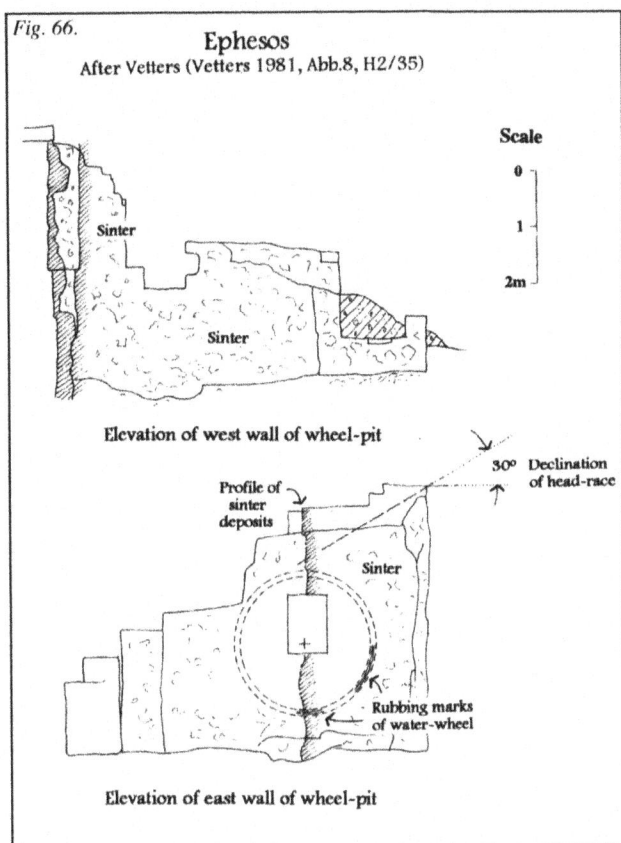

Fig. 66.

Ephesos
After Vetters (Vetters 1981, Abb.8, H2/35)

Scale

0

1

2m

Sinter

Sinter

Sinter

Elevation of west wall of wheel-pit

30° Declination of head-race

Profile of sinter deposits

Sinter

Rubbing marks of water-wheel

Elevation of east wall of wheel-pit

enjoy high stone speeds. If we assume that new top stones were four times the weight (approximately 18 cm thick) working with an MR of 4 to 1, and allowing some 9% of the wheel shaft power for the friction of bearings and gears, a 0.305 m (12 in.) deep head-race would drive the stones at 86 rpm, and a 0.229 m (9 in.) deep head-race, at 55 rpm.

24. Ephesos, Turkey.

At *Ephesos* a series of at least ten Late Antiquity water-mills has been identified and their construction dated to the early 7th c. A.D.[264]. Unfortunately the published excavation reports do not provide enough detail to determine their design and arrangement, so even a rudimentary analysis is not possible. The drawings show two water-wheels, both 2.6 m in diameter which has been established from clear score marks made by the rims of the wheels in the calcium deposits. A section is provided of one of the wheel-pits[265] that suggest a wheel width of *c*.0.65 m allowing for side clearance; another drawing states a width

of 0.8 m inside the sinter deposits[266]. This drawing shows that there may have been a head of water of *c*.1.5 m above the crown of the wheel. If this is accurate, the water would be applied down a slope of 30° from the horizontal, which would be a high level, accelerated head-race. (See Fig. 66.) The size of these wheels and the arrangement of the accelerated head-race are very similar to that in the *Baths of Caracalla* Later Mills. (See site no. 22 above.) The hydraulic analysis of those wheels suggests that these *Ephesos* wheels probably had radial floats, providing that the flow rate was sufficient.

25. Nahal Tanninim, Israel.

Several ancient water-mills were connected to two dams built to raise the water level of Nahal Tanninim to supply water to the city of Caesarea, Israel. On the western dam the remains of both horizontal and vertical-wheeled mills have been identified. During 2002 –2003 excavations were undertaken at the southern end of the western dam on five water-mill sites[267] including one that had been observed by Oleson some years before[268]. (See Fig. 67.) A detailed survey of the many rock-cut channels and building foundations shows that all six of the water-mills, M1-M6, including one M5 that was purposefully left unexcavated[269], operated with vertical water-wheels driving two pairs of millstones. This evidence of duplex drive arrangements provides us with a radical shift in our knowledge of Roman water-mill technology and power transmission. The water for these mills passed through sluices into a channel approximately 3 m wide that fed five head-races. Mills 2 and 4 were in series served by a common head-race and Mill 6 may be an earlier structure, as suggested by separate smaller channels coming from upstream[270]. The main channel serving the mills reduces in width as the head-races spur off indicating, as has been suggested, that these water-mills were planned and built as one unit. This would appear likely for Mills 1, 3 and 5 although Mills 2, 6 and perhaps 4, had origins earlier than the common head-race.

In each mill the lower levels were cut from solid rock with the upper levels built above ground. Little remains of the built elements except for the foundation trenches for the

264 Vetters 1981, Abb. 6, 8; 72, Abb. 5-11. Vetters 1982, 151, Taf XXXI.
265 Vetters 1981, Abb. 7, H2/40.
266 Vetters 1981, Abb. 8, H2/35.
267 Ad, *et al.*, 2005.
268 Oleson 1984a.
269 To allow for future research – a commendable decision.
270 Ad, *et al.*, 2005, 161. The ground plan also suggests that Mill 2 may have had an earlier supply channel.

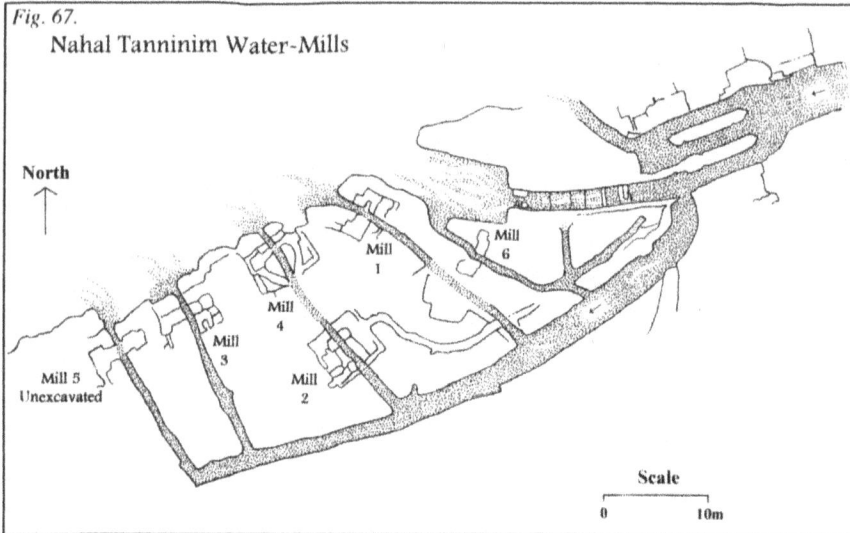

Fig. 67.
Nahal Tanninim Water-Mills

North

Mill 1

Mill 6

Mill 4

Mill 3

Mill 2

Mill 5
Unexcavated

Scale

0   10m

emplacement, rectangular cavities have been cut in the rock to create gear-pits, in some cases separated by a wall *c.*1 m thick with an aperture through which the wheel-shaft passed. (See Fig. 69.) The archaeologists state that in three of these mills the walls show traces of marks made by the revolving water-wheel, indicating diameters between 2.0 and 2.4 m. The published drawings do not facilitate an accurate determination of the width of the wheels, although plan of Mills 3 and 4 suggest that they could not have been more than 0.5 m[271]. This group of mills, although physically close and integrated by a common head-race network, do not display a uniform design as evident at *Barbegal*. We may therefore be looking at mills that were created by different builders and modified over time. The dam has been securely dated to the early 4th c. A.D. providing a building date for the mills not earlier than this. The final stage of their use, identified from pottery found in

walls. (See Fig. 68.) However the man-made cavities show that in most cases the water was applied to the wheels by sloping channels indicating an 'undershot arrangement' where the power was generated by impulse. The angle of the slope varies from mill to mill. In Mill 4 a step exists 2.3 m high, indicating that the water was most likely applied to the top of the wheel, and that the power was generated by weight rather than impulse. Either side of the wheel

Fig. 68.

Nahal Tanninim

Mill 4 looking upstream towards Mill 2

271 Ad, *et al.,* 160, Fig. 4a.

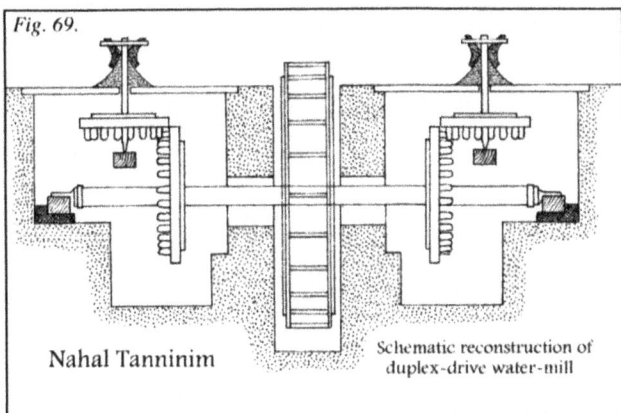

Fig. 69.

Nahal Tanninim   Schematic reconstruction of duplex-drive water-mill

them, is mid. 7th c. A.D.

The contribution that these duplex-drive water-mills have made to our knowledge of Roman water-power technology is undoubtedly valuable, but they have provided evidence of another equally surprising development. In mills 1 and 4, and elsewhere in the excavation, parts of basalt Pompeian-type millstones were found with the *meta* (the lower stone) having central vertical holes showing that they were under-driven. They all had within the rim of the *catillus* two grooves opposite each other, emplacements where the horizontal rod or mill-rynd registered and turned the top stone. The archaeologists identified several different types of upper stones suggesting technological change and development supporting the notion that this site was probably in general use for over three centuries. Neither the dimensions nor the weight of these millstones are published making it difficult to ascertain a meaningful figure for the power they required for operation. The photographs suggest relatively small stones which are also depicted in the schematic reconstruction and repeated here as part of Fig. 69. The MR of the mills is very debatable, for whilst we have some idea of the power generated by the water-wheels, whether by impulse or weight, we do not know if these Pompeian-style stones would have been run at speeds similar to those of disc millstones.

26. Lösnich, Germany.

At *Lösnich*, during 1978, archaeologists found evidence of two water-power sites, 85 m apart, on the same small steeply graded stream, close to a Roman villa-farm-

stead which has been dated as being occupied from late 1st c. to early 5th c. A.D.[272] The villa, which is the focus of the settlement, is the nearest building to the mill sites, being 160 m from the upstream site and standing 30 m higher. The two water-power sites are therefore not remote from the cluster of buildings spread over the flanks of the hillside above the stream. Both of the water-mill sites have been related to the nearby Roman buildings by inference; no clear dating evidence was found, probably because the occupation horizons were eroded away in this steep-sided ravine-like valley. The two water-power sites have strong similarities, both being cut into solid rock with the head-race accelerated by declination. This suggests that they were built in the same period, but whether operating simultaneously or sequentially we cannot tell.

At the Lower mill site[273] the rock face has been cut to create an accelerated head-race, whose profile on the axis of the stream is concavo-convex, 5.84 m high; this provides a strong indication where the wheel stood[274]. (See Fig. 70.) Neyses illustrates a 5 m diameter undershot wheel, which is relatively large within the Roman corpus, but is not out of place within the profiled rock face, and our thoughts on size should be influenced by the reconstruction of the upper site, discussed below. This wheel created power solely by impulse from an accelerated high-velocity head-race, delivered by a wooden chute supported by an emplacement cut into the rock face above the wheel. Neyses speculates that a smaller undershot wheel may have existed, served from the tail-race of the larger wheel, which he has demonstrated existed at the upper site, but there is no evidence of this at the lower site.

At the Upper site[275], only the concave water-wheel emplacement some 3 m deep exists, and all traces of the upper rock profile have disappeared. (See Fig. 71.) The rock face had been cut to form a wheel-pit, of trapezoidal section, 0.6 m wide at the bottom and 1.18 m wide at the top. In one side-wall of this pit, opposite the end of the wheel-shaft, an emplacement has been cut to receive the outer bearing. The opposite rock face has also been cut to allow the driver gear to be installed. A longitudinal section on the axis of the stream shows that the cavity made for the wheel created a hydraulic head of 6.5 m. This evidence allows Neyses to propose with confidence that a relatively large 6.0 m diameter wheel, approximately 0.5 m wide, operated here. A few metres downstream, he identifies

272 Neyses 1983.
273 Neyses 1983, Untere Mühlen XV.
274 Neyses 1983, 211, Abb 2, D.
275 Neyses 1983, 211, Abb 2. Obere Mühlen XIII.

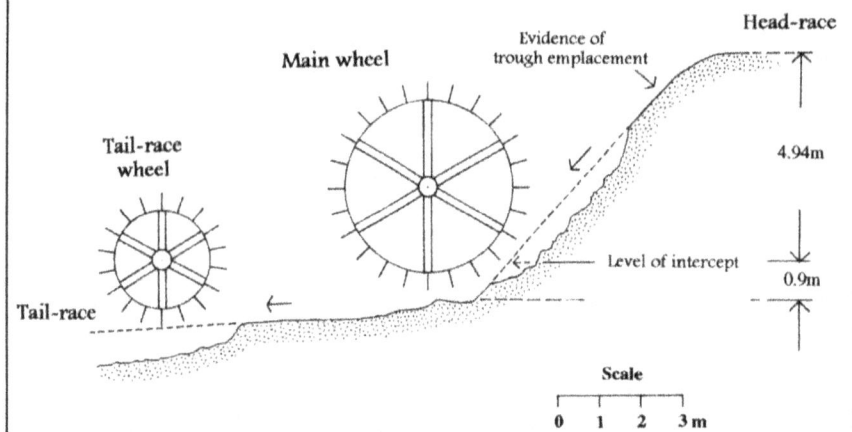

Fig. 70

Lösnich Lower Mill

Neyses records the modern flow rate of the stream as a maximum of 10 l/sec after prolonged rain, and recognizing this as a diminutive flow rate even for an overshot, believes that these mills were served by mill-ponds in the Roman period. He suggested that rock workings that he found on each side of the stream above the mill-sites might have marked the position of such storage ponds. Of course, the flow rate in earlier periods may well have been greater, which is so often the case in many other landscapes including England, but the suggestion of storage is supported indirectly by another observation. What significance should we give to the apparent absence of a 'bypass' channel, a means to divert water from the water-wheels, especially at the upper site with its conjunction of wheels? There is no apparent way for the water to be diverted from the tail-race wheel. A storage system with its interruptible delivery could have facilitated the control normally provided by a diverting bypass. If this suggestion is correct, this is the only Roman vertical water-wheel presently known to us that was served by a stored water system[277].

(from a cavity in the rock bank where a pit-gear had operated) the position where another water-wheel had been placed, driven by the tail-race of the larger wheel. The rock bed between these two wheels had been cut to create a narrowing head-race and an accelerated flow into the lower wheel that Neyses depicts as a 3.1 m diameter impulse wheel with radial floats. Although Neyses concludes early in his analysis that the larger wheel at this upper site was a 'middle-shot' (breast) application, he subsequently debates the merits of undershot and overshot[276] and finally depicts an overshot in his drawings, with inclined buckets. The writer disagrees with this interpretation.

It is very clear that the gradient of this valley, a 45 m drop in 125 m distance in the region of these mill sites, lends itself very well to an overshot application. With such a very steep gradient it would be easy to elevate a head-race serving a large wheel. But there are two rather compelling reasons why this would have been an undershot application. *First*, why else would the builders have cut, from solid rock, a wheel-pit having a trapezoidal radial section and a concave profile to suit a wheel? *Second*, it is clear from the position of these two wheels, that the downstream one could not have operated successfully if its neighbour was overshot. The water from an overshot would have dropped much too close to the lower wheel, creating such turbulence that the velocity of entry into it would have been reduced. With an undershot application on the upstream wheel the efficiency of application of the downstream wheel improves greatly. We should therefore conclude that the larger upstream wheel was of the same form as existing at the lower site, an impulse wheel with radial floats.

The profile of the Upper mill wheel-pit shows that the declination of the head-race, as a tangent to the concavity, was very steep, at 18° from vertical. If we assume, for the purposes of exploring velocities and potential power, a head-race approaching above the wheel 0.6 m wide by 0.15 m deep, the flow rate would be 0.16 m³/s and the velocity of application with a fall to the intercept with the floats of 4 m, works out as 8.68 m/s allowing for the resistance of the head-race trough. This would produce a wheel speed when generating maximum power of approximately 12 rpm. Allowing for a driver gear of the diameter indicated by the rock cavity, this suggests that the driven gear, almost certainly a lantern-gear, was probably slightly larger than the six-stave Zugmantel specimen. For example, an eight-stave lantern-gear would produce a stone speed of 150 rpm[278].

At the Upper mill site part of a sandstone bedstone 1 m in diameter was found. If we accept that the water flow was say 0.1 m³/s, then the potential power generated by the

276 Neyses 1983, 215.
277 With the exception of a possible Roman Tide-mill in London. See Spain 2004.
278 This allows for a cog pitch of 0.06 m, which was proved by the Westree experiment to be necessary for proper engagement of the Zugmantel lantern gear, which was replicated in the rig. See Spain 1992, 88-90. Neyses explores the gear ratios and possible millstone speeds but they are based on the water-wheel being overshot and revolving at 5 rpm.

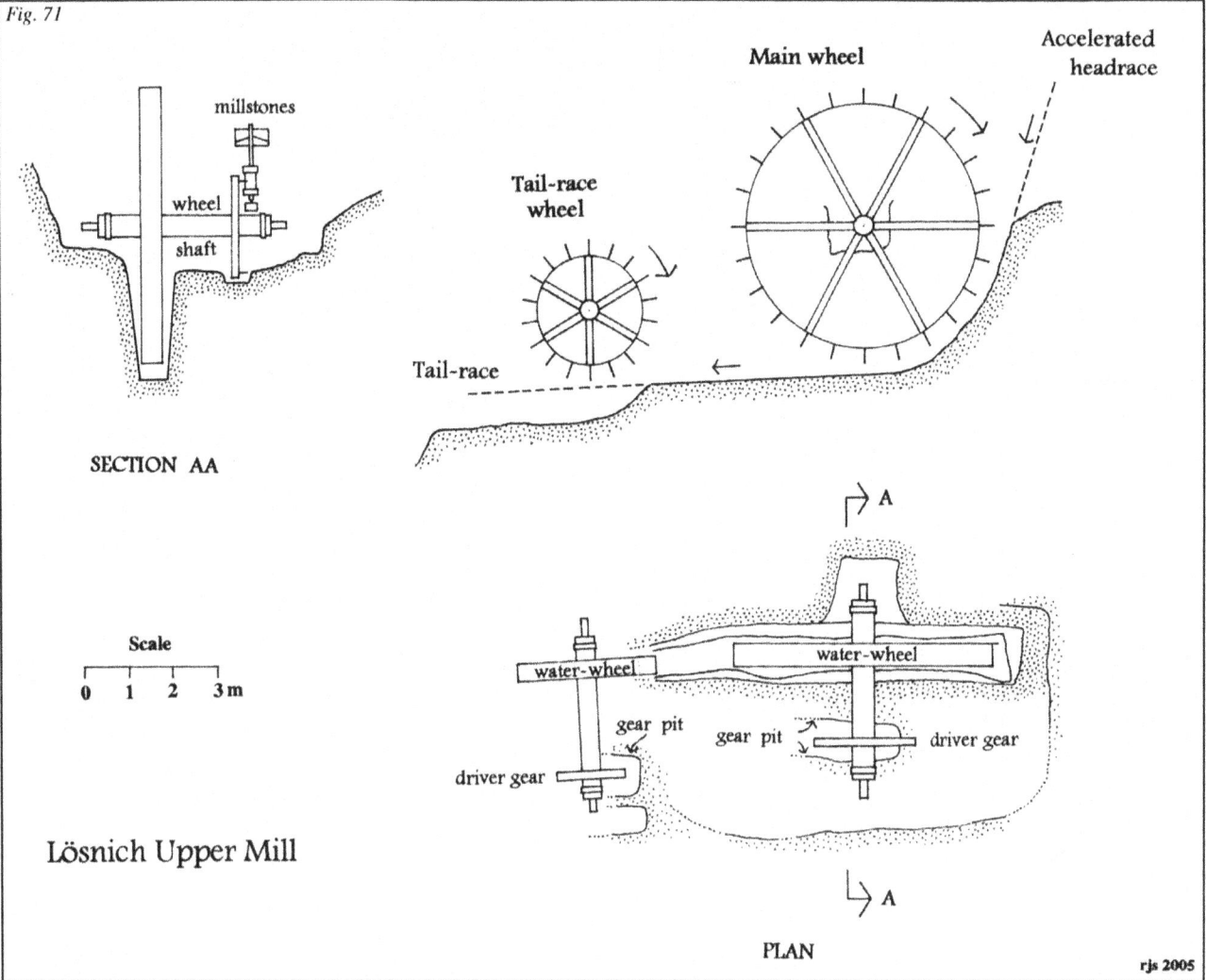

Fig. 71

millstones

wheel

shaft

SECTION AA

Main wheel

Accelerated
headrace

Tail-race
wheel

Tail-race

Scale

0 1 2 3 m

A

water-wheel

water-wheel

gear pit

gear pit

driver gear

driver gear

Lösnich Upper Mill

A

PLAN

rjs 2005

larger wheel at the upper site was 3.82 HP, ample power for such a millstone. With a total hydraulic head of 6.5 m, this represents an efficiency of 27.5%. At the Lower Mill site, the diameter of the main wheel, 5 m as proposed by Neyses, is entirely speculative because we have no evidence of its wheel-shaft position or accurate wheel-pit profile. If we accept the wheel as being 5 m diameter, the declination of the accelerated head-race at 42° from the vertical places the intercept with the floats at a position having a 4.94 m hydraulic head. Thus, although the slope is less than that of the Upper Mill main wheel, the greater head produces a greater impact velocity. Allowing for the resistance of a wooden chute, and the same flow rate of 0.16 m³/s, the impact velocity is theoretically 9.47 m/s, a very fast stream. This wheel would have revolved at approximately 15 rpm.

Within this hydraulic analysis, the approaching head-race is assumed to be 0.6 m wide and 0.15 m deep; this relates to

the flow rate of 0.16 m³/s. At the point of impact, this stream would be c.3.0 cm thick if it was maintained at a width of 0.6 m. Such a fast-moving stream would require very accurate projection onto the floats of the wheel, and, more significantly, would require the wheel to run probably within a very close-fitting head-race trough so as to create and maintain an impact. However, the writer holds the view that a far more effective and practical arrangement would have been used, whereby the width of the delivery trough would have narrowed as it approached the wheel to create a deeper jet of water. This flow rate could have produced a jet having a cross-section of 13 x 13 cm that would have certainly been more effective if directed towards a mid-float position. But this is speculative; nonetheless these unusually high velocities at Lösnich do suggest conditions conducive to the development of water jets and narrow wheels.

27. Venafro, Italy.

Jacono's report[279] of the *Venafro* wheel deserves greater attention than historians have given it. The original facts provided by him in 1938 have somehow become distorted by a series of historians to such an extent that all published versions in English are now misleading if not wholly wrong. The distortions, which appear to have been caused by inaccurate interpretation or translation of Jacono's words, relate to two matters, the position of the site and the date of the artifacts. Let us first examine the evidence for the dating of the *Venafro* artifacts.

The only reference made to the date of the site relates to limestone deposits in which the two millstones and water-wheel impressions were found. A literal translation of the relevant words is, *'they called in Professor Bassani and found out that 2000 years which had passed were sufficient to make up the limestone stratum'*[280]. No corroborating dating evidence is given in the report, which, we should remember, was published thirty years after the finds were discovered. Approximately two years before the *Venafro* finds were published, Parsons had corresponded with Jacono and had apparently accepted them as Roman[281]. The only other evidence that has been published came from Inspector Cimorelli who visited the site,[282] but this does not add anything significant to the evidence provided by Jacono. We are therefore dealing with a single opinion, of unattested repute, whether in archaeology, geology or petrology, which had apparently claimed that a particular limestone deposit had been made during the last 2000 years. The quality of this dating evidence is, as Moritz has said, *'that it is not at all accurate'*[283]. However Forbes has accepted it without question[284], as did many other historians including Reynolds. At present the only other clues on dating come from the millstones and the dimensions of the wheel itself.

The diameter of the millstones, their material and, as Wikander suggests, their slightly conical shape, suggests an Early Imperial date[285]. In the original publication of the *Venafro* finds there is no mention of corroborating evidence, such as coins and pottery, to support the early date claimed

for the site. With regard to the dimensions of the wheel, Jacono noted that it was 100 digits (digit = a sixteenth of a Roman foot) in diameter (1.85 m) and its width and depth of shroud was one Roman foot (0.3 m). Although the wheel is slightly smaller than most other Roman water-wheels, both primary dimensions are met with in the current corpus.

The other mistake about *Venafro*, which is commonly found in the literature, relates to the position of the site. Both this and the dating problem appear to be related to the same source of error, namely the nature of the deposits under which the artifacts were found. Jacono states that the millstones and the impression of the water-wheel were found in limestone deposits but later says that they were in calcium carbonate[286], which was also reported by Parsons;[287] but Forbes has it in tufa[288] and Reynolds as lava[289]. The clue to Reynolds' misunderstanding occurs in his statement that the *Venafro* wheel had been found near Pompeii, covered by the eruption of Vesuvius late in the 1st c. A.D[290]. It would seem that he derived the date from the false assumption that the wheel was covered in lava, but he may not have been the first historian to do so. In fact *Venafro* is 80 km north of Vesuvius, so why have Reynolds and others gone wrong? There appear to be two possibilities. The obvious answer may be that because the model of this water-wheel is in the Museum at Naples, it is mistakenly thought to belong among the Roman archaeological finds identified with and dominated by Vesuvius. Parsons may have further misled people by calling it the Naples wheel. The second and more likely reason is that Jacono's Italian text has been misinterpreted because both lava and Pompeii are mentioned, but that is in context with the millstones.

How was the water applied to this wheel and what was the head? Jacono states that the millstones were discovered 3 m from the surface of a bank made up of limestone deposits. Then the wheel impression was found *'a short distance from these millstones and on the same bank of the river further down in the limestone bed'*. He goes on to say *'the remains of the walls of a Roman canal which could be seen just below the surface'* which we can take as being the head-race. Jacono's single reference to the head of water says *'The extent to which the water ran down H, we can work out approximately bearing in mind the date of the*

279 Jacono 1938.
280 Jacono 1938, 850.
281 Parsons 1936, 70, footnote 2.
282 Cimorelli 1914.
283 Moritz 1958, 137-8.
284 Forbes 1955, 90.
285 Wikander 1985.
286 Jacono 1938, 850, 852.
287 Parsons 1936, 76.
288 Forbes 1956. Tufa, (geology = tuff) a stony coating left by hard water when it evaporates, known also as travertine or cancerous (limy) tufa. Limestone consists of calcite (calcium carbonate) discoloured by impurities, which can vary greatly in colour and hardness.
289 Reynolds 1983. Reynolds may have been misled or confused by tuff, a rock formed from volcanic ashes.
290 Reynolds 1983, 18, 30, 36.

excavation, as being approximately 4m'. This rather abstruse statement suggests that Jacono did have the benefit of measured site levels. From this evidence, such as it is, it is not possible to speculate with much advantage. It is quite possible that the millstones and the wheel were found in the position that they had worked in, with the wheel ' *a short distance away at a greater depth'*. This could have been confirmed if the stones were on the line of the wheel-shaft and within say, 2 m of the wheel. If they were positioned like this, then the centre of the wheel would have been 0.6 to 1.0 m below the millstones. With the bed of the head-race at say, 0.3 m below surface, the head of water was close to 2.4 m to 2.7 m above the wheel, on the basis that the millstones were found under 3 m of deposits. If we assume that the wheel was undershot and the water was applied at a height, say of one quarter of the wheel diameter above the bottom of the wheel, the head would have been approximately 3.75 to 4.1 m, which agrees with Jacono's figure. If overshot and applied to the crown of the wheel then the head was say, a quarter of wheel diameter plus 2.4 to 2.7 m. Whatever we make of these figures, the head of water is unusually high and so also would have been the velocity of impact on the wheel.

There is no indication from the report as to how the position of the watercourse relates to the water-wheel, which might have helped us to decide how the water was taken and applied to the wheel. The few words that Jacono devotes to this are not very helpful. '*Bearing in mind that there is no sort of internal seal between the inside ends of the fins*[291], *it seems to me that this must have been a side wheel on which the water pushed the bottom section'*. What is clear from this is that Jacono's ideas on how the water was applied stems from the design of the wheel and not site evidence of water flow. Although this suggests a lack of evidence, it does give us a clear field for speculation. Both Reynolds and Forbes declare the wheel as undershot, presumably influenced by Jacono's words, but a re-examination of this unusual wheel is worthwhile.

In the *Venafro* wheel we do not know the direction or point of application of the head-race to the wheel; neither do we know if the direction of the water could be varied by a pivoted trough or nozzle. Jacono does not appear to state directly whether or not the wheel was undershot although it is implicit in his suggestion that the wheel 'was pushed from the bottom section'. However, the point is that we do not know for sure the arrangement that existed[292].

The *Venafro* wheel shows distinct features of an unusual design, (See Fig. 72.) which are;-

[a] There are only three different elements used in its construction, radial floats which are morticed in a solid shaped hub and side shrouds – a very simple but strong design.

[b] The solid hub and radial floats are relieved on the sides, which gives a 'dished' appearance to the wheel. This was presumably to allow some or all of the water to pass through between the floats and out of the sides of the wheel.

[c] The unusually high head combined with a small diameter wheel shows that the wheel was capable of running at a very high speed.

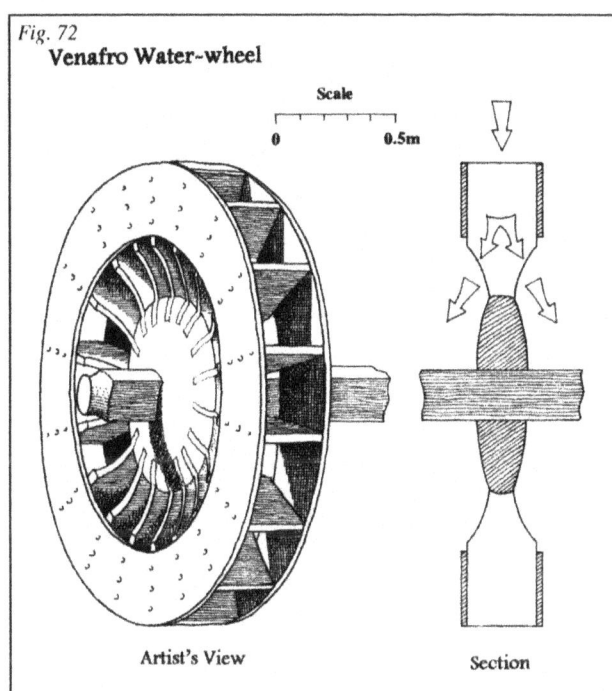

Fig. 72
Venafro Water-wheel

Scale

0   0.5m

Artist's View   Section

All of these features can be identified with an impulse wheel or turbine. Although a sole plate is absent we can recognize the shrouds as having provided greater effect by partial confinement. An interesting feature of the design of this wheel is that when a jet of water is brought to bear on the wheel on an axis tangential to a circle inside the rim, virtually all of the water strikes the radial floats at an angle, which causes a deflection towards the centre of the wheel. The angle of deflection becomes particularly noticeable when the stream is directed towards the middle of the floats.

291 He alludes to sole boards.
292 If any of the excavator's site notes exist they might shed light on this point and other critical features.

In this position the deflection is approximately 120 degrees. If sole boards were present, this deflection would cause violent turbulence and, significantly, a reversal of flow and the laminar conditions of the approaching water would be destroyed. This phenomenon would occur at whatever position around the wheel the impact was made, because the velocity of application is so great.[293] Now we can begin to see an advantage in not having sole boards. Furthermore, the dished effect, produced by the curved edges of the floats morticed into the elliptical sectioned solid hub, would have provided a natural relief for the water flowing into the wheel. As the water coursed through each of the float chambers and passed by the shrouds, it was bifurcated by the curved rim of the hub and discharged through the two open ports, one in each flank of the wheel. The shrouds would have provided strength and stability to the wheel that would have been receiving considerable shocks and stress from the high velocity water. They also helped to constrain and guide the water inwards towards the shaft. This is a form of inward-flowing vertical impulse turbine, which was not met again, according to our present knowledge, until the nineteenth century.

The only historian after Jacono who appears to have studied this wheel, Reynolds, does not recognize these unusual design features as being progressive or advanced. Indeed, he condemns the design saying that the hub was very large and heavy and may have impaired the wheel's effective operation[294]. He saw the shrouds as impeding the exit of the water after impact. The elliptical section of the hub is surely a balance of strength in its juncture with the shaft combined with the hydrodynamic shape necessary to encourage the bifurcation and exit of the water; why otherwise have curved surfaces over the whole of the hub? Neither a clasp-armed wheel or alternative radial armed wheel would have provided such free egress for the high velocity water, because the additional structural elements at the junction of the arms and shaft would have generated violent dispersion and agitation of the water. Reynolds summarises his opinion of the wheel as indicating that Roman technological knowledge in the area of hydropower may have been seriously incomplete.

Let us now consider at what position the water was applied to the wheel. First let us avoid the complexities of geometric variation of stream and float inclination and simplify our view; the lower on the wheel the water was

applied, the greater the head and the higher the velocity and torque generated. When the Romans created accelerated head-races they must have been aware of some basic hydraulic behaviour, certainly of how velocity increased with the height of fall. Whether or not they understood why this occurred or the natural laws that related to this phenomenon matters not. We might also credit them with recognizing that with increased velocity came greater pressure or force, and that the same effect could be produced by increasing the weight or volume of water flowing. They may not have had an understanding of the relationships between velocity, mass and the energy they can produce, but this does not mean that they were not conscious of such forces. Their everyday use of such things as pile-drivers and battering rams would have provided them with an understanding of the effects and relationships between velocity and mass. All this was within the daily experience of artificers. Faced with the *Venafro* evidence we cannot avoid concluding that the builders purposely sought to create a high velocity stream and water-wheel. Other high-velocity Roman water-power sites support this conclusion. Therefore it seems very likely that the wheel received its water low down rather than near the crown. To do otherwise would have wasted some of the head that they had created. This produces a head close to 4 m, which agrees with Jacono's figure.

Jacono appears to be the first historian of technology to have attempted a hydro-mechanical analysis of a water-mill. He calculates that the flow rate was 0.093 m^3/s which equates to a cross sectional area on the headrace of 1.0 ft^2 and a velocity of 1.0 m/s. The report does not mention the size of the head-race but it is reasonable to assume that its width was similar to that of the wheel. The writer has adopted the same flow rate, which we could view as being a minimum to simplify comparison. Jacono puts the velocity of impact at 29 ft/s (8.85 m/s) and the speed of the wheel, assuming a rim velocity of half, at 46 rpm[295]. The calculation did not allow for the resistance of the inclined head-race[296], that if we assume to be 45° produces an impact velocity of 24.3 ft/s (7.4 m/s) and a wheel speed of 39rpm[297]. The values and interaction of the numerous variables are not critical; the important point is that this wheel was very fast, a fact recognized by Jacono.

Jacono states that two millstones were found, 0.8 m dia. and about 0.25 m thick. We do not know if the thickness applied

293 How interesting it would be to test a model of this wheel in a hydraulic laboratory to explore its operating characteristics.
294 Reynolds 1983, 43.
295 Jacono 1938, 582-83.
296 He believed the wheel to have been undershot and surely could not have assumed a vertical drop onto the wheel.
297 Adopting a rim velocity 0.425 of the water impact and assuming the jet, which has a thickness of approximately 2in (0.05m), strikes the outer edges of the floats.

to one or both, and whether top or bottom stone. He does mention that the grinding faces were inclined, and his reported stone thickness, which would be thick for a top stone, may have been the overall thickness. A top stone of this size would absorb 1.0 hp when revolving at 38 rpm. With the head-race delivering 0.093 m^3/s, the power generated by this wheel is theoretically approximately 1.87 hp. Allowing for bearing and gearing friction, a balance of 1.7 hp could be applied to the stones that, having the appropriate MR, could revolve at 64.5 rpm. The output of these stones would therefore be 199 lbs/hr (90.5 kg/hr)[298]. The total theoretical kinetic energy for this quantity and head of water is 5.5 hp so that the efficiency of this wheel with this flow rate using gross generated power is 34%.

28. Roman Tide-mills – The Fleet Tide-mill.

It would be a weakness of this study if some mention were not made of the subject of water-power generated by tidal flow. None of the principal Greek or Roman writers of the ancient world mention tide-mills, although several clearly had knowledge of water-mills[299]. However, it has been claimed that attempts were made in classical times to harness the tidal currents of the Euripus channel separating Boeotia and Euboea, and in the Evrepos Strait in Cephalonia[300], but the writer has been unable up to date to identify the classical source for this assertion. In both the Euripus and Evrepos channels there is a vicious rip, caused by differing tides at either end, which changes direction several times a day[301]. Such mills that are driven by tidal currents are not true tide-mills in the modern meaning of the term, where the power is derived from the hydraulic head created by the rise and fall of tides. If these water-mills existed, they may have been floating mills, which we know to have been used to great effect when Rome was besieged by the Goths in A.D. 537. Alternatively, they may have had wheels in a fixed position that could effectively engage, like river mills, large masses of flowing water with negligible changes in water level. The tidal range of the Mediterranean is small, at a maximum of 0.8 m at Gibraltar and as little as 0.2 m along the French coast. Although we have modern examples of tide-mills that have worked with relatively small ranges[302], it seems improbable that tidal-power was

discovered and developed prior to the expansion of the empire to the Atlantic coast. The opportunity to exploit tidal-power may have been realized when the newly founded Carthaginian empire in the Iberian peninsula fell to Rome after the Second Punic War (218-201 B.C.) or later, Gaul. Their conquest of Gaul in 58-50 B.C., would have brought substantial lengths of the Atlantic coast within their control and with it, we may presume, a fraternization with the maritime tribes having a far better working knowledge and understanding of tides.

We know the Romans had a good understanding of tides from the writings of Strabo[303] (64 B.C. to A.D. 21) and Pliny the Elder (A.D. 23 to 79). Their accounts reveal knowledge of diurnal and monthly tides, and the equinoctial/solstitial inequality that causes the springs to reach their highest levels around the equinoxes twice each year. Their intellectual enquiries may have revealed to them that every four and a half years the spring tides were exceptionally high, a phenomenon which we now know to be due to coincidence with perigee, the closest approach of the moon to the earth, when *perigean* tides occur. But whether or not this knowledge of tides provided them with an alternative source of water-power is the question that this study is facing.

We have seen in the above study examples of wheels where the power was harnessed from rivers and streams and the flow rate was relatively large but the velocity slow. Some of these might be called river mills, where the undershot wheel was immersed in the mill-stream and the volume of water entering the wheel was such that there was no need to accelerate it by grading the bed or aligning the walls of the approaching head-race. It was these slower moving wheels that would have required higher MR's in their gearing to achieve satisfactory millstone speeds. It is this type of machine, with a slow moving water-wheel and high gear ratio that comes closest to the hydro-mechanical requirements of a tide-mill. We could speculate that the engineering experience and innovative capabilities demonstrated by the wide range of examples within the corpus of water-mills, that the Romans would have had no difficulty in recognizing and harnessing the power potential within a tidal estuary.

During the years 1988 to 1992 archaeologists discovered two hitherto unknown islands on the east side of the Fleet estuary in London, that during the early Roman period were

298 Syson thought that the stones could deliver 180 kg/hr and Forbes 150 kg/hr with the stones running at 46 rpm. Syson 1965 24; Forbes 1955, 90.
299 See Olsen 1984b, for a summary and interpretation of these texts.
300 Charlier 1978, A1-2.
301 *Pers. comms.* from Dr. Michael Lewis.
302 RupelmondeFleet Tide Mill on the Scheldt, Belgium with a tidal range as low as 0.9 m; Mystic River Tide Mills, near Arlington, Massachusetts with a tidal range of 0.6 to 0.9 m. See Proceedings of an International Conference on Tide Mills.
303 Strabo Geography. See also Cartwright 1999.

Fig. 73.

The Fleet Tide-mill
Showing areas of excavation (black)
and watching brief (shaded)

River
Fleet

Northern
Eyot

Southern
Eyot

NORTH

Scale

0   20   40   60
metres

River Thames

rjs 2002

Fig. 74.

The Fleet Tide-mill
Principle features from excavations
Early Roman period

Roman road

NORTH

Scale

0   20
metres

River
Fleet

Drainage
ditch

NORTHERN
EYOT

Channels

Watercourse

Building

Timber structure

Dock

Ludgate
Roman road

Bridge
abutment

SOUTHERN
EYOT

Warehouse

Jetty

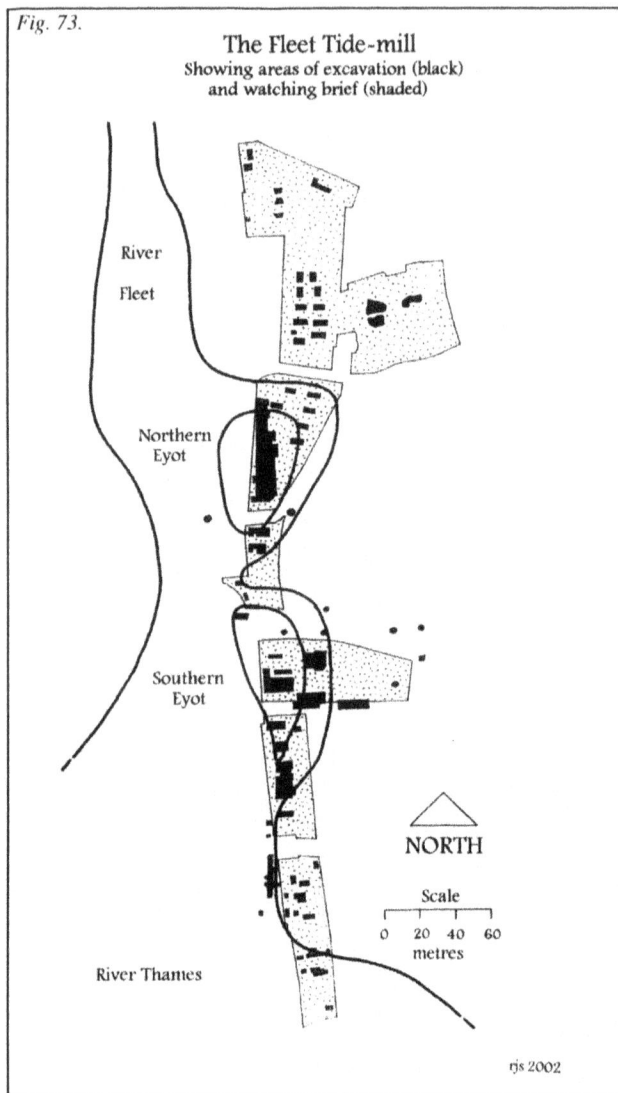

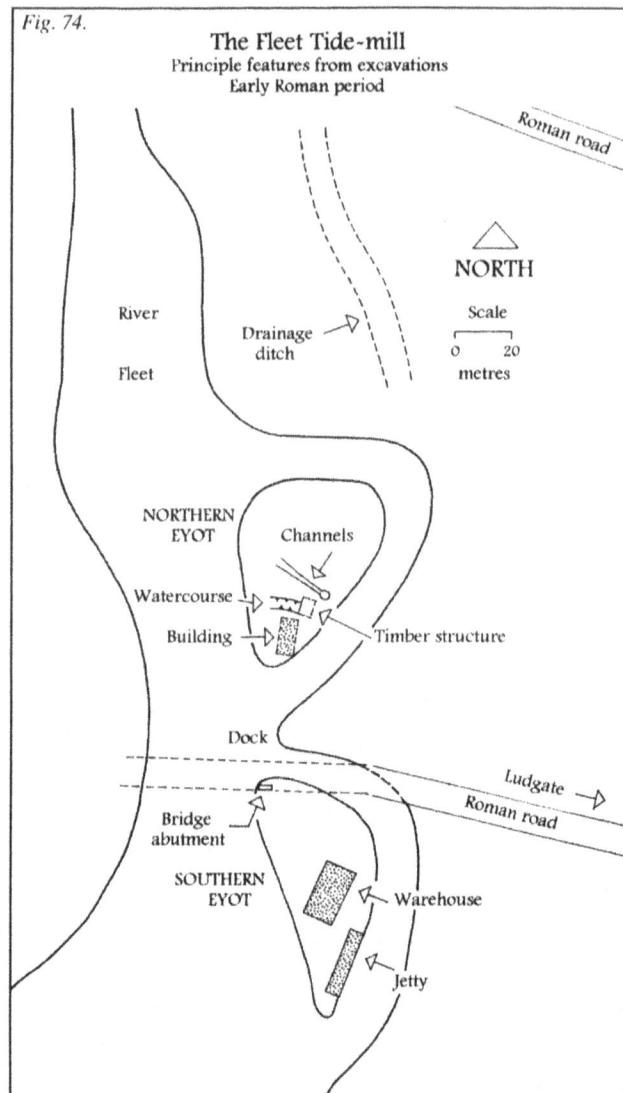

developed and used for industrial purposes[304]. (See Fig. 73.) From the Roman structures and artificial channels found they concluded that a probable tide-mill operated on the north island[305]. (See Fig. 74.) Numerous earth-fast posts, aligned on rectilinear axes, were found adjacent to a man-made water-course cut through the northern island, whose layout and position within the estuary has been interpreted as a probable tide-mill. (See Fig. 75.) The timber structure was dated by dendrochronolgy to A.D.*c*.116 The archaeological reports state that the water-course was not *'bottomed out'* but that it was at least 2 m deep and the *'levels in the mill-race'* are given as 1.48 m to -0.38 m OD[306]. Furthermore we do not know its full width, but if we assume that the limit of excavation, close to post P1, revealed a minimum half width of approximately 2.3 m, and that the channel section was roughly symmetrical, then the

total width may have been in the order of 4.6 m, or perhaps 5.0 m. Mindful that the section of the channel may have been influenced by deposition and erosion, and that the slope of its sides is steeper towards the east[307], if a water-wheel worked in this area, it lay to the east of the structure beyond the edge of the excavated area. Unfortunately the structural remains do not allow us to suggest a size for the wheel and therefore it is not possible to determine the power potential, so our deliberations are limited primarily to formulating a picture of its operational life-cycles and hydraulic head.

One of the reasons why corn-milling operations have been suggested for the northern eyot[308] was that large quantities of charred spelt wheat, chaff and possibly barley, were found in the artificial channel and adjacent areas. The

304 The archives of this very large series of excavations, known as the Fleet Valley Report, have not yet been published but are now available for public research. The London Archaeological Archive and Research Centre (LAARC) ref. VAL 88 volumes 1-54 hold them. The work is summarized in vol. 54, Final Interim Report edited by Bill McCann, May 1993. See also Archaeology in the City of London 1907-1991, The Archaeological Gazetteer Series vol.1 (MoL 1998), 283/4.
305 Spain 2004.
306 VAL 54, 4 Period 1, Early Roman AD 43-200, 26, 34.
307 VAL 49, Abstract, Phase E4, Zone E, 20.
308 Eyot, a variation of ait, a small island especially in a river. This term prevails throughout the archaeological reports of this site and is henceforth adopted by the writer.

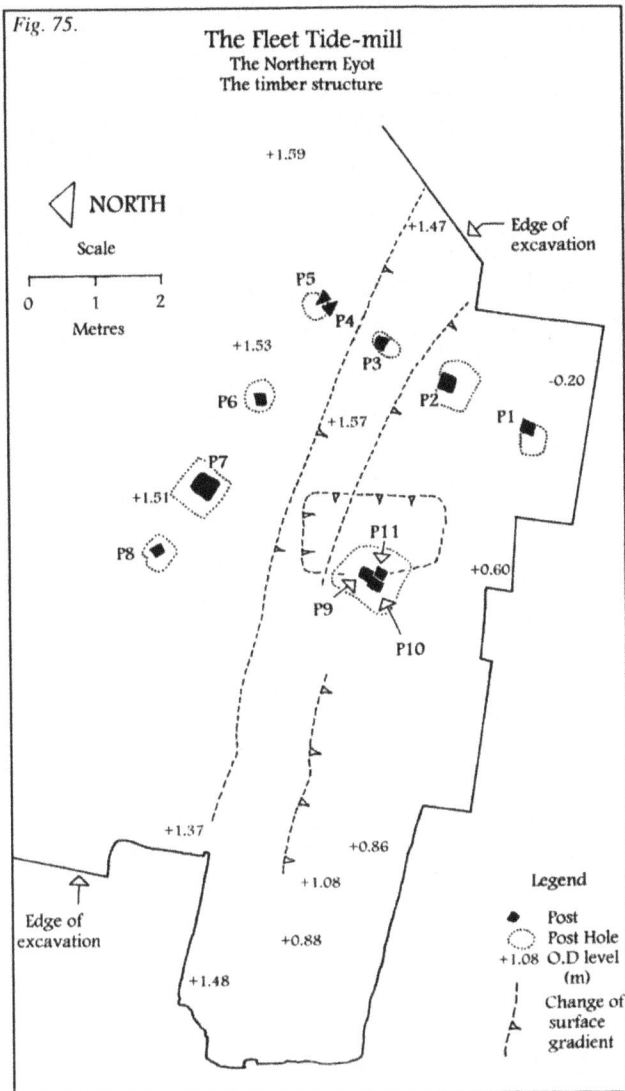

Fig. 75.
The Fleet Tide-mill
The Northern Eyot
The timber structure

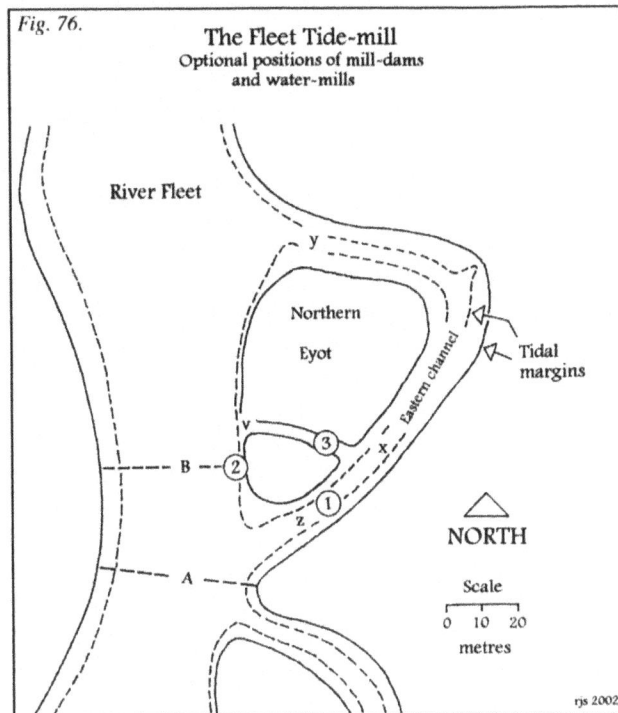

Fig. 76.
The Fleet Tide-mill
Optional positions of mill-dams
and water-mills

rjs 2002

parching implied by the charring is interpreted as the final stages of grain processing, used to make the inner glumes brittle and therefore easily separable from the grain by milling[309]. Finds of burnt and parched cereals on Roman sites suggests that grain drying was common practice and probably integrated with bulk milling using animate or water-power[310]. It seems very likely, as suggested by the archaeologists, that these operations were carried out in the building(s) on the eyot. A large fragment of a quern-stone was also found on the northern eyot, original diameter 0.4 m, which supports the suggestion of milling. The quern itself would not have been the primary method for grain reduction, but several Roman water-mills have yielded querns alongside millstones[311], which suggests they were used for ancillary functions[312].

If a water-mill existed on, or adjacent to the northern eyot, it was clearly positioned in either a natural or artificial channel, which was estuarine – subject to the tides. To be effective, the undershot water-wheel of a tide-mill needed to be (a) at a level so that it could use the stored water whilst the ebb-tide continued to drop away from the underside of the wheel, and (b) in a position so that its head-race and tail-race allowed unimpeded flow downstream from the mill-pond to the lower estuary. In a tide-mill, all of the pond water above the level of the bottom of the wheel can, in theory, be usefully used for powering the wheel, which, in this estuary situation, is a combination of tidal water and flow from the Fleet River. Only by building a mill-dam could a head of water be created to ensure that flow would occur through the head-race to the wheel.

When considering a tide-mill either within the northern eyot or on its banks, the mill-dam cannot be downstream of, and unattached from the eyot (see Fig 76, position A), which would put the mill upstream of the dam in an unworkable situation. The question has been asked – could the mill-dam have been integrated with the river bridge that crossed the northern end of the southern eyot? The major problem with this suggestion is that the water from the mill can only be taken downstream using the channel to the east of the southern eyot, if the dam was extended between the two

309 Parching is essential for stabilizing large batches of grain following a wet harvest or shorter drying season and was also a means of killing pests such as weevil. Drier grain, although slightly harder, is easier to mill and feed into the stones. The parching of wheat using drying kilns was a common feature in landscapes having a temperate climate dominated by the north Atlantic, particularly in northern and western British Isles.
310 Milne 1995, 46, 64.
311 For example Haltwhistle Burn Head, Ickham and the Athenian Agora water-mills.
312 Most likely for testing grain to establish its condition in readiness for milling. Querns might also deal with small volumes of different grains, pulses or seeds from customers. They might also have provided further refinement of a product or a quality control datum for the main milling work.

Fig. 77.

The Fleet Tide-mill
Theoretical spring and neap tide curves
River Fleet estuary c. 100 A.D.

ORDNANCE DATUM (m)

- +1.5
- +1.0
- +0.75 — W_H →
- +0.5 — W_M →
- +0.25 — W_L →
- 0
- Bed of millrace →

Neaps

Springs

-0.5

FLOOD —— EBB —— FLOOD

-4   0   4   8   12

Hours

Fig. 78.

The Fleet Tide-mill
Graph of river levels in the City of London showing
tidal regression during the Early Roman period
(After Watson, Brigham and Dyson 2001)

- +2.0
- +1.0

Activity ceases on northern eyot

Ordnance

W_L →

0

Level of headrace bed →

Datum (m)

MHWS

-1.0

MHWN

Watercourse cut through eyot →
Dendro. date of structure →

-2.0

MLWS

80   120   160   200

Years A.D.

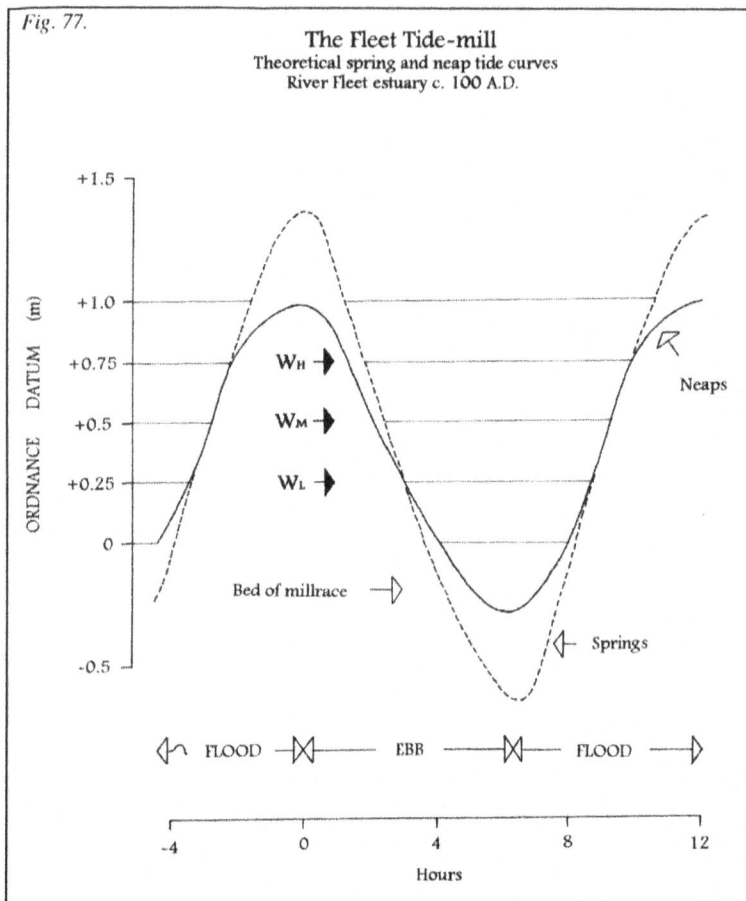

eyots. This impractical arrangement, which would involve a doubling of the length of the dam, would mean that the boats using the southern jetty and the dock had to work against the flow coming from the mill. The suggestion of integrating the dam with the river bridge is therefore rejected.

It is concluded that the main dam has to be in position *B* to be effective. Moreover, it has to be supplemented by another dam in the channel to the east of the eyot. If the artificial channel was a mill-race, that is either a tail-race or a head-race, the supplementary dam had to be positioned somewhere between *y* and upstream of *x*, where the mill-race entered the eastern channel.

There appear to be three alternative positions for the tide-mill, indexed 1, 2 and 3 on Fig. 76. If the water-wheel was at position 1, we are unable to explain the function of the artificial channel, having regard to the natural eastern channel that existed between *y* and *x*. The next option, position 2, suggests that the water-wheel emplacement was integrated with the main mill-dam running between the west bank of the eyot and the west bank of the Fleet. The best position for this would be at the east end, where the mill-house could be built on the bank of the eyot at position 2. With the mill at this position, a supplementary dam would be required at *z*. With the wheel in this position the artificial channel serves no purpose because a bypass or overflow, where water in excess of the mill's requirements could circumvent the wheel, could easily be provided on the dam. Once again the existence of the artificial channel renders position 2 untenable. Position 3 within the artificial channel, in conjunction with dams at *B* and *y*, appears to be the only practical situation for a tide-mill, but we need to examine the level of the channel in relation to the tidal range that existed.

The high tide area of the mill-pond upstream of the suggested dams *B* and *y* is substantial

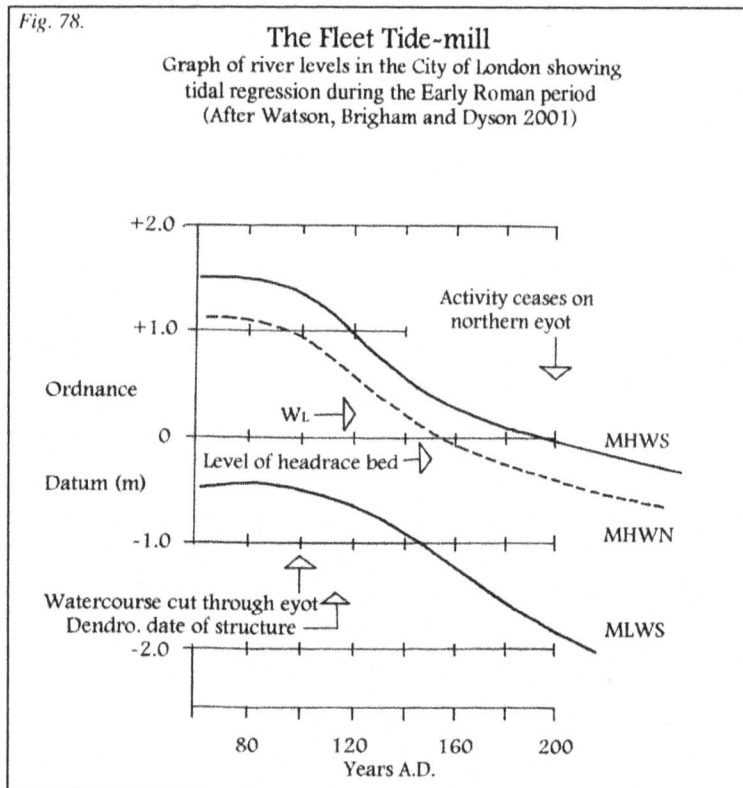

measuring 11,500m^2. With the River Fleet feeding the mill-pond with ample water for one or more water-wheels, we must ask the question was the tide needed to fill the pond? The answer is no, in theory. But the level of the bed of the water-course (0.38 m below OD) equates to mean low tide, which indicates a strong case for the channel to have been tidal. Why otherwise dig it so deep? Why not avoid the difficulties of excavating a tidal channel and build the water-wheels at a higher level? The answer seems unavoidable; they chose to use the tide for power, not the river.

Using the accepted view that the River Thames in Londinium was tidal and that its range mid. 1st c. A.D. was $c.+1.5$ m OD (MHWS) to -0.5 m OD (MLWS)[313], theoretical spring and neap tide curves have been generated for the estuarine lower reaches of the River Fleet for .A.D.$c.$ 100.[314] (See Fig. 77.) The tidal level in relation to the mill-race level has facilitated operational cycles for an undershot water-wheel to be proposed for different levels of the wheel. (See Table O.)

Table O – Operational cycles

Level of bottom of wheel (m. OD)	Mill work (hours)		Idle period (hours)	
	Springs	Neaps	Springs	Neaps
+ 0.75 m W_H	8.3 [9.1]	8.9 [9.4]	4.1 [3.3]	3.5 [3.0]
+ 0.50 m W_M	7.2 [8.2]	7.5 [8.0]	5.2 [4.2]	4.9 [4.4]
+ 0.25 m W_L	5.9 [7.2]	5.9 [7.0]	6.5 [5.2]	6.5 [5.4]

[ ] Denotes time periods that include for running the wheel in backwater.

The level of the water-wheel is unlikely to have been at +0.75 m OD, position W_H on Fig. 77, because the head of water was less than 0.25 m during neap tides. Level +0.50 m OD, position W_M, would allow theoretically an average working period across all tides of 8.1 hours. In this position the head of water is improved, varying from 0.85 m maximum to 0.50 m minimum. Lowering the wheel further to position +0.25 m OD, position W_L, reduces the average working period to 7.1 hours across the tides but greatly increases the head from between 0.73 m to 1.10 m. This position also enjoys the maximum storage of water in the mill-pond. Below this level, as the wheel position is

lowered, the working period rapidly reduces, particularly at neap tides, and so it is considered unlikely that the bottom of the wheel was below +0.25 m OD. From this analysis, the favoured position that brings a balance between working periods, head of water and storage is W_L. At this position the axis of the shaft and bearings of a 2.5 m diameter water-wheel would be 150 mm above the spring tides. A slightly larger wheel would keep the shaft and bearings above virtually all water levels, though the pit-gear would probably run partly immersed.

Archaeology of the Roman water-front in London has identified a tidal regression or progressive fall in the river level of 1.5 m between A.D.$c.$50 - 300[315]. This suggests that this regression of the tide interrupted the miller's working, day and night, so that by A.D.$c.$150 the tidal power became spasmodic and had virtually disappeared by A.D. 160. (See Fig. 78.) During this period and thereafter, the miller would have increasingly used the flow of the River Fleet itself for power.

The wheel of a Roman tide-mill would have had radial floats and was probably not shrouded. Planks would have lined the bed of the wheel-pit and the first few metres of the tail-race, for without such protection the water would have quickly scoured the bed of the mill-race, thus allowing the water to pass under the wheel without having a positive effect on the floats. The same principle of constraint applies to the sides of the wheel-pit, where, we can imagine, the builders realized the obvious advantage of close-boarding the walls so that the wheel was a reasonable fit in the emplacement. On the question of sole-boards we need to be more cautious. In many ways a tide-wheel is similar to a river wheel, where the body of water has considerable volume but low velocity, and the floats can operate quite deep, indeed, wholly immersed in the water. When there is plenty of water - as must have existed at this site – and the wheel operates within an emplacement, the advantage gained by having sole boards is minimal. Indeed, there is a danger that sole boards could constrain the water surging into the wheel and cause an upward thrust that could unseat the journals in the bearings. Light upward thrusts or vibrations could easily be checked by top covers or straps above the journals, which would probably be present anyway, but the forces that might occur with freak waves or flash floods could have had catastrophic results. We can conclude that sole boards were unlikely to have been

313 Milne 1985, graph 50.
314 These tide curves have been based on those that exist at London Bridge, which is currently the nearest tide-gauge to the River Fleet 1.08 miles upstream. Their shape has been transposed on to the tidal range that existed in the Early Roman period. Hopefully the asymmetry of the profiles reflects the influences that occur in this estuarine situation. See Spain 2004, 18, 19.
315 Watson, Brigham and Dyson 2001, 53.

present in the wheel.

There are really too many variables to consider in attempting to ascertain what power this water-wheel could have generated. The diurnal and lunar tidal variations in conjunction with the early Roman tidal regression produce a complicated and ever-changing operational life for the miller. Suffice to say that with the suggested hydraulic head range of 0.73 – 1.10 m when the mill was built in A.D.*c.*100, we can confidently assume that the large mill-pond, combined with the flow of the River Fleet, would have provided ample potential power at the site. With a typical pair of Roman disc millstones needing 1.0-2.5 HP, it is entirely possible that more than one prime-mover may have existed in this area. The assumption that this is the site of a tide-mill is founded largely on circumstantial evidence, strengthened by our inability to sustain an alternative and secure interpretation of the northern eyot's building structure and man-made water-course.

Two other possible Roman tide-mills are known. At Le Yaudet near Ploulec'h, Britanny, there are the remains of a massive dam some 5 m thick, made of large dressed stone blocks stretching across a natural river-fed bay, having three identifiable sluice positions cut through and where a millstone was found close by[316]. Clear evidence of a tide-mill, and although this is adjacent to a major Roman site, as yet no evidence has been found indicating the date of the structure. Also in Britanny there is another similar structure, some 4 m wide on top with corbelled sluice openings, called the Pont Crach, near Aber Wrac'h[317]. A Roman road reaches the coast at this point, but as yet, the Pont Crach has not been dated.

29. Roman Floating Mills.

In the history of technology, there is an often-quoted example of Roman innovation concerning water-power. When the Goths besieged Rome in March A.D. 537, they cut off all the aqueducts serving Rome and thereby brought to a halt the water-mills on the *Janiculum Hill*. Procopius informs us that Belisarius installed floating mills on the Tiber to help restore the milling demands of the city[318]. This account states that the boats supporting the mills were moored in pairs tied with ropes to both river banks, below one of the vaults of a bridge that Wikander identifies as the Pons Aurelius-Antoninus[319]. Behind the first pair of boats Belisarius tied similar pairs of coupled boats, one after the other in a long line. A water-wheel was slung between each pair of boats. These boats, which were apparently installed very quickly within the first month of the siege, were small river craft that were adapted for this unusual purpose. Procopius says that Belisarius moved milling machinery from the Janiculum to the boats; that would have certainly included the millstones and possibly the gears but not the wheel-shafts and the water-wheels. Most of the *Janiculum Hill* wheels were overshot, and new wheels would have been needed to harness this novel undershot application, with their size and shafts being tailored to suit the physical situation. Procopius states that the boats were moored two feet apart, which Wikander has taken to mean the distance between each pair, thereby limiting the width of the wheels. The writer suggests an alternative interpretation that this distance was between successive pairs of boats and not between the pairs, for two reasons. First, the limit of two feet for the width of a river wheel is quite impractical. To generate reasonable power the floats need to have substantially large submerged faces, and to achieve this their width is the most valuable dimension. The second reason relates to the transportation of materials. With a series of pairs of boats moored behind each other in a long line, the transportation of materials to each pair would surely not have been facilitated using a number of parallel bridges, which would seem ergonomically and structurally unnecessary. The simple solution is that each pair is positioned close enough to its neighbours to allow labourers to carry sacks upstream and downstream from boat to boat. The writer therefore believes that Procopius' comment about the distance between the boats refers to their separation upstream and downstream and not across the water flow. With the upstream pair of boats secured to the road bridge, the 'floating bridge' could have communicated with the boats further downstream, thereby giving some stability to the position of the whole line of boats.

Placing the head of the floating mills below the vaults of a bridge makes considerable sense. Mariotti Bianchi[320] considers that the boats would have needed to be moored

316 The writer is most grateful to Prof. Barry Cunliffe for bringing this site to his attention. Cunliffe and Galliou 2002, Fig. 1.
317 I am indebted to Dr. Michael Lewis for bringing this site to my attention.
318 Procop. Goth. 5. 19. 19-27.Wikander has made a valuable study of Procopius' description of this event. Wikander 1979, 29-32.
319 Wikander 1979, 31.
320 Mariotti Bianchi 1976, 47-8.
321 Mariotti Bianchi 1976, 47-8, tav. 4, 8, 10-12.

near one bank of the river for transporting the grain and meal to and from the mills, and therefore supposes that Procopius' description of their position is inaccurate[321]. Establishing a bridge between the bank and one of the near-side boats would have presented no difficulty to Roman engineers, who could have used pontoons or other boats to support the structure. But placing the water-wheels near the centre of the river makes unquestionable sense because they would experience the greater velocity of the river flow and therefore maximum power. Acquaroni's engraving of c.1820 showing a floating mill on the Tiber, and illustrated by both Mariotti Bianchi and Wikander[322], depicts a permanent wooden bridge between one bank and the floating mill. Although the wheel is very wide, this bridge arrangement puts the wheel very close to the centre of the river. Being beneath the vault of a bridge would bring the advantage of tending to accelerate the flow between the piers or abutments and into the wheels. Moreover, if Wikander's sensible comments concerning the diminution of the flow in drier seasons holds true, the wheels would have been less affected by lower water levels. The other influence on position is navigation, which later floating mills could not have obstructed, but during the siege of A.D. 537, was irrelevant. The bridge would also bring the advantage of providing an upstream anchor for the whole boat assembly, and critically important, support either a floating boom or a chain to intercept floating debris that would smash the water-wheels. Such a protective barrier would be essential to thwart attempts by the besiegers to break the wheels with floating tree-trunks or baulks of timber.

With regard to the structure and arrangement of each of the floating mills, our thoughts are largely speculative and influenced by our experience of later floating mills and common sense mechanical practicalities. The water-wheels had to be placed between two boats for there is no other way of supporting the bearings at each end of the wheel-shaft. To ensure that the bearings remained aligned on the same axis so that each journal remained fully seated and supported by the bearing, each pair of boats had to be firmly secured to each other with wooden frames so that they 'pitched and tossed' as one rigid body. In creating a rigid twin-hulled floating mill, the wheel-shaft journals could be held firmly in position at an exact distance apart, and the side clearances of the wheel could be reduced so as to maximize its width between the boats.

In calculating the impulse power generated by a submerged float an assumption has to be made of the impact velocity of the water, but the writer must admit to being unfamiliar with the flow rates and velocities of the River Tiber, and therefore the following analysis must be treated with some caution. Because the hydraulic conditions are unknown and they probably varied through the year, the approach has been to determine what size paddle is necessary to generate 1.0 hp (considered a minimum either for very slow normal sized stones or smaller diameter millstones operating at normal speeds) and 2.0 hp (considered a near average demand for a pair of working millstones). Using this approach of determining the power by the change in velocity of a body of water[323], the diameter of the wheel can remain undetermined[324].

What does affect the result is the depth of the paddle, but this is not too difficult to evaluate. We should assume that the whole of the paddle is submerged when it is at its lowest, with perhaps a few centimetres of water above it. A depth of 0.3 m is thought to be reasonable, but in our quest to seek a greater potential perhaps a limit of 0.4 m depth could be taken. Making the paddles much deeper would have incurred a risk of their grounding, especially if they projected beyond the bottom of the boats, remembering that they were small river craft. They may have been flat-bottomed to reduce their draught especially if the flow of the Tiber changed much over the seasons. It would have been catastrophic if there were a risk of the boats grounding, with the bottom of the wheels close to or below the level of their keels – another reason for positioning the boats in deep water, mid-stream. The water velocity is something of a guess. The study of modern boat-mills on the Tiber shows that it was a slow-moving river, and to compensate for this the water-wheels were several metres wide[325]. A velocity of 1.0 m/s is rather feeble and produces some ridiculously wide wheels even with a paddle depth of 0.4 m and power of 1.0 hp. Two values have been adopted for the impact velocity of this exercise, 1.5 m/s and 2.0 m/s. The following table gives the width of wheels necessary to generate theoretically both 1.0 and 2.0 shaft horsepower. (We should remember that nearly 10% of the shaft horse-power would be absorbed by the friction of the bearings and

322 Mariotti Bianchi 1976, tav. 8; Wikander 1979, 30.
323 See Part One, Section 3 above, for the formula.
324 Nonetheless, the writer will hazard a guess on the diameter. Allowing for a fully immersed float and freeboard on the boat sides, a wheel diameter of not less than 3.0 m is favoured. A slightly larger wheel would bring the advantage of less water surging over the floats as they dipped into the river.
325 Wikander 1979, 31; Mariotti Bianchi 1976, 48.

the gears.)

Table P – Width of water-wheels (m)

Paddle depth (m)	One hp		Two hp	
	Impact 1.5 m/s	Impact 2.0 m/s	Impact 1.5 m/s	Impact 2.0 m/s
0.3	3.0	1.27	6.0	2.54
0.4	2.26	0.95	4.52	1.9

Bury interpreted Procopius' words as meaning that each wheel drove two sets of mills on each boat, i.e, four mills altogether[326], but Wikander understandably questioned this and sought for an alternative explanation[327]. The most likely one seems to be that a 'pair of stones' (= 1 mill) has been interpreted as a 'pair of mills', thus inadvertently doubling the reality. Confusion may also have occurred when each pair of boats was structurally locked together to form one floating vessel. The analysis shows that even using the deeper paddle (0.4 m) and a fairly high impact velocity (2.0 m/s), the wheel would have to be over 2.0 m wide to generate 2.0 hp at the millstone spindle[328]. If, as the later evidence of floating mills suggests, the Tiber was slow moving and liable to seasonal variations, then even wider water-wheels would have struggled to drive two pairs of stones simultaneously. Of course, it is entirely possible that one pair could have been disconnected at times when there was insufficient river velocity, and then brought into action when the flow increased. But we can suspect, that for much of the time, the stones operated at slower speeds.

326 Bury 1889, 392.
327 Wikander 1979, 31/2.
328 Allowing 9% for the friction of the bearings and gears in accordance with the allowances defined in Part One above.

PART THREE - SUMMARY AND CONCLUSIONS.

Let us now take an overview of this catalogue of ancient mill sites, and try to assess how much hydro-mechanical analysis can contribute to the study of Roman water-power technology. First, we must look at the productive output and efficiency of the early mills, and at their locations, distribution and dates, bearing in mind certain natural phenomena which are embodied in the laws of mechanics and hydraulics and which, in the writer's opinion, must have been encountered by the builders and operators of early water-mills. We may then perhaps be able to shed some light on the very difficult questions concerning the origins and evolutionary development of these prime movers.

1. Mill production.

The great advantages gained by the introduction of rotary motion into the corn milling process were most fully realised with the invention and use of the water-mill. The substitution of water-powered millstones for animate powered stones created an immediate potential quantum leap in production. Even the advantages of scale possessed by the Pompeian mill over a disc millstone of the same diameter were completely overtaken by the potential of water-power. Using the friction coefficient determined by the Westree experiment, a direct comparison can be made between the power absorbed by a typical pair of Roman style disc millstones, and that absorbed by a typical Pompeian mill of the same diameter[329]. If they both operate at an animal driven speed of say, 6 rpm, a Pompeian mill can produce 3.5 times as much as the disc millstone. (This assumes, as we have determined above, that the production is proportional to the power absorbed by the working stones.) The main reason for this difference is the much greater weight of the Pompeian mill combined with its larger grinding face area[330]. However, when we allow for the much greater speed of the water-powered disc millstones, let us say 120 rpm, then the same diameter stones would

produce 5.7 times as much per hour as the Pompeian mill. Although this comparison was based on a diameter that is small for both water-powered millstones and Pompeian mills, readers can apply the comparative analysis to larger diameter stones and use different speeds, but the result will remain a considerable advantage to the faster disc millstone.

This comparison between the two types of millstones has been greatly stimulated by the *Nahal Tanninim* mills with their water-powered duplex-drive, Pompeian stones (see site 25 above). When comparing the behaviour of these different stones we have the advantage of a substantial body of modern operational experience relating to disc millstones, but our knowledge of the working of Pompeian stones is negligible. Whilst we know that disc millstones can happily rotate at speeds of 120 rpm and more, we do not know the behaviour of Pompeian stones at speeds greater than that relating to animate power. It would require full-scale replication and testing to determine the operational characteristics and efficiency of a Pompeian *catillus*. In a disc water-powered millstone the grain is fed under gravity, usually with the aid of vibration, into the eye of the stone from a stationary hopper suspended above. In a Pompeian *catillus* the stone itself usually serves as the hopper so that the grain it contains is spinning and subject to centrifugal force. Under this condition the gravity feed of the grain into the eye of the *meta* could be adversely affected at higher speeds, possibly creating a throttling affect on the flow. This suggests that mechanically-driven Pompeian stones may not have had the operational speed range of disc millstones. Another factor that may have influenced the application of water-power to Pompeian-style millstones is their stability at higher speeds. The centre of gravity of the *catillus* is much higher above the bell-shaped grinding face, when compared with the equivalent property of a pair of disc stones. If the *catillus* wears unevenly as it ages, its rotating mass becomes unbalanced, creating increasing centrifugal forces and vibration that can damage the stones, reducing their grinding efficiency and shortening their life. Although we have identified that Pompeian stones have the inherent advantage of greater output compared with the same diameter of disc stones, they were not widely adopted for water-power corn-milling. Probably the main reason for this is that the making of Pompeian stones required considerably more stone and labour than that required for disc stones and their greater bulk made transportation more

---

329 For this analysis the design illustrated by Moritz in 1958 and reproduced by White in 1984, taken from a mill in the Casa di Sallustio, Pompeii, has been used. The size indicates that this was a donkey-driven mill as distinct from the larger type driven by horses or mules. Moritz 1958, 75-6, Fig. 8; White 1984, 65, Fig. 54.

330 For the full analysis see Spain 1992, 259-262, Appendix A, 284-5. The maximum diameter of the grinding faces in both mills was 0.56 m (22 ins.). The disc millstone rim thickness was taken as 12.7 cm (5 ins.), which is assumed to be approximately half-life thickness.

costly. Discoidal top stones also had the advantage as acting as bed-stones late in their lives, thus achieving a greater utilization of the stone. A comparative measure of their popularity is provided by the Britannia evidence; only three recorded specimens of Pompeian stones are known compared with several hundred known disc millstones.

The present corpus of Roman water-mills shows that disc millstones prevailed throughout the whole of Europe, North Africa and Asia with the exception of the *Nahal Tanninim* sites. In the Eastern Mediterranean in the Hellenistic period, Pompeian-type mills preceded rotary hand-mills, and the existence of Pompeian-style stones at the water-powered *Nahal Tanninim* sites has been interpreted as a local survival from earlier periods.[331] If this theory is sustained the appearance of duplex-drive water-mills with Pompeian stones in Israel should be viewed as temporary and exceptional rather than a significant development in the evolution of roman water-power machinery. No other archaeologically proven examples of duplex-drive exists in the corpus of Roman water-power corn milling, although a variation of power transmission that could be viewed as 'duplicity' has been realistically interpreted at the *Jarash* stone-sawing mill.

The Westree experiment has shown that a pair of lava millstones having their grinding surfaces dressed in typical Roman design yielded a throughput of 117 lbs/hp.hr. (53.0 kg/hp.hr.). As we have seen above, this production/power ratio can be extrapolated and applied to any water-mill where the production is unknown, but the power generated by the water can be determined. Although derived from lava stones, the ratio probably has reasonable validity for other types of stones having similar grinding properties and dressing. It must be remembered, however, that the production/power ratio relates to the power actually absorbed by the working stones, and so in cases where the generated power has been determined using hydraulic analysis, an allowance has to be made for the loss due to friction of the bearings and gears. Thus the relevant figure to which the production/power ratio should be applied is the shaft horsepower at the millstone spindle.

Assuming that the average consumption per head of population is equivalent to 900 g of wheat-meal per day and that 90% of the mill's product is for human consumption[332], a graph can be generated to show the number of people that a water-powered corn mill could serve. (See Fig. 79.) The

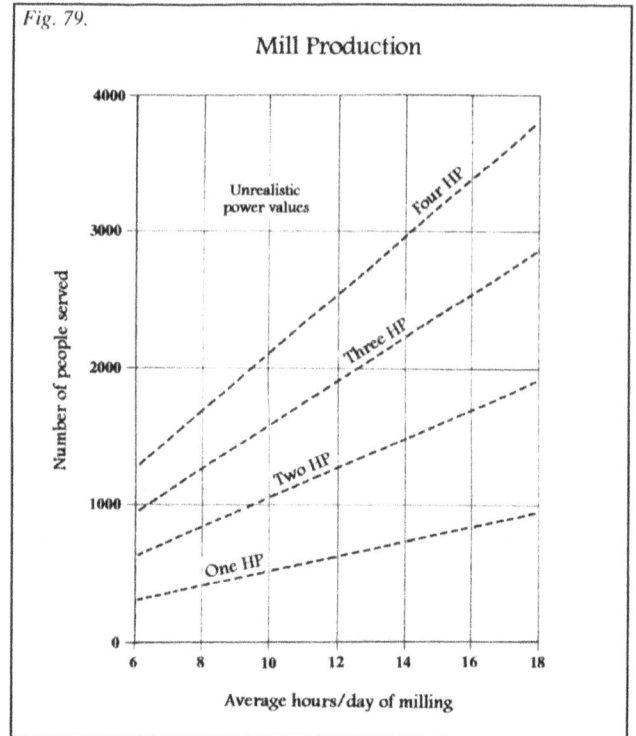

Fig. 79.

Mill Production

base line of the graph is the average number of hours per day that the mill is assumed to work, and its application should reflect all variables affecting mill-work (e.g, seasonal influences such as water shortage, harvest yields; domestic demand patterns; illness and absenteeism of the miller; wars and social strife; stoppages due to maintenance of machinery and millstones; rest days etc.). It is probably best to view the hours/day as an average for the whole year, rather than relating to a working week of seven days or less. The choice of the hours/day is not easy, and can be confounded if the water-wheel in question is one of a series, where some of the variables affecting production take on different values. For instance, we can imagine that the scale and intensity of work at *Barbegal* and the *Janiculum* factories would influence some of the factors to increase the average hours/day of mill work.

But let us put aside these multi-wheel complexes for the moment, and view Fig. 79 as applying to single water-wheel sites that represent the vast majority of Roman water-mills. The major difficulty in using the graph is how to decide what value to put on the average hours/day for the mill-work. Perhaps we should admit that we have little idea of the working life of a miller in ancient times, except for three observations.

First, we now have good evidence of how the Romans

331 Ad *et al.*, 2005, 169.
332 It is reasonable to suppose that following sieving, a proportion of the husks and pollards was removed and consumed by animals.

controlled the feed of grain from the hopper. This was a tapered iron spindle, lodged on top of the millstone spindle, and inserted into the base of the grain hopper above. Raising or lowering the hopper adjusted the feed rate, and the rotation of the spindle provided the vibration necessary to ensure continuous flow[333]. This would have ensured continuous automatic operation, so the miller need not have been in permanent attendance.

The second observation is that working times would have surely varied between provinces and cultures, influenced by climate and local demands. Some water-mills would have served villas, others, the potentially greater demands of urban populations or military markets. Readers may therefore wish to place their own values on the graph, both for horsepower and average hours of work per day, but it is the writer's view that the great majority of Roman water-wheels were generating net power to the millstones of between 1.0 to 2.5 hp and perhaps working an overall average of say 7 to 9 hours/day. The obvious exceptions to this generalization of theoretical output would be the multi-wheeled sites, where the average operational periods were probably extended, perhaps substantially, by shift working within the factories. At other times in history the burgeoning demands of urban population, especially during periods of strife and war would have placed great demands on the miller. During such periods the miller had only one effective way of increasing output, namely by increasing the hours of work[334].

The third observation to be made on the question of the operating hours concerns the life and maintenance cycles of the machines' components. It is important to remind ourselves of the fallibility and limited durability of the machines that we are dealing with. In later centuries vertical water-wheels were capable of driving two or more pairs of millstones simultaneously. In the Roman mill with disc millstones this did not occur, as we have seen above; each wheel was coupled to one pair of stones. There was no standby or duplication of the power transmission elements. If any part of the machine failed, (water-wheel; wheel-shaft; shaft bearings; gears; millstone spindle or footstep bearing; or millstones) production stopped. All of the moving parts and stationary elements of a water-mill which were subject to wear must have had life cycles of maintenance and replacement.

Probably the two components causing most production interruption were the millstones and the wooden cogs of the gears. Our evidence of Roman millstones suggests that most were dressed with furrows, which would mean that regular maintenance of the grinding faces occurred, involving the regeneration of the furrows and the harps[335] as the stones wore away. This would require periodically stopping the mill and lifting off the top millstone and re-dressing both faces – a process which would have taken many hours of work. At the same time, if the stones were badly worn away the cavity for the mill-rynd in the underside of the upper stone would require deepening, to prevent the rynd from touching the face of the bed-stone and scoring the surface. As this process was repeated and the top stone became thinner, the risk of breakage increased, especially as the mill-rynd cavity penetrated near to the top surface of the upper millstone. A great many top stones have been found that have obviously fractured in use, and then been abandoned. But there is another reason for abandonment – at least as a top stone – which is, that prolonged wear may make them insufficiently heavy to grind the corn effectively. We now have a number of examples from different sites that show the top stone being re-positioned and acting as a bottom stone (e.g, *Ickham, Fullerton* and *Barbegal.*). When this occurred, the miller had to re-shape the old top stone and create a fresh convex grinding surface to mate with a new top stone.

The iron rungs of the lantern gear would have lasted a lifetime but the engaging wooden cogs were a different matter. Their design, material and method of mounting (taper driven; wedges or nailing) would all affect the life of the gears. Generally, the wear of a cog is directly related to the number of engagements that it makes in unit time, but this could be mitigated by rotating, exchanging or renewing cogs. The miller would probably hold spare cogs ready for emergencies so that he could replace individual cogs when they became dangerously weak, and on occasion install an entire new set. But at other times an accident might occur that would strip several of the cogs in an instant – for example if the water-wheel suddenly jammed say, from a floating branch or, if a stone entered the millstones and jammed them. In either event the momentum of the rotating masses would cause a critical torque on the gears and take out several cogs. This would require shutting down the mill to replace the cogs and attend to the cause of the accident.

333 Baatz, 1994.
334 Fairbourne Mill, Kent provides a good example of the latent potential of the throughput of a water-mill, albeit an eighteenth century mill. During the Seven Years War this small rural mill increased its output by three-fold in 1758-9 in response to the victualling offices at the ports. Spain 1970, 120.
335 See Appendix Two for an illustration of furrows and harps.

2. Incidence.

As time passes and the corpus of Roman water-mills increases the question of incidence of water-power within the whole industry of corn-milling will undoubtedly re-assert itself. The steadily increasing number of sites continues to display a general diffusion throughout the western provinces, except for the Iberian Peninsula. An interesting development during the last two decades of publication is that there is a noticeable increase in the number of Early Empire sites dating from the 1st and 2nd c. A.D. As a result the centre of gravity of the site foundation dates has moved back in time, and it is now considered likely that widespread adoption of water-power occurred in earlier periods than had been previously supposed[336], and as the evidence grows, we need to re-assess our views on the chronology of that development, and of its impact on the corn-milling industry.

By far the greater proportion of the known sites are rural in all provinces, while urban and city water-mill sites remain less common, but we must acknowledge that archaeological evidence is less likely to survive in urban areas. Wikander has drawn the conclusion, and demonstrated by a convincing analysis, that in Rome water-power corn-milling was far from dominant during the first four centuries A.D. even after the *Janiculum* complex became established. In Caligula's time (A.D. 37-42) there were 250 bakeries (*pistrina*) in Rome, nearly all of which had draught animals providing the power source. These animal mills were controlled by the bakers who had formed themselves into a powerful organization (*collegium pistorum*) that may have worked actively against the introduction of water-mills in Rome[337]. It seems likely that this monopolistic situation occurred in other large cities of the Mediterranean, given that it was a symptomatic product of lack of suitable water-power sites combined with growing population. Nonetheless, with the economic advantages that water-power had over muscle-powered mills the monopolies based on the old technology would have been tested and eventually broken by the emerging corporation of *molendinarii*. Cassiodorus, writing in the early sixth century A.D. cites the enormous number of water-mills in Rome in testimony to Rome's size in earlier times[338]. What proportion of Rome's milling demands were provided by water-power is a difficult question to answer, although clearly, the archaeological and written evidence indicates that the proportion coming from water-power increased as time passed. This gradual shift from animate-powered sources to water-power undoubtedly occurred in other cities, occasionally accelerated by the economies of scale created by multi-wheeled factories (e.g *Barbegal*, *Ephesos* etc.). But the greater number of water-mills were located in the countryside associated either with villas, farmsteads or military encampments. In landscapes with abundant streams and rivers water-power could easily be developed and exploited as the great number and wide diffusion of extant under-driven Roman style disc millstones indicates.

These millstones provide additional 'negative' evidence relating to the incidence of water-mills. Although a proportion of these extant millstones is without known provenance, of the great number that are identifiable as top stones, it is the exception, certainly in Britannia, to find an over-driven arrangement[339]. This feature indicates an animal-driven mill as distinct from an under-driven stone, where the mill-rynd cavity occurs in the underside of the top stone (the grinding face), indicating a water-powered stone. We should also note that evidence of only three Pompeian style mills have been found in Britannia, suggesting that this form of animal-powered mill was the exception. Thus the archaeological evidence within Britannia suggests that water-power probably dominated corn milling, certainly within the later Roman period. The number of known water-mills in Gaul is similar to that in Britannia, and particularly strong in the south. But the incidence of under-driven Roman disc millstones is unknown to the writer, and their interpretation is more difficult because of the unusual drive arrangement of some Early Empire stones. Top millstones from *Avenches* and *Martres-de-Veyre*, have cavities on the upper surface, which might suggest that they were over-driven by animals, but in fact they were under-driven by water-power via iron spindles that projected above the stone, split and turned downwards to engage two diametrically opposed cavities[340].

3. Machine efficiency.

When modern man appraises a machine that converts one form of energy into useful work, he will often

---

336 Wikander 2000, 397; Wilson 2000, 236-7.
337 Forbes 1955, 94. Wilson questions that there is any good evidence for this. *Pers. comms.* Wilson.
338 Cassiod. *Var* 11.39. 1-2.
339 An example of over-driven millstones was found at Orton Hall Farm, England. See Spain 1996.
340 If the millstone spindles were one single piece of wrought iron, this unusual drive arrangement would make the de-mounting of the top stone most difficult, unless the top section was socketed onto the lower spindle.

measure its efficiency by comparing the energy entering the machine with that being delivered. During the 18th and 19th c. A.D. numerous experiments and studies sought to explore and improve the design of water-wheels[341]. By the end of the Victorian period various different efficiencies had been ascribed to the basic types of vertical water-wheels invariably reflecting their optimum design. Overshot wheels were considered to be 65-70% efficient, breast wheels 55-60% and undershot wheels 35%. Understandably, historians of technology have used these modern water-wheel efficiency figures in different ways when examining Roman machines, some simply using them for general comparison purposes whilst others have used them in the calculations of power, which is potentially misleading[342].

It is the writer's view that the development of Roman water-power was empirically driven, advanced by practical necessity rather than by search for efficient performance. Whenever possible in the work above, the writer has avoided using general efficiency figures and has calculated generated power from first principles of mechanical and hydraulic analysis. This has only been possible at eight sites, and it is these that allow us to determine an efficiency figure for the wheel arrangement. The following Table Q provides the relevant figures.

A quick comparison of these figures with modern 'traditional' wheel efficiencies shows that they are very different and bear little relationship with them. There are a number of reasons for this. But first we need to agree the appropriate definition of wheel efficiency.

Let us first look to the bucket wheel. We have seen above that the generated power is calculated by resolving the torque generated by each of the buckets holding water, making allowances for the losses due to centrifugal force and splashing etc. The result is the theoretical horse-power delivered by the wheel – the shaft horse-power. To obtain the working efficiency this figure has to be compared with the total potential energy that is proportional to the product of the flow of water (Q) and the hydraulic head (H) at the wheel position. The value of Q is generally determined by the size and design of the wheel, and is, in one sense, self regulating; it cannot be greater than the capacity of the wheel at its 'normal' speed plus allowances for splashing and centrifugal force. If a greater value were given to Q then it would diminish the efficiency of the wheel, since the total potential energy of the head would increase but the power generated would not. But it is the head H that has the greatest influence on the efficiency of these Roman bucket wheels.

Table Q – Machine efficiencies.

Name of water-mill	Type	Efficiency	Velocity of impact (m/s)
Barbegal	Bucket-wheel	43.8 %	Not relevant
Les Mesclans	Bucket-wheel	39.0 %	Not relevant
Baths of Caracalla (Early)	Bucket-wheel	36.0 %	Not relevant
Haltwhistle Burn Head	Impulse u/shot	42.0 %	4.62
Janiculum (North, wheel 1)	Impulse u/shot	37.0 %	11.96
Baths of Caracalla (Late)	Impulse o/shot	34.0 %	4.6
Agora (0.305 m deep headrace) (0.229 m deep headrace)	Impulse o/shot Impulse o/shot	41.0 % 42.6 %	19.0 18.44
Lösnich (upper)	Impulse u/shot	27.5 %	8.68
Venafro	Impulse u/shot(?)	34.0 %	7.4

341 See Reynolds 1983, for a thorough history of the development of the vertical waterwheel.
342 Sellin 1981, 421.

The total hydraulic head H is the vertical distance between the level of the water leaving the head-race trough, and the level of the bed of the tail-race where it receives the water. This assumes that the water leaving the head-race trough is moving at a similar velocity to the rim of the wheel. If there is an accelerated head-race, the velocity will be much greater, and the true level from which the head should be measured will be the top of the inclined trough, or in the head-race where the acceleration begins. With this definition of hydraulic head, the greater the diameter of the wheel compared with the head, the higher the efficiency, since a greater diameter means more buckets carrying the water further and for longer before discharging it. The most effective diameter bucket wheel would be one where the delivery trough is very close above the wheel and the underside of the wheel is just sufficiently clear of the tail-race bed to allow the water to flow away without impeding the movement of the wheel. As we have concluded in the *Barbegal* analysis above, the low theoretical efficiency of the wheels (*c*.43.8 %) is due mainly to the wheel being considerably smaller than the available head. Another effect of the relatively small diameter of the *Barbegal* wheel is that it brings disproportionate losses due to centrifugal force at its operational speed. The diameter of the *Barbegal* wheel (2.1 m) is very much smaller than the average diameter of modern bucket wheels that are often quoted as having 65 % efficiency; this size difference makes a comparison of efficiency futile and irrelevant.

To assess the efficiency of an impulse driven wheel, the generated power of the wheel must be compared with the total kinetic energy of the water applied to it, which is proportional to the product of the velocity of the impact squared (V^2) and the flow rate (Q). As with bucket wheels, so too with impulse wheels; if the volume of the flow (Q) exceeds the capacity of the paddle area, then the efficiency will be reduced. That is to say, when Q is greater than the flow needed to impact the full face area of the paddle plus any allowance for splashing and leakage, then the generated force will be smaller as a proportion of the potential kinetic energy. On the few sites where a hydraulic analysis can be undertaken, assumptions have to be made on the flow rate; they are usually influenced by the capacity of the wheel, and the depth and velocity of flow. In other words the analysis tends to make full utilization of the potential generation but in so doing inadvertently optimises the flow rate Q and thereby the efficiency.

In Table Q above, only the *Janiculum* wheel can be compared with the traditional undershot vertical wheel. All of the others fall outside the modern classification because they have the inherent dominant feature of accelerated head-races. Although wheel efficiency can be calculated for the other five impulse sites, they should not be compared with the performance of modern types, since the operating conditions are not equivalent. The only value the calculation has is for comparison between the sites, but even that is of little use in view of the wide variations between their different arrangements.

4. The natural phenomena which tend to accelerate technological evolution.

The **first phenomenon**, although very basic, has great implications for our enquiries. If a force F created by a flow of water at a constant velocity is applied to the radial floats of a wheel of radius R_1, the power of the wheel is proportional to the product of speed (rpm) and torque (F x R_1). (See Fig. 80.) If the same force F acting at the same velocity is applied to a smaller radius R_2, the torque reduces to (F x R_2), but the speed of rotation increases. In fact they balance each other exactly, so that theoretically, the power generated is constant. This means that a smaller diameter impulse wheel can theoretically generate the same power as a larger wheel when receiving the same flow and velocity. But the reduction in wheel diameter brings distinct constructional and operational advantages. The smaller wheel involves less material and labour in its making, and being lighter, has less bearing resistance. Its higher speed

Fig. 80.

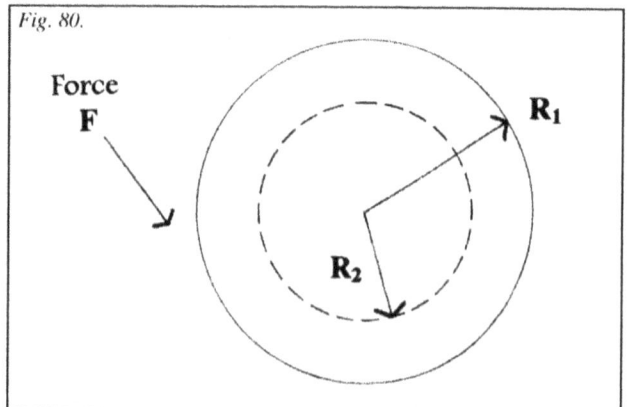

Force
F

R_1

R_2

facilitates either greater millstone speed or, more likely, a lower MR to achieve the same stone speed. Moreover, whereas a larger impulse wheel is likely to occupy most of the available head of water, a smaller wheel in the same situation can be set lower and thereby enjoy a greater impact velocity from the steeper slope of the headrace.

Now let us turn to the **second phenomenon**. Fig. 81 is a graph showing the theoretical potential horsepower of water flows impacting against paddles that are normal to the axis of flow. The results are based on the formula horsepower (hp) = 1.341 A V(V-v)v[343], where A is the area of impact (m²) and v (m/s) is the average velocity of the paddle taken as 0.425 of V, the velocity of the water at impact (m/s). (The factor of 0.425 has been adopted in our previous calculations and should be seen as empirically rather than theoretically ascertained.) It is the writer's view that virtually all Roman water-wheels that are powered solely

by impulse would be positioned on the graph between the power values of 0.5 and 2.5 hp. Note that the unusually high theoretical impact velocities for *Venafro* (7.4 m/s) and the *Lösnich Upper* sites (8.68 m/s) lie beyond the adopted margins of the graph. The generation of the graph reveals two important features of the power formula. First, and perhaps rather obvious, is this; when the flow rate (Q) is increased, the power generated increases by exactly the same proportion. The second feature has much greater significance to our study. If Q is held constant and the velocity of impact is doubled, the power generated is quadrupled[344]. Thus a considerable advantage is gained by accelerating the headrace.

The third observation that we can make – not really a phenomenon but nonetheless a natural manifestation – concerns the spatial or positional flexibility of waterwheels in generating power by impulse. When flowing water is accelerated into a small-sectioned stream or jet, the surface that it impacts against is necessarily normal, or nearly so, to the axis of flow. However, the axis of rotation of the wheel holding the paddles is not determined or influenced by the direction or physical arrangement of the water jet. Even if the axis of the flow is inclined, which it often is, the transfer of energy to the wheel can still be effective, regardless of the position of the axis of rotation. In other words, the water-wheel can be either vertical or horizontal; the effectiveness of the hydraulic arrangement is exactly the same with either. But the mechanical efficiency does change – with advantage to the horizontal wheel (vertical axis), which we will examine later. Both the first hydro-mechanical phenomenon and the second demonstrate and confirm the advantages of adopting smaller diameter vertical impulse wheels and accelerated headraces. The question that we have to ask is, were the Romans aware of these phenomena?

The corpus of vertical impulse wheels includes several specimens whose diameter is relatively small including *Barbegal* (2.1m), *Venafro* (1.85 m), *Caracalla (Late)* (2.18 m), *Ickham (Early)* (2.0 m), *Janiculum (North)*

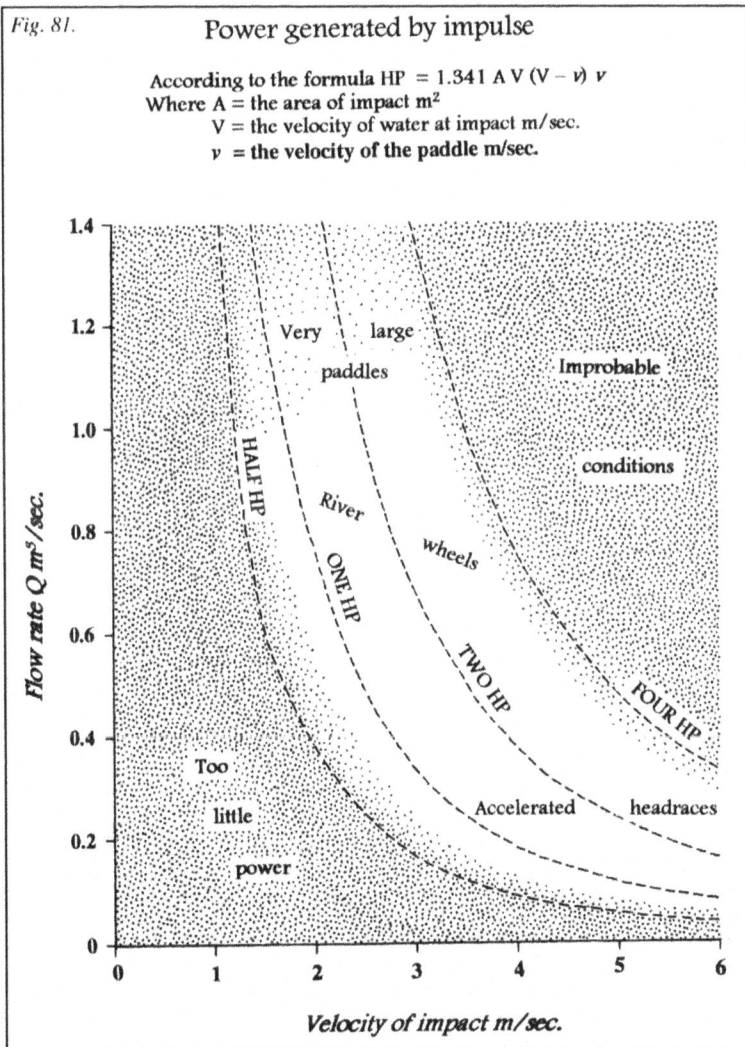

Fig. 81.

Power generated by impulse

According to the formula HP = 1.341 A V (V – v) v
Where A = the area of impact m²
V = the velocity of water at impact m/sec.
v = the velocity of the paddle m/sec.

343 Industrial Archaeology of Watermills and Waterpower, 56.
344 When V is doubled and Q held constant, the impact area (A) is thereby halved, so that the equation resolves to a quadruple increase in power.

(2.3 m), *Ickham (Late)* (2.4 m) and *Hagendorn* (2.15-2.3 m). Most of these are dated to the 2nd and 3rd c. A.D. and having regard to their widespread distribution throughout the Empire suggests that the advantage of using small diameter impulse wheels was recognized and well practiced by that time.

Concerning the adoption of accelerated headraces, the evidence is unquestionably strong for we have several examples of where the builders took considerable care to create a high impact velocity such as at *Oderzo* and *Haltwhistle Burn Head* (4.62 m/s) and at *Caracalla (Late)* (4.6 m/s) where the physical conditions were more carefully contrived. The best-known example of an accelerated headrace is Parson's *Athenian Agora* mill (5.8 m/s) but the most outstanding and enigmatic specimen is *Venafro*, which we calculate to have had an impact velocity of 7.4 m/s. But even this velocity is exceeded by the potential of the *Lösnich* site, where the upper site main wheel could have worked with an impact velocity of 8.68 m/s, and the lower site main wheel 9.47 m/s. The wide range of building dates of these water-mills combined with the high velocities that were created, surely supports the notion that the practice of accelerated headraces was an entrenched technique within Roman Early Empire water-power technology.

The evidence from the *Baths of Caracalla* supports this notion. The original mill A, probably one of a pair, is thought to have been built between A.D. 212 and 235, and the construction of the later mills has been placed between A.D.*c*.275 and 300. If we accept these dates we have an example of technological change that occurred over a period of from 40 (minimum) to 88 years (maximum) within the 3rd c. A.D. The entire arrangement of both installations is artificial and displays great ingenuity, not only for the way it was integrated in this great aqua-leisure centre but also the manner in which it was subsequently modified. Of particular note to the historian of technology is the fact that this example involves a single site in Rome itself which was unaffected by any extraneous traditions. When this opportunity for change occurred, the builders created a higher head of water and installed faster wheels utilizing impulse power. They also duplicated all machinery in a clever arrangement of lapped water-wheels so that the available space was efficiently utilized and there was improved access for wheel maintenance. Nor should we lose sight of the fact that these mills were in the nexus of the

empire, and although in the subterranean chambers of this vast establishment, must have been well known to many of the visitors and clientele. Palladius, a Roman writer on agriculture, may have seen the *Caracalla* mills, for he recommended that when there was an abundant supply of waste water from public baths it should be used to drive water-mills[345]. In such circumstances we should view the *Caracalla* specimens as examples of technological advance. There is also slight evidence that a water-mill may have operated in the Baths of Mithras at Ostia[346].

Of all of the water-mill sites where it is possible by analysis to determine the type of power source, there are very few sites where the power was generated solely by weight. Nearly all of them use impulse and perhaps half of those that do so have accelerated head-races and relatively small wheels. Although our corpus of study represents rather less than half of all known probable mill sites[347], this preference shown for these design features of relatively fast wheels is surely meaningful. We can now propose with some confidence that during the formative years of mill technology the Romans observed a variety of different installations, and came to recognize two natural hydro-mechanical phenomena, namely:

(1) That a small impulse-driven wheel can deliver the same power as a larger one with the same water-flow and velocity, but at a higher speed of rotation.

(2) If the flow rate is held constant and the velocity is doubled, the power generated is quadrupled.

The recognition of these two phenomena clearly influenced design and arrangements of successive water-wheels and can be viewed as an accelerator in the evolution of the technology.

The growing body of archaeological evidence shows that the dominant industry using water-power was corn-milling. This is especially true if we take into account the number of water-mill sites that are inferred by circumstantial evidence, combined with the incidence of millstones of unknown provenance. A few decades ago our knowledge of Roman water-power technology was shaped and influenced by our interpretation of Vitruvius' description of a water-mill. It has since advanced in a very piece-meal fashion, driven by the incidence of archaeological discovery. The Romans' understanding and development of hydro-mechanics is clearly demonstrated by the evidence. The experiences

345 Palladius, *Opus agriculturae*, I, 41, (42).
346 Schøiler 1973, 138, Fig. 99, no. 6.
347 Wikander 2000, 372. The number of archaeological well authenticated sites up to A.D. 700 probably exceeds 56. Several new sites have now been added to the list.

coming from the generation and transmission of water-power in numerous alternative physical arrangements displays a confidence in adapting to markedly different landscapes. A wide range of engineering skills embracing both carpentry and smithing was being applied to the building, operation and maintenance of both slow and fast moving water-mills. The evidence of their machinery design, especially water-wheel construction, gearing, shafts and bearings is slowly revealing itself, but the picture emerging is that this technology was well established and exploited. A growing body of specialized empirically driven skills can be identified with a new body of artisans, the *molendinarii*, whose engineering discipline in later centuries was identified with millwrights. As Lewis points out, we know little about them but they certainly existed[348].

The Romans show considerable ingenuity and versatility in harnessing the natural forces of the very different landscapes of the Empire's provinces. Where rivers existed close by the mill sites different methods could be employed to bring the water to the wheel. Bridge structures gave the advantage of integrating the wheel emplacement with the foundation structures *(Chesters Bridge)* including abutments *(Willowford Bridge)*. These were high volume low velocity arrangements. In other cases where the builders sought greater hydraulic heads, a man-made head-race could be created by diverting the river water over a considerable distance *(Fullerton)*. Where greater velocity was sought the head-race bed could be sloped to create acceleration into the wheel *(Haltwhistle Burn Head)*. An alternative and apparently well understood innovation was to accelerate the head-race by narrowing its width on approach to the wheel *(Oderzo; Avenches)* or further contraction of the head-race was achieved by inclining the bed immediately before the wheel *(Oderzo)*. Sometimes the natural features of the landscape could be used with great benefit in providing a head such as scarp slopes *(Barbegal)* and steep ravines *(Lösnich)*. Their probable tide-mill in the estuary of the *River Fleet* shows that they were capable of creating a substantial storage pond in conjunction with nearby dock facilities. One wonders if the evidence of the substantial tide-mill at *Le Yaudet* of un-proven date, might be another example of Roman ingenuity.

We have several examples of water-wheels operating in series *(Janiculum North; Lösnich Upper; Ephesos)* where the same water passes successively through the wheels.

These are sites where the wheels are in such close proximity as to suggest that they were under one roof or at least were under common management. Where there was enough water to allow a bifurcation to exist and create two parallel head-races, this gave the opportunity to maximize the utilization of space. *Barbegal* is the outstanding example of this, but parallel arrangements also existed at *Janiculum* and *Caracalla* (both phases). These three sites also provide good examples of space utilization, but in slightly different forms. At *Barbegal* the proximity of the wheels was probably determined by the incline of the scarp slope rock face, whilst at *Janiculum (North)* the series of wheels were set as close as practically possible, even to the extent of adversely affecting the mill-race velocity and downstream wheel speeds. A final example of spatial utilization was the design of the *Later Caracalla* mill, where the two water-wheels served by parallel head-races, were lapped. This demonstrates a carefully planned and executed design with the two machines closely integrated ergonomically in the confines of the subterranean chamber.

Our evidence of Roman vertical water-wheels shows us that nearly all of them generated power using impulse, and that bucket wheels driven by weight of water were the exception. This high incidence of impulse wheels is present in those sites established in the 1st and 2nd centuries A.D. suggesting that it was an accepted and commonplace form of prime-mover in early Roman water-power technology. Although our archaeological evidence of horizontal water-wheels during the Roman period is scant, we can be sure of one fact; without exception, they were all impulse driven or fully-flooded reaction prime-movers. Our vertical water-wheel corpus therefore displays the same impulse generation feature inherent within horizontal wheels. Is this a coincidence? *Barbegal* is the earliest known example of a weight-driven bucket wheel, but it is inconceivable that this was the first use of this wheel type. The builders would surely not have risked a new unproven design in such a large multiple-wheeled establishment. No, *Barbegal's* bucket wheels were based on antecedents which archaeology has yet to find. But for the moment, the evidence tells us that mill sites having bucket wheels were greatly outnumbered by impulse driven wheels.

348 *Pers. Comms.* There are epitaphs of Euchromeios at Sardis and Benignus at Arles. Oleson 1984b, 38, 45.

5. Theories of evolution.

Having concluded that the Romans had recognized these hydro-mechanical phenomena and applied that knowledge to their technology, we can now approach the question of how they may have influenced evolution. But first, let us remind ourselves of the factors or variables that trigger evolution. These are essentially the interaction between, on the one hand, the variables affecting power generation, and on the other, the opportunity for change as determined by life cycles, frequency of operation and the intensity of the distribution of the artefact[349].

An artefact that has relatively short life will present more opportunities for change and innovation than one having a longer life. Let us therefore first look at the primary element in a water-powered corn mill, the millstones. There would not be a critical speed that the miller would seek for the millstones. Modern (19th c.) corn milling with disc millstones shows that the usual maximum speed equated to a peripheral velocity of 460 m/minute above which the meal becomes heated, with adverse and sometimes dangerous results. But the average size Roman disc millstone, say between 0.6 and 0.9 m, which was noticeably smaller than 'modern' millstones, could therefore have revolved considerably faster before product degradation occurred. During their life, as the millstones lightened, they would tend to speed up if driven by an impulse wheel, and the same phenomenon would have occurred with a bucket wheel under certain circumstances. Thus over the years the miller would experience different operational speeds and performances. During these millstone life-cycles, the miller would surely gain knowledge of the interaction between the gear ratios, the weight of the top millstone and the water flow rate. He would learn how these three variables affected the balance of power, and develop his knowledge and expectation concerning operational performance. At sites where there was a multiplicity of water-wheels (*Barbegal, Janiculum, Ephesos etc*) the simultaneous operation of the machines would have accelerated the miller's learning. Several centuries of a developing and expanding industry, empirically driven, would ensure an increasing awareness of such operational improvements and advantages as could be provided by the adoption of smaller and faster impulse wheels. Such progress was inevitable; our only doubts should relate to the speed of change and diffusion of the technology.

In 1992, the writer proposed an evolutionary model for the vertical water-wheel that was developed using hydro-mechanical analysis including the natural phenomena examined above[350]. The model related to the advantages of accelerating the head-race and proposed a development from open to closed head-race channels, and finally to applications generated by fully-flooded pressure heads. Increasing the inclination of the head-race led to the discovery of the advantages of tapering and boxing in the trough and the inevitable discovery of a flooded outlet, served by a column and reservoir of water, the *'arubah'*. A succession of development phases were identified; first, slow moving vertical wheels where the power was generated wholly or mostly by weight of water, through further development to smaller, faster vertical wheels driven mainly by impulse, and finally, to a wholly impulse-driven wheel that can apply to either horizontal or vertical-wheeled arrangements. The model suggested that speciation[351] of the horizontal wheel did not occur until a fast vertical impulse wheel had evolved and the accelerated head-race was in use. The most logical development would then be to change the axis of rotation from horizontal to vertical and gain the constructional and operational advantages of a simpler, gearless machine.

Most historians of technology have proposed an evolution of vertical and horizontal water-wheels. A simplified view is either that one type of wheel was the progenitor of the other, or, that they both came from unrelated origins[352]. Only Moritz and Wilson[353] have suggested that the horizontal developed from the vertical wheel, whilst the majority of those that suggest that they were directly related, believing the horizontal to be a more primitive machine, propose that it was the progenitor of the vertical wheel. With the exception of Lewis, all of these views appear to be supposition based on subjective examination, theories that hang loosely on the logic of comparative form and function. None of the historians of technology, who have written on the origins of the water-wheel, have demonstrated or supported their theories with any form of functional or theoretical analysis. Instead they have relied on imaginative resolution and conjecture. The writer's evolutionary model is therefore different from all the others, because its foundation was based on dynamic analysis and is demonstrable using hydraulic laws.

Hitherto, the majority of scholars date the invention of the

---

349 For a discussion of technological evolution see Spain 1992, 249-256.
350 Spain 1992, 256-297.
351 In technological evolution speciation is the appearance of a new energy form, an improved process or mechanism.
352 Smith has suggested that the horizontal mill might be an independent invention. Smith 1983/4, 73. Landels also suggests an interesting hypothesis for the independent origin of the vertical overshot wheel. Landels 2000 20, 21.
353 Moritz 1958; Wilson 1995, 505.

water-mill to the late 1st or early 2nd c. B.C., but more recently, Lewis has confidently proposed that both the vertical and the horizontal-wheeled types were invented at approximately the same time in the mid. 3rd c. B.C.[354]. This contribution to the debate concerning the origins of water-power, which is a fresh interpretation of contemporary Hellenistic treatises, is new and persuasive. Lewis believes that the horizontal-wheeled water-mill was invented at or near Byzantium by c.240B.C., and that the vertical wheel was perhaps invented at Alexandria slightly later. His thesis supports the general consensus of historians that water-mill technology moved *from the simple to the more complex machine*.

In 1997 Lewis commented that in Roman archaeology the predominant water-wheel type was the vertical one and questioned why the horizontal wheel is so poorly represented in Europe, but recently several new sites have come to light in Gaul[355]. At *La Calade du Castellet* [356], a stone-lined chamber with a vaulted roof, served by a narrow steeply inclined head-race, has been identified as a water-power site[357]. The paucity of the calcareous deposits within the wheel chamber suggests a relatively short operating life prior to abandonment of the site dated to the 5th or 6th c. A.D. More recently, four additional horizontal-wheeled Roman water-mills have been identified[358]; [1] *la Croix de Fenouillé/Les Croisées*, Castillon-du-Gard (30); [2] *St Martin*, Taradeau, Var. (2nd to 3rd c. A.D.) [3] two mills at *Forum Voconii*, Le Cannet des Maures, Var, (5th c. A.D.). At *St. Doulchard*, several structures dated to the first half of the 1st c. A.D. together with the discovery of two small wooden paddles, has prompted the suggestion that this might have been a water-mill. The above analysis has shown that for the paddles to be effective in generating power, an impact velocity of at least 4 m/s would have been required. Such velocities had been achieved on other Roman water-mill sites (e.g, *Haltwhistle*, *Hagendorn*, *Agora*, *Lösnich* and *Venafro*). However, the suggestion that the paddles could have come from a horizontal wheel, primarily because of their shape and small size, whilst

possible, is admittedly, speculative. In addition, the lack of circumstantial evidence such as millstones and a well defined mill-race, weakens the proposal of a mill. This evidence clearly shows that both types of machine, with vertical or horizontal wheels, co-existed, certainly within Gaul.

Elsewhere in Europe the evidence for horizontal-wheeled water-mills is weaker. The 1st c. B.C. site at Bolle, Denmark[359], appears to have been securely dated but its interpretation, as a horizontal mill is not convincing. At *Worgret*, Dorset, evidence for a probable horizontal mill is slightly stronger[360]. This site was provisionally dated as 3rd and 4th c. A.D. but has been revised by dendrochronology to a foundation date of A.D.c.664[361]. A large, shaped timber ground-beam set across two parallel water-courses has been identified by the writer as a possible ground-plate for a double-penstock horizontal water-mill. In this arrangement the mill houses two independent horizontal water-wheels in parallel, each having its own head-race. This interpretation relies solely on comparison with all other known Irish double-penstock horizontal mills dating from post 7th c. A.D. sites[362]. The *Ickham* evidence is equally tantalizing and again has been identified as a possible horizontal mill by comparative analysis with the corpus of Irish double-penstock ground-plates. At *Ickham* the two timber ground-plates and associated water-course have been dated to A.D.c.260-400. Both the *Worgret* and *Ickham* evidence, if accepted as relating to horizontal mills, support Lewis' comment that the Irish mills are most easily seen as borrowings from Roman practice in England[363].

It is interesting and rather strange that the evidence for Roman horizontal mills in North Africa and the Middle East also suffers from uncertainty, but unlike the seven European sites mentioned above, it is generally their dating rather than the identification of type, that is insecure. Wilson has provided a valuable overview of the North African archaeological evidence of possible Roman horizontal water-mills. These include the unusual sophisticated helix-turbine mills at *Chemtou* and *Testour*[364], which have not

354 Lewis 1997.
355 Lewis 1997, 123.
356 Amouric, *et. al.* 2000.
357 The conjectured design shows paddles with concave faces, typical of later periods. These may have evolved from flat faced, inclined paddles, of which the St. Doulchard 1st c. A.D. evidence might be an example. Lewis considers that flat paddles are found only in the 'Norse' mill as adapted by the Vikings from their Irish model and disseminated to Scotland and Scandinavia. *Pers. comms.*
358 Site [1] was the subject of a paper presented at Colloque International D'archeologie at Site Pont du Gard 20-23 September 2006; sites [2] and [3] *Pers. comms.* from J-P Brun.
359 Steensberg 1952, 52-63.
360 Maynard 1988, 77-98. Large quantities of iron slag were found on this site together with a quernstone (millstone?). Watts sees this as a vertical-wheeled mill. Watts 2002, 81.
361 Hinton 1992, 258/9. The dating of the Worgret site is intriguing. The parallel ditches approaching the structure were probably filled in by the end of the second century, but the structure has been dated to 7th c. A.D. (Maynard 1988, 96). At least one of the ground plates was re-used and another was dated by dendrochronology to a felling date not earlier than A.D. 664 (Hinton 1992, 259). A later phase of work has been identified where additional stakes were installed (one radio carbon dated to A.D. 470-590) to counter movement of the ground-plates. My thanks to Prof. Andrew Wilson for his comments on this matter. Holt has suggested that a vertical water-wheel might have operated here (Hinton 1992, 259) in a later period with an elevated head-race, but the building foundation and layout does not support this suggestion.
362 Spain, *et. al.* forthcoming.
363 Lewis 1997, 59.
364 Wilson 1995.

been scientifically proved as Roman. The *Chemtou* turbines are axial-flow fully flooded reaction turbines, of an unusual design, currently not met again in the history of technology until the 16th c. A.D.[365] In the corpus they are isolated examples that are unsupported by either prototypes or earlier developmental types of wheels. In the course of time, archaeology may provide other similar specimens that will then cause a paradigm shift in our understanding of Roman water-power development and evolution, but until we have confident scientific dating for such machines it is advisable that we exclude them from our corpus of evidence. Where provisional but unsecured dating has been possible, it shows that none of these North African mills pre-date the 2nd c. A.D.

Back to the hydro-mechanical phenomena. If we accept that the phenomena probably caused change and acted as stimulants or accelerators in the process of technical development and evolution, do they indicate the *direction* of change? Is it from the simple to the complex, or the reverse? A feature of modern technical development is that it often has a hierarchy of ascent from the simple to the complex, which as we have noted, is the view of most historians concerning the evolution of water-power technology. But ancient technology does not always display this ascent of complexity, and the refinement of the complex is just as likely to occur[366]. Two views support this. The first is that when a function is to be performed the simplest way of effecting it will be naturally sought. A second view is that when stasis[367] is approached, it tends by its very nature to search for the most economic combination of resources. Furthermore, we should remember that technical evolution could suffer reversion. In some environmental circumstances man may revert to an earlier form or development. If a technical development occurred more than once in the history of a culture, a reversion must have occurred. Moreover, one culture may miss out a technical development that another used to reach the same point on the evolutionary scale.

Both of the phenomena involving diminution of wheel diameter (first phenomenon) and higher impact velocities (second phenomenon) lead to smaller faster wheels, that require less materials and thereby a greater economy of resources[368]. In the context of these water-power machines, they can be interpreted as influences that cause change from the complex to more simple technology. The development of smaller faster vertical wheels facilitated lower gear ratios and thereby smaller gears. With this development, there would come a time when the velocity of the accelerated head-race could drive a wheel at a rotational speed similar to that required by the millstone for satisfactory grinding. Thus, a gearless direct drive was possible, simply by changing the axis of the water-wheel from horizontal to vertical.

The hydraulic analysis of the sites has shown that several of the water-wheels were served by very high velocity head-races. At *Venafro* and *Lösnich (Upper and Lower)* where the impact velocities theoretically ranged from 7.4-9.47 m/s, we can confidently envisage that the head-race, as it approached the wheel, would have narrowed, in order to create a thinner stream or jet of water onto the wheel. These high impact velocities were such, that unless the water flow was concentrated, the stream of water striking the wheel would have been so thin as to make it less effective in generating thrust when striking the face of the floats, particularly if it was directed against a wheel running within a trough, where a proportion of the water would pass beneath the floats. Thus we can imagine a series of gradual changes and improvements that would advance the evolution of these prime-movers or hydraulic motors.

On this subject of water-wheel size, it is a fascinating fact that the smallest water-wheels invariably occur in horizontal motors. The diameters of horizontal and vertical wheels fall within two different bands that rarely overlap. Roman vertical wheels are apparently not less than 1.85 m diameter[369] while horizontal wheels, which can be most appropriately represented by the post 7th c. A.D. Irish corpus and later medieval examples, rarely reach *c*.1.2 m diameter[370]. This tells us that very small prime-movers can only take the horizontal form, although the reasons for this are not obvious and appear not to have been examined by historians of technology[371].

365 Wilson 1995, 499.
366 Smith 1983/4.
367 Stasis – perfection of function; stagnation; a state of motionless or unchanging equilibrium. Stasis in Greek means standing.
368 The wheel construction involves less time and material and its design can be simpler; the loads on the wheel-shaft and bearings less; the foundations of the mill building, particularly the wheel and gear pits, can be smaller.
369 The reconstruction of the Dasing water-wheel, although of later date (7th and 8th c. A.D.) is shown as 1.6 m diameter. But this should be treated with caution, because it was based on a fragment of an annular wooden rim that could have suffered distortion. Czysz 1994, 154, Abb. 5.
370 The reconstructed La Calade du Castellet horizontal wheel is shown 0.88 m diameter but the head-race axis suggests that it was closer to 1.1 m diameter. Amouric et. al. 2000, 264, Fig. 4; 268, Fig. 8. In later periods, however, larger diameter horizontal wheels occur. Those of 17th c. A.D. Provence and Dauphiné regularly reached 2.1 m diameter. *Pers. comms.* Dr. Michael Lewis.
371 There are two approaches to this question, why are there no ancient horizontal wheels over 1.2 m diameter and why are there no vertical wheels less than 1.85 m diameter? A survey of the horizontal corpus suggests that there is nothing to be gained by having a larger diameter wheel. The construction becomes heavier and the morticed paddle joints demand a higher standard of craftsmanship to ensure that they will endure. A manifestation of this strength problem is the presence of an annular wood or iron rim on some of the larger horizontal wheels. A larger heavier wheel means a greater bearing load and resistance, and more energy is needed for acceleration and maintaining motion. The development of horizontal wheels shows that although their paddles and blade take a variety of forms, satisfactory power is generated with wheels that are approximately 1 m diameter. Turning to the vertical wheel, there is no apparent reason why they could not be made smaller; horizontal wheels prove this, suggesting that the reason is not related to construction. As the wheel gets smaller and becomes faster, the MR can be reduced to achieve the same stone speeds and the rotating masses decrease.

Table R – ROMAN VERTICAL WATER-WHEELS – Chronology of types

Name	Design Date Century E=early M=mid L=late	Water-wheel Size Dia x Width (m)	Water-wheel Type B=Bucket R=Radial float	Water-wheel Arrangement	Hydro-mechanical analysis Power (per wheel) HP	Hydro-mechanical analysis Wheel Speed [372] (rpm)
St.Doulchard	E1	?	R	Remains of small wooden paddles suggest a high velocity impulse wheel.	-	-
Avenches (Early)	M1	? x 1.4	R	U/shot low head, headrace accelerated by reduced width.	-	-
(Late)	M1	? x 1.1	R	U/shot low head, headrace accelerated by reduced width.	-	-
Lösnich (Lower)	L1?	5 x ?	R	Very fast accelerated headrace and wheel.	-	c.15
(Upper main)	L1?	6 x 0.5	R	High head u/shot operating in trapezoidal section pit – possibly fed by storage pond.	3.82	12
(Upper tailrace)	L1?	3.1 x ?	R	U/shot fed by tailrace of upstream wheel.	-	-
Barbegal.	E2	2.1 x 0.75	B	16 aqueduct fed o/shot wheels in two parallel series.	2.04	11.6
Les Mesclans	2	3 x 0.25	B	O/shot wheel fed from aqueduct spur.	1.13	11.0
St.Pierre/Les Laurons	2	2.6 x 0.5	?	Probably o/shot.	-	-
Oderzo	2	? x 1.4	R	River -wheel, unusual accelerated headrace.	-	-
Venafro	2?	1.85 x 0.3	R	High head accelerated headrace; very fast wheel of unusual turbine-like design.	1.7	39
Martres-de-Veyre	L2	1.8 x 0.7	R	Accelerated headrace into curved breast u/shot.	-	-
Hagendorn	L2	2.15 x 0.23	R	Very fast high head accelerated headrace – shrouded paddle wheels.	-	Fast
München-Perlach	L2	2.3-3.1 x 1.45	R	Accelerated headrace u/shot.	-	-
Caracalla (Early)	E3	2.28 x 0.53	B	Two identical o/shot wheels served by overflow from baths.	2.05	16.6
Ickham (Early)	E3	2.0 x 0.56	R	Low velocity high flow rate u/shot	-	Slow
Janiculum (North)	E3	2.3 x 1.5	R	3 probably 4 identical u/shot wheels, close-set in series fed by aqueduct spur.	0.5-3.2	11-25
(South)	E3	3.2-3.8 x 1.5	R	U/shot wheel fed by aqueduct spur parallel to the north branch.	-	Slow
Caracalla (Late)	M3	2.18 x 0.53	Inclined non-radial	Two identical high head lapped wheels served from overflow of baths.	c.0.8	Fast
Haltwhistle	3	3.6 x 0.35	R	Very fast accelerated headrace; fed by spur from nearby river.	1.51	11.4
Chesters Bridge	3	3-3.6 x 0.6-0.9	R	River-fed u/shot in base of tower.	-	Slow
Willowford Bridge	3	2.7 x 1.5?	R	River wheel.	-	Slow
Fullerton (Early)	3	2 x 0.8-0.9	R	Low head u/shot fed by 250m spur from river.	-	-
Nettleton	3?	2.6 x 0.36	R	River wheel; splayed intake with inclined sluice-gate; curved breasted pit; dating insecure.	-	-
Ickham late (Phase One)	M3	2.4 x 1.1	R	Low velocity high flow rate u/shot.	-	-
(Phase Two)	E4?	2.4 x 0.9	R	Low velocity high flow rate u/shot.	-	-
Nahal Tanninim	E4	2.0-2.4 x 0.5	5R + 1B	Six duplex-drive water-mills served by a common headrace.	-	-
Fullerton (Late)	4	2 x 0.6	R	1m head u/shot; power generated by weight and impulse.	0.5-1.1?	-
Agora	M5	3.24 x 0.49	R	High head accelerated headrace o/shot.	1.3-2.05	14.1-14.5
La Bourse	L5	2.0 x 0.2	B	U/shot low breast with wheel trough.	0.28	5.0
Jarash	M6	4-4.5 x 0.5	B	Stone-sawing mill.	-	-
Dasing	7	1.6 x 0.225	R	U/shot accelerated headrace. Radial paddles morticed into annular rim.	-	-
Ephesos	L7	2.6 x 0.65	R?	Series of ten water-wheels.	-	-

372 Where calculations have suggested a wheel speed this is given, otherwise a general category is given e.g, slow, fast, etc.

On the enigmatic question of evolution, let us examine the vertical wheel corpus for evidence that might indicate either, that there existed earlier forms or developments of the technology which could have led within a short time to the introduction of the horizontal wheel or, which might suggest that its development had already occurred. (See Table R.)

This table has been generated primarily to illustrate the variation of water-wheel arrangements in chronological order. The sites are given in *time order of commencement of working*, which reflects the date at which a design was implemented. For comparative purposes, only the briefest physical data is provided and, where hydro-mechanical analysis has been possible, performance figures. Although the physical data of millstones, known for many of these sites has featured in the hydro-mechanical analysis of these machines, it is considered that they are not critical or directly related to the development and evolution of the vertical water-wheel. Millstones are therefore excluded from the table. Of greater relevance are the brief descriptions of each arrangement that demonstrates the great range of designs, both in scale and physical arrangement within different landscapes. The chronological evidence together with the diffusion of these innovative arrangements suggests that the adoption of water-power was well-advanced and widespread in the Early Empire, and that the formative years of this technology had occurred earlier. Let us also look to the question of stasis of the vertical wheel.

In a vertical-wheeled water-mill, the horizontal shaft provides the opportunity of duplicating the pit-gear (driver gear) to power two sets (pairs) of millstones. In the *Fullerton (Early mill)* evidence, the structural arrangement raised this possibility of a duplex-drive, but the analysis suggested that it was unlikely, though not impossible, because of insufficient power for working two pairs of stones simultaneously. Aside from the *Janiculum* (north millrace) and *Nahal Tanninim* (a duplex-drive with small Pompeian-style stones), neither the hydro-mechanical analysis nor the archaeology has brought to light any wheel capable of effectively powering two pairs of disc millstones simultaneously. Although they could have easily built larger and more powerful wheels – we have examples of both large diameters and widths, but not occurring together – it is quite clear that common practice was to couple a water-wheel with a single pair of millstones. In the history of corn-milling technology, multiple millstone drives from a single vertical prime-mover apparently did not appear until many centuries later in post-medieval Europe. In this respect, the evidence suggests that the vertical-wheeled corn-mill had reached *stasis* from at least as early as the 2nd c. A.D.[373].

Horizontal wheels generally required higher impact velocities than vertical wheels but it is interesting to note that we have several examples of vertical wheels having very high impact velocities, well within the horizontal wheel range of velocities. We may conclude therefore that whilst high impact velocities are a pre-requisite for horizontal wheels, Roman vertical wheels had the flexibility of working the entire range of velocity and flow rates. Moreover, vertical wheels had the singular advantage of generating greater power, which was critical in the application and development of water-power to industries other than corn milling. Vertical wheels of small diameter also share another design feature with horizontal wheels. They both have radial paddles made from a single piece of wood. Paddles of this type occur in the *Hagendorn* and *Venafro* specimens, and also the *St.Doulchard* site, if the elements found were in fact parts of a water-wheel. All three of these are small diameter wheels dated to the first two centuries A.D.

One other design development for which we have some evidence and can confidently relate to the combination of diminishing wheel diameter and single-piece radial paddles, is the change from wheels with two side frames to radial single-armed paddles, first shrouded then un-shrouded. Although we have little evidence of how large diameter Roman water-powered wheels were constructed, we can be fairly confident that most, if not all, were built with two parallel side frames, like all Roman drainage wheels. Indeed, no practical alternative can be suggested for wheels over say 0.75 m wide. We can also conclude that most vertical water-wheels had radial arms rather than clasp-arms. The next development from two parallel side-frames would be a single set of radial arms supporting the paddles between shrouds, such as at *Hagendorn* and *Venafro*, but this form of construction can only be applied to a smaller diameter wheel because the single set of radial arms does not have the strength and rigidity provided by parallel frames. An alternative arrangement for a single set of radial

373 We must note however, in the Jarash water-wheel, built A.D. 527-65 or shortly after, which Seigne has confidently interpreted of driving simultaneously two stone-sawing frames, the power required is unknown, but clearly within the power of an averaged-size Roman wheel. Seigne 2000c.
374 Czysz 1994, 154, Abb.5.

arms is for the paddles to be morticed into an annular wooden rim, as illustrated by the *Dasing* evidence[374]. The final sequence in this development is a relatively small diameter wheel having radial single-piece paddle arms morticed into the shaft or hub. Such a wheel might operate within a straight or curved (*Hagendorn*) wheel trough to improve the efficiency of application. Although the *St.Doulchard* evidence may well have been an example of a final form of this development sequence, it is the more complete *Venafro* wheel, which, although it retains the shrouds from the penultimate stage, displays the most advanced design of a very fast turbine wheel. All of these horizontal wheel design features found in later horizontal wheels – smaller diameter combined with single-piece radial paddle arms on un-shrouded and shrouded wheels – are present in the vertical wheel corpus dating from the Early Empire; this demonstrates that the Early Empire engineers had an experienced grasp of water-power technology. Their ability to adapt to variations in physical geography to generate water-power, by means of innovative arrangements of head-races and water-wheels, in single or multiple units, is also convincingly demonstrated by the corpus. More importantly, this body of *anno domini* evidence, suggests that we are probably examining the remains of a technology that had already experienced the invention and development of the horizontal-wheeled machine.

The little evidence we have of the horizontal-wheeled machine in later European archaeology could be explained by its having been displaced by the more powerful vertical wheel, which appears to have dominated the water-powered corn milling industry. This imbalance of evidence of the two types will probably be sustained or increased as evidence of the application of the vertical wheels to other industries requiring reciprocating linear motion and greater torque increases[375]. The European archaeological evidence shows that the vertical machine was the prevailing type of water-power generator, certainly from medieval times onwards. If we accept that the horizontal machine was known and used in earlier periods, then it may have been eclipsed by the vertical machine and not introduced into some provinces. Alternatively, regression of its technology may have occurred, so that in some areas, its re-appearance depended either upon re-discovery or subsequent repeated geographic diffusion. The writer's hypothesis is equally valid, both for the re-appearance of the horizontal machine

following regression as it is for its original invention. Thus, it is possible for both hypothesis, Lewis's and the writer's, to have validity.

If the origin of these two machines is really as close in time as Lewis proposes, archaeology will surely never prove it, for the window of history is much too narrow. In spite of a noticeable increase in water-mill discoveries in recent decades, none have yet been found dated to before Christ[376]. Why is this? The present corpus of archaeological evidence reflects the interaction of two influences, one ancient, and the other modern. The most obvious feature of the corpus is that it reflects the formative years of the European provinces of the Roman Empire, where the diffusion of technology is essentially limited to the expanding boundaries of the Empire. We would not expect to find evidence of this technology within Gaul prior to its conquest of 58-50 B.C. nor within Britannia prior to A.D. 43. The corpus reflects this; nearly all of the evidence from Gaul is 2nd c. A.D. and that of Britannia 3rd c. A.D. The second and 'modern' influence, we have already identified. It is the fact that modern archaeology does not extend evenly across the entire ancient world. The distortion that this is causing to our view of the history of this technology is damaging to our progress. Until archaeology makes inroads on the Early Empire provinces, where hopefully we may discover older examples of both vertical and horizontal machines, the probability of demonstrating the evolutionary relationship between the types and their diffusion is faint. The present corpus shows how difficult it is to interpret the technological developments from a body of archaeological reports that vary greatly in detail and value from one province to another. If the emerging archaeological evidence continues to favour the north-west provinces of the Empire, supported by minimal evidence from the Iberian peninsula and other Mediterranean provinces, then our interpretation of the history of water-power technology will be sporadic both in terms of time and geographical spread, and liable to distort our views. There is a danger that a historical palimpsest may develop, which could be complicated by the possibilities of evolutionary regression, re-invention and diffusion patterns influenced by geographic and cultural factors.

And so in conclusion, we have two hypotheses concerning the evolution of these machines. Lewis's, developed from a fresh interpretation of classical written sources, and the

375 Marble-sawing, (Seigne 2000c); mining, (Lewis 1997, 106-10; Wilson 2002, 21-23). Metal-working clearly took place at the Ickham (Later mills) site and in spite of an interesting shaped hammer head being found, use of water-power for forge work cannot be suggested with confidence. Spain 1984, 121.
376 The writer has examined the report of the earliest claimed water-mill site dated to the early 1st c. A.D. at St Giovanni di Ruoti, but does not agree with the interpretation. It is probably a latrine. Small & Buck 1994.

writer's, based on the interpretation of physical laws. The latter assumes that man, when exploring water-power, is likely to have discovered and then utilized certain natural phenomena in a predictable order which in turn resulted in smaller faster prime-movers. This hypothesis has been suggested as an explanation of how the horizontal mill evolved from the more complex vertical mill. Its validity, if accepted, is not confined to the origins of the horizontal mill. If in a culture using both machines, regression occurred and the horizontal mill disappeared for whatever reason and knowledge of its use was lost, then its re-discovery could occur under the same conditions of a developing empirically-driven water-power technology. Such evolution could have occurred in different cultures at different times, within or outside the Roman Empire.

APPENDIX ONE

Gear Ratio Changing Options

There are several places in this study where the possibility of changing the MR, or gear ratio of a mill, is met with. The different options available to a miller and their implications on the changes to the machinery need to be discussed.

The MR of a vertical-wheeled water-mill is determined by the relative sizes of the driver gear (in modern molinological terms the pit-gear) mounted on the wooden wheel-shaft, and the driven gear mounted on the vertical iron millstone spindle. The ratio is calculated by the number of cogs they each have, with the driver being larger than the driven so that the top millstone rotates faster than the water-wheel. We need to be aware of the physical and structural implications of altering one or both of the gears to effect a change in the gear ratio.

Although our knowledge of Roman gear design is very limited, common sense and modern millwrighting experience tells us that a disproportionate gear ratio will evolve with the smaller driven gear having iron for its engaging elements (teeth, cogs or rungs) with the larger driver gear using wood. The reason for this is obvious; if the cogs on both gears are made of wood, their wear from use is inversely proportional to the number of cogs on the gear in question. Thus, if the MR was 4 to 1 (driver to driven) the cogs on the smaller gear will suffer four times the engagement of the cogs on the larger gear, and therefore the wear would be four times as much. The solution, to avoid short life cycles and maintenance of the smaller gear, is to use iron for the engagement. For greater strength and durability the smaller gear can take the form of a lantern gear, and the Zugmantel specimen is an exemplar of this design (See Fig. 1).

For the purposes of this exercise it is assumed that the driven gear takes the form of a lantern-gear, having wrought-iron staves held between two parallel hardwood discs bound with shrunk-on iron hoops. This gear would be

377 Jacobi 1912. For a discussion on this see Spain 1992, 85.

tightly wedged on the square-section vertical wrought-iron millstone spindle. A six-stave lantern gear may well have evolved as the standard, because six registers is surely the minimum to effect reasonably smooth transmission. If the number of staves is less than six, the angular velocity of the lantern becomes unsteady, fluctuating as each stave passes through the engagement sequence. Whilst the rotating mass of the top millstone acts as a flywheel and tends to dampen the variations in angular velocity and torque, the stresses on the driven cogs becomes greater as does the likelihood of breakage. With a spindle of sufficient length the lantern could be re-positioned up or down on the spindle to engage with different diameter driver gears. With the driven gear in the form of a lantern-gear, the driver gear has to take the form of a face gear, with contrate pin shaped cogs. Such cogs could be made of iron, but most likely of hardwood, which would wear and bed in to provide a smooth and quieter transmission. It is possible that the driver cogs could take the form of rectangular-shaped projections as depicted by Jacobi in 1912, but this is considered unlikely[377].

The following three options A, B and C, are considered to be the most practical methods of changing the gear ratio to achieve a change in millstone speed. See Fig. 82. In each of these options only one of the gears is replaced. There is a fourth option, not illustrated, whereby a new gear ratio could be achieved by replacing both gears, but as this would involve more work it is considered an unlikely scenario. In Option A the driver gear is changed for one having a different number of cogs and therefore a different diameter, whilst the lantern-gear remains unchanged but is repositioned up or down on the millstone spindle to maintain engagement. In this option the positions and axes of the spindle, the millstones and the supporting bridge-tree, do not change. In Option B the driver gear remains unchanged, but a different diameter gear, mounted in the same position on the spindle, replaces the lantern-gear. This means that the millstone spindle, the millstones and the bridge-tree supporting them, have to be moved. Option C is where a new different sized lantern-gear is installed but the millstone spindle and bridge-tree remain in their original position, whilst the unchanged driver gear is repositioned on the wheel-shaft to maintain engagement.

None of these options would present insurmountable difficulties to the miller and their relative advantages and disadvantages were probably marginal, influenced by the accessibility of the machinery, maintenance life-cycles and structural considerations. Option B has the disadvantage of requiring structural alterations and moving of the millstones and grain-feeding arrangements, but aside from that, little meaningful can be said concerning the choice of options because we would be speculating on the physical situations that would probably have varied from mill to mill. Whether or not some millers practiced changing their gear ratio during the life of a top millstone to maximize the efficiency of production, as briefly discussed above in the *Barbegal* study (Site 1), is questionable. If they did, it may only have occurred in larger milling complexes such as Barbegal, where a multiplicity of working millstones existed. Otherwise the reasons for changing gears would have been either the life-cycle of the gears themselves, or, a radical change in the weight of the driven millstone. Two other influences could have affected which option to adopt. First, if a larger driver gear was to be installed, the gear-pit needs to be large enough to accommodate it. This might not be a problem in a timber-framed mill, but in a stone-lined or bed-rock pit the builder's work could be troublesome. We will recall that this problem was met at the *Baths of Caracalla* (Later Mill). Secondly, the work relating to driver gear changes required only carpentry skills, whereas the driven gear, with its iron rungs and hoop bands, required the skills of a smith.

It is interesting to note that the Westree experiments determined that the pitch of the Zugmantel lantern gear was 64.75 mm. Provisional calculations show that the minimum pitch-circle diameter of the driver gear to engage with a Zugmantel style lantern-gear, allowing for a wheel-shaft of say, 230 mm diameter, and a bridge-tree of 75 mm depth, is close to 385 mm. Such a gear would need 37 cogs and therefore create an MR of 6 to 1. having regard to the wheel speeds that we can propose at several of these water-mill sites, this MR would result in millstone speeds of between 65 and 100 rpm.

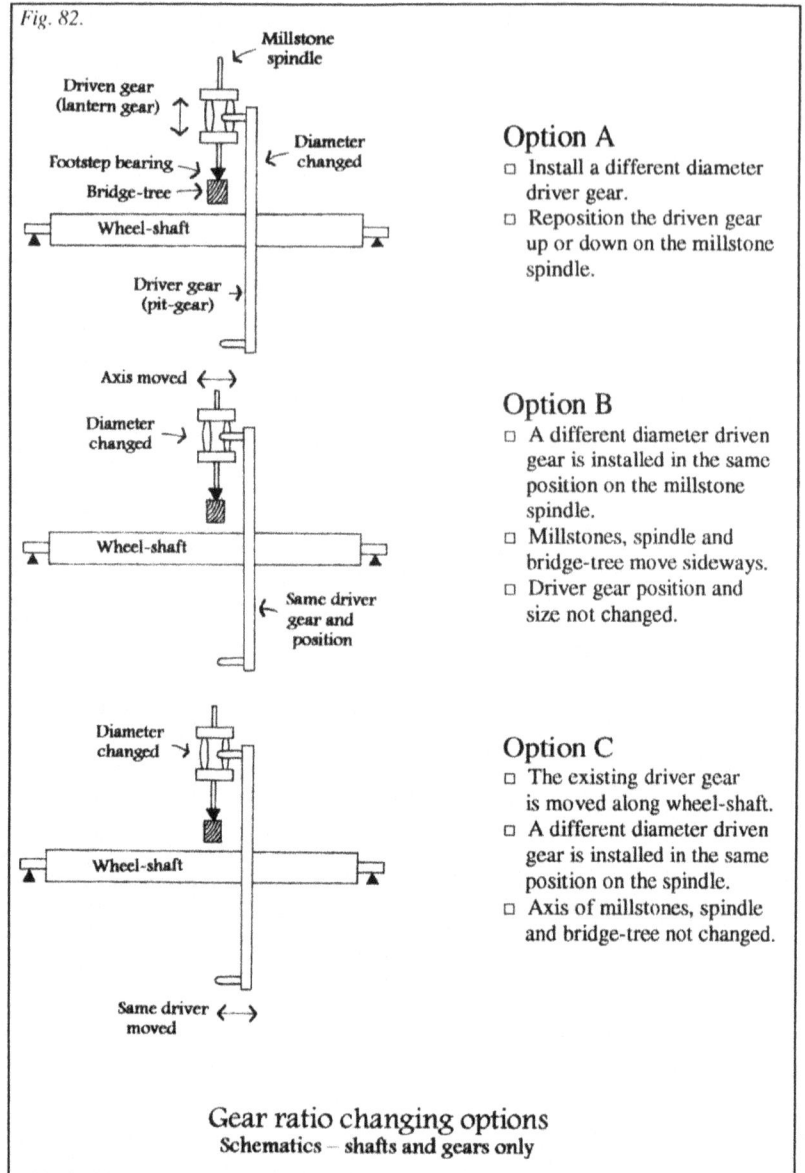

Fig. 82.

Option A
- Install a different diameter driver gear.
- Reposition the driven gear up or down on the millstone spindle.

Option B
- A different diameter driven gear is installed in the same position on the millstone spindle.
- Millstones, spindle and bridge-tree move sideways.
- Driver gear position and size not changed.

Option C
- The existing driver gear is moved along wheel-shaft.
- A different diameter driven gear is installed in the same position on the spindle.
- Axis of millstones, spindle and bridge-tree not changed.

Gear ratio changing options
Schematics – shafts and gears only

APPENDIX TWO

Roman Millstone Dress

Fig. 83.

Showing a pair of typically dressed millstones having parallel furrows and seven harps. Both grinding faces are dressed the same and when the top-stone is inverted onto the bottom-stone it rotates clockwise when viewed from above.

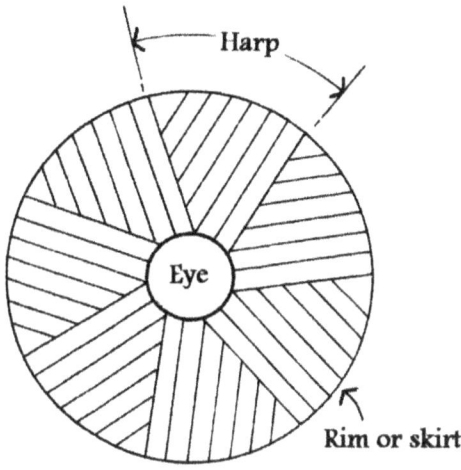

Harp

Eye

Rim or skirt

Bottom millstone
(Bedstone–stationary)

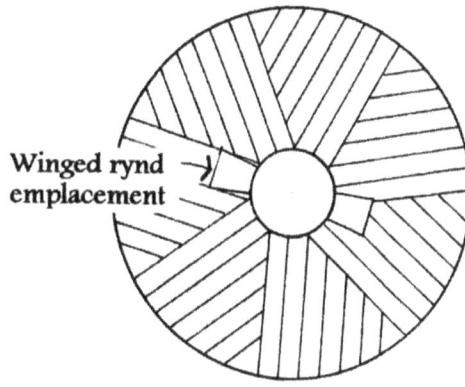

Winged rynd emplacement

Top millstone
(Runner–moving)

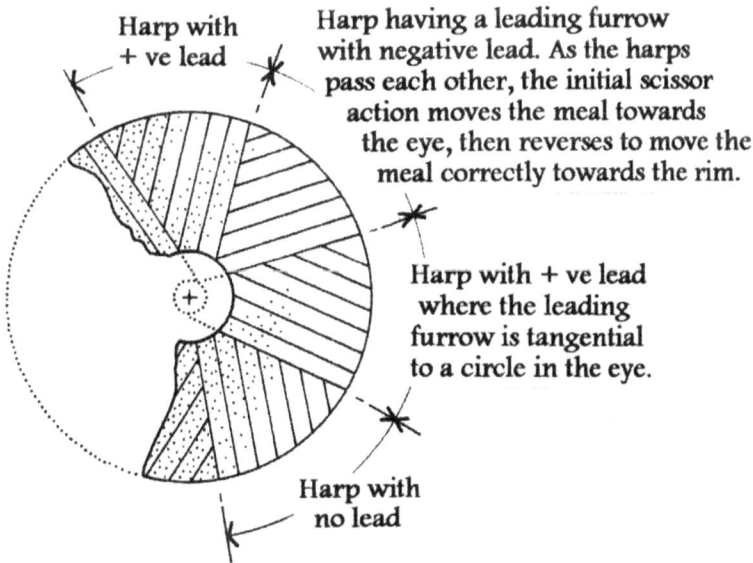

Harp with + ve lead

Harp having a leading furrow with negative lead. As the harps pass each other, the initial scissor action moves the meal towards the eye, then reverses to move the meal correctly towards the rim.

Harp with + ve lead where the leading furrow is tangential to a circle in the eye.

Harp with no lead

APPENDIX THREE

Terminology

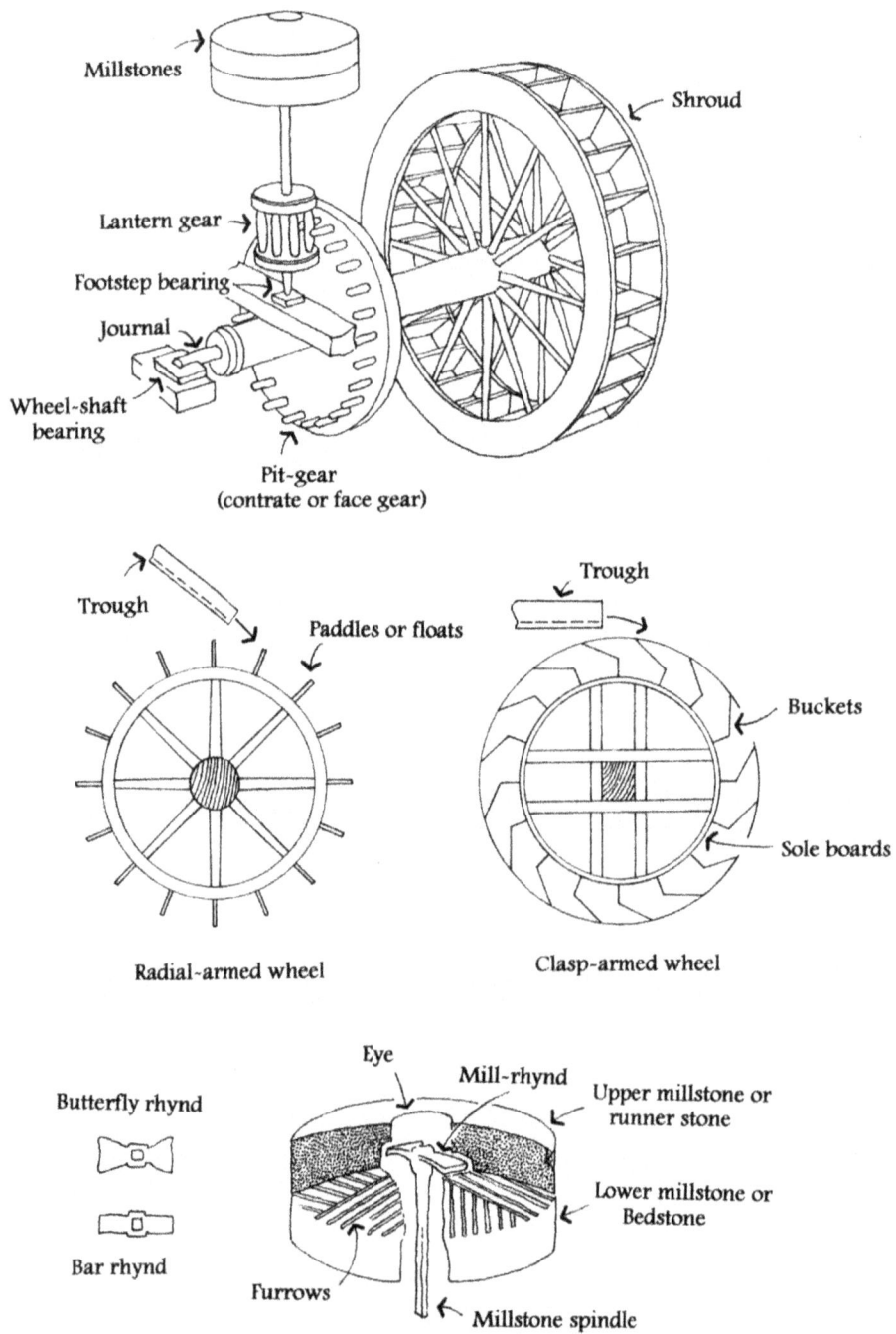

Fig. 84.

Millstones

Shroud

Lantern gear

Footstep bearing

Journal

Wheel-shaft bearing

Pit-gear (contrate or face gear)

Trough

Paddles or floats

Trough

Buckets

Sole boards

Radial-armed wheel

Clasp-armed wheel

Butterfly rhynd

Bar rhynd

Eye

Mill-rhynd

Upper millstone or runner stone

Lower millstone or Bedstone

Furrows

Millstone spindle

APPENDIX FOUR

Ancient sources on rations to slaves, soldiers and plebs.

Slaves

Early 2nd c. B.C., Cato, *Agr.*56:

Winter ration 4 modii of flour/month	= 27.24 kg	= 908 g/day
Summer ration 4$^1/_2$ modii of flour/month	= 30.64 kg	= 1021 g/day
Overseer's ration 3 modii of flour/month	= 20.43 kg	= 681 g/day
Chained slave's ration 4 Rom. lb bread/day	= 1.311 kg	= 874 g/day flour
Ditto, heavy labour, 5 Rom. lb bread/day	= 1.64 kg	= 1093 g/day flour

A.D.*c.*50 Seneca, *Epist.* 80.7:

Ration 5 modii of flour/month	= 34.05 kg	= 1135 g/day

Soldiers

*c.*150B.C., Polybius 6.39. 12-14:

Ration $^2/_3$ Attic medimnus flour/month	= 20.43 kg	= 681 g/day

Plebs

78 B.C., Lex Lepida and 73 B.C., Lex Terentia Cassia:

Ration 5 modii of flour/month	= 34.05 kg	= 1135 g/day

Flour dole replaced by bread 270-5 in Rome, early 4th c. B.C., in Alexandria 369 A.D. Codex Theodosianus 14.17.5:

Ration 20 *panes sordidi* (= rolls?) /day or		
6 biscuits of 160 g each/day	= 960 g	= *c.*900 g/day flour?

Conversions:

1 modius of wheat = average 15 lb imperial = 6.81 kg (Moritz 186, based on Pliny)

Assume bread as being $^2/_3$ flour and $^1/_3$ water

Roman lb = 0.722 lb imperial = 0.328 kg

1 medimnus = 4.5 modii

The range of the above figures is between 681 and 1135 g/day. The figure of 900 g/day for each person has been adopted in the above study.

BIBLIOGRAPHY

Ad, Uzi. 'Abd al-Salam Sa'id. and Frankel, R. 2005 "Water-Mills with Pompeian-Type Millstones at Nahal Tanninim," *Israel Exploration Journal*, 55, 156-171.

Amouric, H. Thernot, R. Vacca-Goutouli, M. and Bruneton, H. 2000 "Un Moulin á Turbine de la fin de L'antiquité, La Calade du Castellet (Fontvieille)," *Études Archéologiques de Quelques Sites, Milieu et Sociétés dans la Vallée des Baux*, 261-274.

André, J. 1961 *L'alimentation et la cuisine à Rome*, 73-4.

Annales Institut National Agronomique 1910 2nd series, lx.

Archaeologia Aeliana 1861; 1865, 2, vi.

Archaeology in the City of London 1907-1991, The Archaeological Gazetteer Series vol.1, Museum of London 1998, 283-4.

Aubuisson de Voisins, J.F.d'. 1852 *A Treatise on Hydraulics, for the use of Engineers* Trans. Joseph Bennett (Boston).

Baatz, D. 1994 "Eiserne Dosierkegel, Ein Beitrag zur Römischen Mühlentechnik", *Saalburg Jahrbuch* 47, 19-35.

Bélidor, B.F. de. 1819 *Architecture hydraulique; ou, L'art de conduire, d'élever, et de ménager les eaux pour les différens besoins de la vie...*, edit. with notes by Navier, C.L.M.H., new ed., I (Paris).

Bell, M, III. 1994 "An Imperial flour mill on the Janiculum," *Le ravitaillement en blé de Rome et des centres urbains des débuts de la République jusqu'au Haut Empire*, (Collection Centre Jean Berard, 11), 73-89 (Naples and Rome).

Benoit, F. 1940 "L'usine de meunerie hydraulique de Barbegal (Arles)," *Revue archeologique* 15.1, 19 80.

Blaine, B.B. 1966 *The Application of Water-Power to Industry During the Middle Ages,"* (Ph.D. diss., University of California)

Box, T. 1882 *A Practical Treatise on Mill-Gearing, Wheels, Shafts, Riggers, etc for the Use of Engineers* (London).

Bradley, F.A. 1912 *Pumping and Water Power.*

Bruce, J. Collingwood. 1867 *Roman Wall* (London).

Bruce, J. Collingwood. 1966 *Handbook to the Roman Wall* xii, edit. Sir Ian Richmond.

Brun, J.-P. and Borréani, M. 1998 "Deux Moulins Hydrauliques du Haut Empire romain en Narbonnaise. Villae des Mesclans à La Crau et de Saint-Pierre/Les Laurons aux Arcs (Var)," *Gallia* 55, 279-326.

Buchanan, R. 1814 *Practical Essays on Mill Work and Other Machinery*, with notes and additional articles by T. Tredgold , 3rd. edit. with additions by G. Rennie 1841 (London).

Bury, J.B. 1889 *A history of the later Roman Empire, from Arcadius to Irene (395 A.D. to 800 A.D.)*, I, (London).

Cartwright, D.E. 1999 *Tides – A Scientific History.*

Casado, C.F. 1983 *Ingenieria Hidraulica Romana* (Madrid).

Cassiodorus *Var* 11.39. 1-2.

Castella, D. *et al* 1994 "Le moulin hydraulique gallo-romaine d'*Avenches* "En Chaplix". (Aventicum VI) Fouilles 1990-91 *Cahiers d'Archéologie Romande* 62 (Lausanne).

Cato, *Agr.* 56.

Champagne, F., Ferdière, A. and Rialland, Y. 1997 "Re-découverte d'un Moulin à eau augustéen sur l'Yèvre (Cher), *Revue Archéologique du Centre de la France*, 36, 157-60.

Charlier, R.H. 1978 '*Tidal Power Plants : Sites, History and Geographical Distribution'*, BHRA Fluid Engineering, *Proceedings of the International Symposium on Wave and Tidal Energy*, Canterbury (Cranfield), 1, A1-1 to A1-6.

Cimorelli, G. 1914 "*Nel territorio di Venafro-Una importante scoperta archeologica*" (Venafro).

Clayton, J. 1861 "The Roman Bridge of Cilurnum," *Archaeologia Aeliana*, vi, 80-86.

Coadic, S. and Bouet, A. 2005 "La chaîne à godets des thermes de Barzan (Charente -maritime) : une première approcje," *Aquam Altum Exprimere, Les Machines Élèvatrices D'eau Dans L'antiquité*, 31-44. Bouet edit. Ausonius Éditions, Scripta Antiqua 12.

Codex Theodosianus 14.17.5.

Coles-Finch, W. 1928 *Life in Rural England.*

Crawford, O.G.S. and Röder, J. 1955 "The Quern Quarries of Mayen in the Eifel," *Antiquity*, 29, 68-75.

Cunliffe, B., and Galliou, P. 2002 *The Le Yaudet Project, Twelfth Interim Report on the excavations 2002.* Institute of Archaeology, University of Oxford and Centre de Recherche Bretonne et Celtique, University of Brest.

Czysz, W. 1994 "Eine bajuwarische Wassermühle im Paartal bei Dasing," *Antike Welt.* Zeitscht. F. Archäol. U. Kunstgesch. 25, 2, 152-54.

Czysz, W. 1998 *Die ältesten Wassermühlen – Archäologische Entdeckungen im Paartal bei Dasing*. (Thierhaupten).

Dedrick, B.W. 1924 *Practical Milling*.

Droysen, J.G. 1958 *Historik*, 4, 22.

Euzennat, M. and Salviat, Fr., 1968 *Les dècouvertes archèologiques de la Bourse à Marseille*, Marseille, Centre regional de documentation pédagogique. 48.p.

Fairburn, W. 1871 *Treatise on Mills and Millwork*, 3rd edit. 2 vols (London).

Farey, J. 1827 *A Treatise on the Steam Engine, Historical, Practical and Descriptive* 2, David and Charles 1971 (London).

Finley, M. I. 1985 *Ancient History: Evidence and Models*.

Fleet Valley Report, The London Archaeological Archive and Research Centre (LAARC) ref. VAL88 vols. 1-54.

Fleming, S. 1983 "Gallic Waterpower: the Mills of Barbegal," *Archaeology* 36:6, 68-9, 77.

Forbes, R.J. 1955 *Studies in ancient technology*, vols. 2 and 3 (Leiden).

Forbes, R.J. 1956 "Power," in C. Singer *et. al.* eds. *History of Technology* 2, 589-622.

Freese, S. 1971 *Windmills and Millwrighting* (Cambridge).

Gähwiler, A. and Speck, J. 1991 "Die römische Wassermühle von Hagendorn bei Cham ZG. Versuch einer Rekonstruktion," *Helvetia Archaeologica* 22, 86, 33-75.

Ghislanzoni, E. 1912 "Scavi nelle Terme Antoniniane," *N.Sc.*, 5, 9.

Gibson, A.H. 1930 *Hydraulics and its Applications* (London).

Guéry, R., and Hallier, G. 1987 "Réflexions sur les ouvrages hydrauliques de Marseille antique retrouvés sur le chantier de La Bourse," De Réparaz, A. (ed) *L'eau et les homes en Méditerranée*, Actes du Colloque du GIS 1984, CNRS, 265082 (Paris), 265-82.

Hinton, A, 1992 'Revised dating of the Worgret Structure' *Dorset Natural History and Archaeological Society Proceedings* 114, 258-9.

Hodge, A.T. (November) 1990 "A Roman Factory," *Scientific American*," 263, 5, 58-64 (New York).

Industrial Archaeology of Watermills and Waterpower, 1975, Project Technology Handbook, 11. Schools Council Project Technology Series.

Jacobi, H. 1912 "Römische Getreidemühlen," *Saalburg Jahrbuch* 3, 75-95.

Jacono, L. 1938 "La ruota idraulica di Venafro," *L'Ingegnere* 12, 15 Dec., 850-3.

Jasny, N. 1944 "Wheat Prices and Milling Costs in classical Rome," *Wheat Studies of the Food Research Institute*, xx, 4, March 1944, 135-70.

Journal of Roman Studies 1965, lv.

Keay, S.J. 2003 "Recent Archaeological work in Roman Iberia (1990-2000)," *JRS*, xciii.

Kiechle, F. 1969 "Sklavenarbeit und technischer Fortshrittim römischen Reich," *Forschungen zur antiken Sklaverei* 3, eds. J. Vogt and H.U. Instinsky (Weisbaden).

Klemm, F. 1954 *Technik. Eine Geschichte iher Probleme* (Freiburg).

Kozmin, P.A. 1921 *Flour Milling* (London).

Lanciani, R. 1891a "L'itinerario di Einsiedeln e l'ordine di Benedetto Canonico," *Monumenti antichi pubblicati dall' Accademia dei Lincei* 1.3, 436-552.

Lanciani, R. 1891b *L'Itinerario di Einsiedeln e l'Ordine di Benedetto Canonico* (Rome).

Lanciani, R. 1910 *Forma Urbis Romae* (Rome).

Landels, J.G. 2000 *Engineering in the Ancient World* (London).

Lea, F.C. 1916 *Hydraulics for Engineers and Engineering Students*, 3rd edition.

Leveau, P. 1996 "The Barbegal water mill in its environment: archaeology and the economic and social history of antiquity," *JRA*, 9, 137-53.

Lewis, M.J.T. 1997 *Millstone and Hammer : The Origins of Water Power* (Hull).

Machinery's Handbook 1944, 12.

Mariotti Bianchi, 1976 *I molini del Tevere* (Roma).

Maróti, E. 1975 "Ueber die Verbreitung der Wassermühlen in Europa," *Acta Archaeologica Academiae Scientiarum Hungaricae* 23, 225-80.

Maynard, D. 1988 "Excavations on a pipeline near the river Frome, Worgret, Dorset," *Dorset Natural History and Archaeological Society Proceedings* 110, 77-98.

Milne, G. 1985 *The Port of London*, 7, 79-86.

Milne, G. 1995 *Roman London*.

Moritz, L.A. 1958 *Grain-mills and flour in Classical Antiquity* (Oxford).

Neyses, A. 1983 "Die Getreidemühlen beim römischen Land- und Weingut von Lösnich (Kreis Bernkastel-Wittlich)," *Trierer Zeitschrift* 46, 209-21.

Oleson, J.P. 1984a "A Roman water-mill on the Crocodilion river near Caesarea," *Zeitschrift des Deutschen Palästina-Vereius* 100, 137-52.

Oleson, J.P. 1984b *Greek and Roman Mechanical Water-Lifting Devices : The History of a Technology* (Toronto).

Palladius, *Opus agriculturae*, I, 41, (42).

Parsons, A.W. 1936 "A Roman water-mill in the Athenian Agora," *Hesperia*, 5, 70-90.

Polybius 6.39. 12-14.

Proceedings of an International Conference on Tide Mills, held on 11th September 1999, organized by The International Molinological Society.

Procopius. *Goth.* 5. 19. 19-27.

"Discoveries per Lineam Valli," *Proceedings of the Society of Newcastle-upon Tyne*, 3, iv, 167.

Rialland, Y. 1989 "La détection des sites en milieu alluvial: l'example de la Rocade ouest de Bourges, commune de saint-Doulchard," *Cahiers d'Archéologie et d'Histoire du Berry*, 98, 11-18.

Reynolds, T.S. 1983 *Stronger than a hundred men: A history of the vertical water wheel* (Baltimore and London).

Richmond, I.A. and Bruce, J.C. 1947 *Handbook to the Roman Wall*.

Röder, J. 1972 "Die Mühlsteinbrüche von Mayen, Geländedenkmäler einer vor-und früghgeschichtlichen Grossindustrie," *Sonderdruk aus Bonner Universitätsblätter*, 35-46.

Romeuf, A.M. 1978 "Un Moulin à eau gallo-romain aux Martres-de-Veyre (Puy-de -Dome)," *Revue d'Auvergne*, 92, 2, 23-41.

Roos, P. 1986 "For the fiftieth anniversary of the excavation of the watermill at Barbegal: A correction of a long-lived mistake," *Revue Archéologique* 327-33.

Sagui, C.L. 1947 "La meunerie de Barbegal (France) et les roués hydraulique chez les anciens et au moyen âge," *Isis*, 38, 225-31.

Schiøler, Th. 1973 *Roman and Islamic Water-Lifting Wheels*.

Schiøler, Th. and Wikander, Ö. 1983 "A Roman water-mill in the Baths of Caracalla," *Opuscula Romana*, 14, 47-64.

Schiøler, Th. 1986 "Power Adjustment before James Watt," *Polhem Tidskrift for Teknikhistoria* Innehåll, Årgång 4, 191-201.

Schoonhoven, J. 1978 "Grinding with Stones," *Trans. Of the International Molinological Society Symposium* 4, 269-83.

Seigne, J. 2002a "Sixth-Century Waterpowered Sawmill," *International Molinology*, 64, July 2002, 14-16.

Seigne, J. 2002b "Une scierie méchanique au VIᵉ siécle," *Archéologia*, 385, 36-7.

Seigne, J. 2000c "A Sixth Century Water-powered Sawmill at Jarash," *Annual of the Department of Antiquities Jordan* 46, 205-13.

Sellin, R.H.J. 1981 "The large roman water mill at Barbegal (France)," *La Houille Blanche* 60, 1981, 413-26.

Sellin, R.H.J. 1983 "The large Roman water mill at Barbegal (France)," *History of Technology* 8, 91-109.

Seneca, *Epist.* 80.7.

Shaw, R.C. 1926 "Excavations at Willowford," *Cumberland and Westmorland Antiquarian and Archaeological Society, Transactions*, 2, 26, 429-506.

Simmons, N.O. 1955 *Compound Milling*.

Simpson, F.G., and Wilson. 1976 *Watermills and military works on Hadrian's Wall. Excavations in Northumberland 1907-1913 by F.Gerald Simpson*, edit. G. Simpson.

Small, A.M. and Buck, R.J. 1994 "The Excavations of San Giovanni di Routi," 1, 47-9, 305-9, 429, review by Greene, K. 1999 *American Journal of Archaeology* 103.3, 577-9.

Smeaton, J. 1759 "An experimental Enquiry concerning the natural Powers of Water and Wind to turn Mills, and other Machines, depending on a circular motion," Royal Society of London, *Philosophical Transactions*, 51, 100-74.

Smith, N.A.F. 1983/4 "The Origins of Water Power: A Problem of Evidence and Expectations," *Transactions of the Newcomen Society* 55, 67-84.

Spain, R.J. 1970 "An Eighteenth-Century Corn Watermill," *Archaeologia Cantiana* 85, 113-122.

Spain, R.J. 1976 *A Mechanical and Hydraulic Analysis of the Roman Watermill at Haltwhistle Burn Head, Northumberland* unpublished report.

Spain, R.J. 1984a "Romano-British Watermills," *Archaeologia Cantiana* 100, 101-28.

Spain, R.J. 1984b "The Second-Century Romano-British watermill at Ickham, Kent," *History of Technology*, 9, 143-80.

Spain, R.J. 1987 "The Roman Watermill in the Athenian Agora: A new view of the evidence," *Hesperia*, 56, 4, 335-53.

Spain, R.J. 1992. *Roman Water-power: A New Look at Old Problems* (unpublished Ph.D. diss. Imperial College of Science and Technology).

Spain, R.J. 1996 The millstones in D.F.Mackreth (edit), *Orton Hall Farm.: a Roman and Early Saxon Farmstead (East Anglian Archaeology Report 76)* 105-13. University of Manchester/Nene Valley Archaeological Trust.

Spain, R.J. 2004 *A Possible Roman Tide-Mill* <kentarchaeology.ac>

Spain, R.J., and Fuller, M.J. 1986 *Watermills; Kent and the Borders of Sussex* (Maidstone).

Steensberg, A. 1952 *Bondehuse og vandmøller i Danmark gennem 2000 år. (Farms and water-mills in Denmark through 2000 years* (Copenhagen).

Strabo *Geography*, 17 vols, trans. Jones, H.L. See book 3, 5, Loeb, 1917-1933.

Sutcliffe, J. 1816 *A Treatise on Canals and Reservoirs, and the Best Mode of Designing and Executing Them...*(Rochdale).

Syson, L. 1965 *British Water-mills* (London).

Thompson, H.A. 1960 "Activities in the Athenian Agora : 1959," *Hesperia* 29, 327-68.

Trovò, R. 1996 "Canalizzazioni lignee e ruota idraulica di età romana ad Oderzo (Treviso)," *Quaderni di Archeologia del Veneto, XII*, 119-34.

Usher, Abbot. P. 1954 *A History of Mechanical Inventions* (Cambridge, Mass.).

Vapeur, Chaudiéres A. 1894 *Cours de Mécanique & Machines*, École National D'arts et Métiers D'aix.

Varoqueaux, C., and Gassend, J-M. 2001 "La roué à aubes du grand basin de la Bourse à Marseille," *Techniques et sociétés en Méditerranée*, Brun, J-P. Jockey, P. and Amouretti, M-C. 529-549.

Vetters, H. 1981 "Ephesos. Vorläufiger Grabungsbericht 1980," *Anzeiger der Österreichischen Akademie der Wissenschaften in Wien, Philologisch-historische Klasse* 118, 137-68.

Vetters, H. 1982 "Ephesos. Vorläufiger Grabungsbericht 1981," *Anzeiger der Österreichischen Akademie der Wissenschaften in Wien, Philologisch-historische Klasse* 119, 62-101.

Vitruvius, 1960 *The Ten Books on Architecture*, Morgan, M.H, trans.

Volpert, H-P. 1997 "Die römischer Wassermühle einer villa rustica in München - Perlach," *Bayerische Vorgeschichtsblatter*, 62, 243-278.

Watson, Brigham and Dyson, 2001 Brigham, T. *The Port of Roman London*.

Watts, M. 2002 *The Archaeology of Mills and Milling* (Stroud).

Wedlake, W.J. 1982 "The excavation of the shrine of Apollo at Nettleton, Wilts (1956 -71)," *Society of Antiquaries London, reports of the Research Committee, 40*, (London).

Weisbach, J. 1877 *A Manual of the Mechanics of Engineering and of the Construction of Machines*, trans. by A.J.Du Bois, 2 (New York).

White, K.D. 1984 *Greek and Roman Technology* (London).

Wikander, Ö.J. 1979 "Water-mills in Ancient Rome," *Opuscula Romana*, 12, 13-36.

Wikander, Ö.J. 1985 "Archaeological Evidence for Early Water-mills – an Interim Report," *History of Technology*, 10, 151-79.

Wikander, Ö.J. 2000 "The water-mill," in *Handbook of Ancient Water Technology*, 371 -400.

Wilson, A.I. 1995 "Water-power in North Africa and the development of the horizontal water-wheel," *JRA* 8, 499-510.

Wilson, A.I. 2000 "The Water-mills on the Janiculum," *Memoirs of the American Academy in Rome*, 45, 219-46.

Wilson, A.I. 2002 "Machines, power and the ancient economy," *Journal of Roman Studies*, 92, 1-32.

Wilson, A. 2003 "Late Antique Water-mills on the Palatine," *Papers of the British School at Rome*, 71, 85-109.

Wulff, H.E. 1966 "A Postscript to Reti's Notes on Juanelo Turriano's Water Mills," *Technology and Culture* 7, 398-401.

INDEX

www.ingramcontent.com/pod-product-compliance
Lightning Source LLC
Chambersburg PA
CBHW061005030426
42334CB00033B/3374